TALES OF A
COUNTRY
DOCTOR

TALES OF A
COUNTRY DOCTOR

Paul Carter

Library of Congress Control Number: 2014905930
ISBN: Hardcover   978-1-4990-0012-2
                 Softcover   978-1-4990-0011-5
                 Ebook   978-1-4990-0013-9

To order additional copies of this book, contact:
Xlibris LLC
1-800-455-039
www.Xlibris.com.au
Orders@Xlibris.com.au
522674

CONTENTS

1. Dave...15

2. Woongarra...29

3. Locals...41

4. Es..51

5. Digby..60

6. Hardy..70

7. Phill...82

8. Clayton..91

9. Edwin..99

10. Show Girls... 108

11. Peter.. 115

12. Domestic.. 125

13. Good Choice.. 140

14. Heather.. 152

15. Neighbours... 159

16. Archie.. 167

17. Famiglia... 178

18. The Letter.. 186

19. Isobel... 193

20. The Swinging Arms 201

21. Beck... 212

22. Walnuts.. 222

23. Helen.. 231

24. Maggie 245

Paul Carter was born in Coventry, England and educated at King Henry VIII School and Guy's Hospital. He migrated to Australia in 1976 and has been a country GP in central Victoria for the last twenty-six years.

He lives with his wife Gillian on a farm in the Macedon Ranges. Apart from writing he also enjoys portrait painting. He has eight beautiful grandchildren, all of whose names he can remember.

For Gilly

But he who kisses the joy as it flies
Lives in eternity's sunrise
William Blake

Acknowledgements

I would like to thank Gordon Thomson for his encouragement, Ali-Breeze King and Julia Stiles for lessons in English and composition, Tor Roxburgh for catapulting me into the world of publishing, Mary Edqvist for showing me the rules of the game, Jennifer Darling, for having faith in a newcomer, and Gillian Carter for fearlessly keeping me on the rails.

Author's Note

There can be few more enjoyable, or indeed privileged, positions than that of being a small country-town doctor and I have enjoyed every minute of it. Not only is the work challenging and varied, but I have also been lucky enough to serve a community that measures its worth by what can be given rather than by what can be taken.

Over the years, in both private and professional capacities, my fellow community members have generously taken me into their lives and opened themselves up to me. They have shared with me their hopes, their fears, their highs and their lows. Now their generosity extends to my sharing all this with a wider audience.

I must point out, however, that this is not a memoir in the strictest sense. Whilst almost all of what follows actually happened, *Tales of a Country Doctor* is also partially born of my imagination. I have mixed true life events with small doses of storytelling, and the final brew is a mix of many things that really took place and a few that definitely never did.

1 Dave

I WAS SPENDING AN evening at home, at the urgent pleading of my accountant, trying to unscramble the pile of paperwork on my desk. It was even vaguely pleasant for I had lit the fire and made some tea, Hardy was curled up at my feet, and heavy rain was pelting on the roof. After some hours of shuffling and sorting, I was actually making headway when the phone butted in. I found myself talking to Sergeant Hogan who ran the local police station. Could I please come out to have a look at someone?

'Are they alive or dead?' I enquired cautiously.

'That's for you to decide.'

'Have you called an ambulance?'

'No,' he replied. 'Not yet.'

'Mmmm,' I said a little suspiciously.

It was late. The rain was bucketing down and the wind was rattling the windows. I was dog-tired and, although I hate paperwork, I wanted to get this particular pile of it over and done with. But the sergeant was persistent.

A few minutes later I had donned my heavy-weather gear, grabbed my sou'wester, backed the ute out of the carport and was driving reluctantly into the squalling rain. There was no moon and I sat hunched forward in my seat as though this would somehow help me peer deeper into the gloom. I splashed my way past fallen limbs and through flooded dips, carefully following the sergeant's instructions. The roads grew narrower and rougher until, twenty minutes or so after leaving home, I found myself on a dirt track which wound its way to a remote spot at the foot of the mountain.

It was not hard to know when I had reached my destination. In a small clearing only a hundred metres or so into the bush below the road, there was a pool of bright light surrounded by a ring of flickering red and blue lights. It was an oasis of vivid brilliance in the blackness of the storm and it looked quite beautiful.

In the centre of the clearing, brilliantly lit by the SES floodlights, stood an old station wagon, encircled, as if to prevent any possibility of escape, by half-a-dozen police and emergency vehicles.

As I left the shelter of the ute the wind almost took my breath away and it was only my lightening reactions that stopped my sou'wester disappearing into the night. Whichever way I turned the rain seemed full in my face.

'Hi, doc, thanks for coming out,' a senior constable shouted above the wind as he lurched up out of the darkness.

'Where's Hogan?' I shouted back.

'At the station,' came the reply. 'He asked us to come and meet you.'

'I bet he bloody did,' I muttered. 'What's happened here?'

'A spotlighter saw the station wagon in amongst the trees, thought it had run off the road and phoned us. When the lads came to check it out, they found someone in the car. And they also found this.' He pointed to the hose from the exhaust and the tape over the back window.

'We need to get you to check him out before we can shift him,' the constable continued. 'Oh, and by the way, he had this note in his hand.'

I stuck the note in my pocket and put my bag down under the car, out of the weather. The driver's door was open and by the flare of the floodlights I could see an ill-kempt middle-aged man slumped backwards in the driver's seat. His face was swollen and discoloured and the rain was running down the side of his neck. I leaned into the car. There was no heartbeat or breathing and his pupils failed to respond to my torchlight.

'Any idea who the poor bugger is?' the constable asked as I finished.

I shook my head, but when I stood back from the vehicle I saw for the first time a large hand-painted fairy on the rear passenger door.

'Yes, I'm very much afraid that I do,' I replied.

In all the years I had known Dave he had only ever had the one car. It was one of those huge early model Holden station wagons which had been built for a different era. I think the car may have started out lime green, but it was hard to be absolutely certain for, by the time I knew it, it had metamorphosed into a startling harlequin pattern in which every panel represented a different part of the rainbow. Even apart from the colour scheme the car did not look healthy: rust was eating away at the bottom of the doors, and the rear window was a spider's web of fractures. Most of the chrome had long since flaked off; the rear-view mirror had disappeared, and in place of the aerial was a tortured coat-hanger. However, despite all of this, what first caught the eye were the large fairies Dave had painted onto the car's rear passenger doors.

Mechanically, the Holden was not much better than it looked either. Although Dave was forever covered in grease and oil from his latest foray under the bonnet, neither the brakes nor the steering ever reached a point the average motorist would call reliable. Thick black plumes of smoke followed the car wherever it went and Dave was constantly needing rescuing or towing. As a result of this, the local boys in blue forever picked him off as an easy target, and he ran up vast amounts in fines, none of which he ever paid, causing him still further problems, and leading him constantly to ask me to intercede on his behalf. I can't remember how many times I asked the police to turn a blind eye to unpaid fines, or to yet another broken deadline for a roadworthiness check.

I did this because that old Holden was a crucial part of Dave's life. It wasn't just his vehicle, it was also his home. A home which he shared with Chess, the love of his life, a large, ugly, black and brown dog Dave always referred to as 'the King of the Mountain' or simply 'the King'. Chess was a bit like the car. He may have started out as a definable breed but you certainly couldn't have picked it by the time I knew him. He had seen a bit of life and wore the scars to prove it. Nevertheless, he was a gentle giant with a lovely disposition and he hung on every word Dave said. They both slept in the back of the vehicle amongst a chaotic pile of clothes, food, bedding, guitars and amplifiers.

I had first met Dave ten years or so before that night on the mountain. The police had phoned the surgery in the middle of a busy morning and asked that I come up to the station straight away to help calm a hysterical woman.

Normally Heather on the front desk can block anything and anybody, especially when I am fully booked and running late. She has done it many, many times over the years and has built up a wonderful range of reasons why I cannot be interrupted. And she does it all with a beautiful soft Lowlands accent that makes her sound like she arrived from Scotland last week rather than twenty-something years ago.

This time, however, Heather had met her match in the station sergeant and only a few minutes later I was plucked out of my comfortable office and sent up the main street to the police station. I discovered that the distressed woman in the interview room was Peg from the newsagency who sold me my Powerball ticket every week.

She was very agitated and her agitation didn't improve as she recited her story. Apparently she had been peacefully driving back from town when she had been forced off the road a few kilometres south of Rushby by some maniac who appeared to be trying to kill her. The motorist coming from the other direction had suddenly crossed the centre line and started flashing his lights at her. She had swerved to avoid him, almost lost control of her car, and skidded to a halt on the edge of an embankment. The other car had screeched to a halt in the middle of the road and the driver had jumped out and run towards her. When he reached Peg's car he had tried to wrench her door open and had started screaming that he was onto her and knew that she was in the secret police. Fortunately at about this time a police car had chanced upon the scene, otherwise who knows what might have happened.

When Peg had finished telling me her story, I prescribed her something to help her sleep that night, organised someone to drive her home and arranged to see her in the surgery the next day.

I was just about to head back to the surgery when Sergeant Hogan put a hand on my arm.

'While you're here . . . ,' he started.

My heart sank.

'Look,' I said. 'I'm in the middle of a busy surgery. I need to get back.'

'As I was saying,' the sergeant continued, tightening his grip, 'while you're here, would you quickly take a look at the other party?'

'Quickly?' I asked sarcastically.

'Yes, quickly,' he replied from behind an expressionless face.

I was led down to the detention room, a bare, windowless, cell with a fixed bench running the length of one wall. Sitting on this bench seat was an extremely dirty man dressed in rags. His name, apparently, was Dave.

'He's all yours,' the sergeant said, and closed the door on me before I could reply.

I was standing there wondering what to do when the small window in the door opened and a voice said: 'Call out if you want anything.'

'Well as a matter of fact . . .' I began, but the window had already closed again.

I sat down on the far end of the bench. 'Hello,' I said a little nervously. 'I'm Paul Carter, the local GP. Can I help you in any way?'

Dave looked up at me with fiercely sparkling eyes set in a filthy tangled ball of hair and beard.

'I have cracked the code,' he said.

'Yes?' I asked, rather puzzled.

'I can tell secret police cars from ordinary ones,' he whispered.

'And how would you do that?' I asked after a small pause.

'From their number-plates.'

'Right,' I said, nodding my head. 'Very handy.'

He reached into the deeper regions of his voluminous coat and handed me a grubby, dog-eared notebook. I opened it and found that every page was covered with car registration numbers. All carefully listed by starting letter and cross-referenced with a chaotic web of lines.

Dave leaned forward. 'There have been a lot more secret police around recently, and that woman is one of them.'

'Actually, Dave,' I said, 'I don't think so. I know her well. She works in the local newsagent.'

Dave was initially unconvinced by Peg's alibi but, after much discussion, and to my enormous relief, he eventually agreed to go to hospital. By lucky chance there was a bed for him and he made the journey to Lockridge uneventfully in the company of a couple of boys from the station.

'Oddly enough,' said the sergeant as I was leaving, 'we *have* had more unmarked cars around the district this month.'

'And is there a code?' I asked with interest.

'I have no idea,' he said. 'But there could well be.'

Dave responded well to medication and was discharged after only two weeks. The discharge was not unconditional, however. He had to agree to take his medication every day and to visit me on a regular basis.

Dave was always very good about keeping his appointments and while he was in the surgery Chess would wait faithfully by the front door, happily putting up with being patted by every child who came and went.

Dave enjoyed flirting with the office staff, all of whom had a very soft spot for him. He was obviously highly intelligent and always had interesting and thoughtful comments to make on current events. I came to learn that, apart from his dog and the Sydney Swans, his real passion was music.

I only ever heard Dave play his guitar once. It so happened that on one occasion he was my last patient for the day. Somehow the talk got round to his music and he asked if I would like to hear him play. I said yes, of course, not thinking it would happen, but when we had finished, Dave went out to his car and brought in his guitar and rest of his equipment. He set himself up at the end of the waiting room with amplifiers and speakers and, by the time he was ready, the floor was a tangle of cables running every which way.

'Would you like to stay as well?' I asked Meaghan who was the receptionist on duty at the time.

'It's either this or go home and cook Mile's tea,' she smiled. 'What do you reckon?'

So we set ourselves up with a couple of chairs and settled in for some entertainment. I am not sure what I had expected but it was obvious from the first note that Dave was very talented indeed. For nearly an hour Meaghan and I sat there open-mouthed at his virtuosity. We had been told how good he was, but nothing had prepared us for his sheer brilliance. I don't claim to be any sort of expert on guitar playing but I knew I was listening to something special. He could so obviously have been professional. But that was not what he wanted. He simply wanted to spend evenings entertaining and jamming with friends. So that is what he did.

From time to time I asked Dave about his family. I was keen to see if it was possible to create a better network of support than the somewhat unsatisfactory and fragmented system that was all I could offer professionally. He did have family—his mother and brother lived in Melbourne—but he hadn't seen or heard from them in ages. There had been a falling-out at a family get-together when Dave had been going through his drug phase.

He told me that enquiries about his health had led to a heated argument about his lifestyle. The discussion had degenerated into fisticuffs with his brother, followed by Dave telling his mother that he hated her. Dave then left and had seen neither of them since. Over the next year or two his mother and brother had frequently tried to make contact by way of calls, letters and even clothes parcels, but he had not responded and had heard nothing from either of them in years.

Dave's funeral was held in one of those neat, cream-brick neo-Norman churches that are scattered across Melbourne's more northerly suburbs. As I entered the church I was handed an order of service. Dave's rather plain coffin stood in front of the altar on two trestles. It was made of light pine with bright silver handles and on the top of it was a large spray of native flowers flanked by framed photographs of his dogs, Angel and Chess, at the head and his Swans scarf at the foot.

It all looked so neat and orderly. Not at all like Dave. Dave had never been into appearance in the slightest. In fact, he had always looked pretty ordinary with his scrawny frame and long straggly hair. He almost invariably sported a few days' growth of stubble, except, of course, on those occasions when he decided to shave or pick half of it off. His smile didn't improve things either, for those teeth that weren't missing were blackened stumps, and it became obvious on warmer days that personal hygiene was not his strong suit.

On top of all this, Dave had no dress sense, in large part due to the fact that he never bought himself any clothes. What clothes he did possess had been donated to him so they invariably didn't fit or match. He looked like a walking scarecrow. The notable exception being when, in the middle of a bitingly cold winter, Heather gave him a brand-new bright blue ski suit. Dave wore that jumpsuit continuously for months on end, winter and summer alike, until it finally reverted to its component parts and became part of Chess's boudoir. Rob, Heather's husband, had kicked up a bit of fuss when he had found out what Heather had done with the ski suit he had treated himself to. Nothing came of the fuss of course. Heather was always good at smoothing Rob's feathers.

When the King of the Mountain died, some two years before, Dave was inconsolable. It had been obvious for months that Chess was dying. He lost a lot of weight and his tummy became more and more distended with fluid. But despite the prolonged illness and the fact that it was Dave himself who took Chess on his final journey to the vet, Dave took the blow hard and subsequently fell ill again. He went through a phase of believing that Chess's death was the result of a plot against him and it took a lot of support to help him battle through this period. But, to his credit, battle through he did, and eventually he saw Chess's death for what it was. No plots, no conspiracy, no codes. Simply a rugged old dog who had come to the end of his rugged old life.

Life without Chess was a lonely one for Dave. They had done just about everything together for years. Time might be a great healer, but Dave's loneliness didn't lessen as the months went by. If anything, his sense of isolation grew worse, and eventually he decided he could endure it no longer. Much as the King was irreplaceable, Dave decided to get another dog.

Once the decision was made it was if a weight had fallen from Dave's shoulders and he was galvanised into a considerable flurry of activity. There was a great deal of to-ing and fro-ing about whether to have a dog or a pup and what breed to get. Should it be pure or should it be crossbred? Should it be 'kennel' or should it be 'rescued'? Dave looked at every possibility from every conceivable angle. There was no room for error in this one. In terms of decision-making, this was the big one for Dave.

Eventually he made up his mind and settled for a pure-bred dingo pup. This decision did, however, cause a few problems, for dingo pups are not only hard to find but are also surprisingly expensive. Dave was a man of small means and it was not easy for him to raise the necessary funds. Nevertheless, he tackled the task with determination, missing meals and saving up his security payments, and within a few months the day arrived when Angel was weaned, paid for and brought to her new home in the back of the fairy car.

No one, of course, could ever be expected to replace the King, but Angel certainly became the second love of Dave's life. He adored her and she appeared to regard him similarly. Like the King before her, she slept in the car with Dave, which was an interesting exercise until she was fully house-trained or, perhaps more accurately, car-trained.

The first time I saw the two of them together was when Dave appeared without an appointment in the middle of a packed morning surgery.

'Dave's in the spare consulting room,' said Heather.

'Does he have an appointment?' I asked.

'Of course he does,' she lied, knowing full well that I could see the entire morning's appointments on my screen.

'Heather . . .' I started to protest.

'This one's for me, please,' she said with a winning smile, so I relented.

'I am so pleased Heather was able to fit me in, Paul,' Dave grinned through his rotten teeth as I entered the room.

By now I had had years of experience of giving in when Dave turned up without an appointment and I bowed to the inevitable. 'If you can get past Heather, then who I am to stand in your way? But please, please, please make it quick.'

'I wonder if you could do me a really big favour,' he said as we sat down.

My heart sank. OK,' I said, 'but let's make it a really quick big favour. Please.'

In reply, Dave said nothing, but appeared to start fighting with his clothing. I looked on startled as arms and jackets went every which way. Then, to my great surprise, Dave reached under his indescribably dirty jumper, pulled out a dingo pup, stood her on my desk and said, 'Could you help her, doc?'

'What? How?' I spluttered.

'Well, as you may know, I only got her a few weeks ago, and I was driving to town to pick up some groceries and she fell out of the car window.'

'Yes?'

'And I think she's hurt her back leg.'

'Yes?'

'And I can't afford the vet.'

'Yes?'

'And I wonder if you would have a look at her.'

'Dave,' I said, 'this is ridiculous. There's a waiting room full of people out there, and besides, I don't know anything about dogs.'

Needless to say, two minutes later the dog was on the examination couch and I was gently feeling an obviously sore back leg.

'She's very touchy below the left hip,' I said. 'We'd better get an X-ray.'

At that time we had a really wonderful radiographer, Ahmed, working at the clinic. Not only did he take great X-rays, but to his credit he didn't even blink when presented with a species that was much smaller and furrier than the usual. He said later that the dog was better behaved than most of the children he irradiated. Angel stood stock-still the whole time and the pictures came out perfectly, showing an undisplaced spiral fracture of the left femur.

I asked Lesley, the sister on duty, to set up a trolley for plastering while I saw another patient. When the consultation had finished and the patient was leaving, she turned at the door and said: 'I hope you don't mind me mentioning it, doctor, but do I detect the smell of dog in here?'

'Impossible,' I said with a straight face and then shot down the corridor to the treatment room where Lesley was standing fully aproned and gloved next to Angel, who was being held on an emergency bed by Dave. Lesley was always wonderful, and no less so on this occasion. Without so much as the faintest hint of any expression on her face she asked: 'And what size plaster will you be requiring?'

The whole exercise turned out to be a great success. Dave was as pleased as punch, and Angel recovered so quickly that the plaster came off only three weeks later. I have no idea whether this is good veterinary practice, but Angel never looked back. She never fell out of the car window again either.

From where I was sitting I could see that the light from the side window of the church fell across Dave's coffin. There must have been a tree outside, for the pattern of light moved and changed constantly. It was as though the coffin was under a tree in the forest rather than inside a church.

In the early days, Dave moved around the district quite a lot, parking his car in a quiet spot and then moving on a few days later. But when he found his campsite in the forest at the foot of the mountain his nomadic days were over. It was quiet, secluded, a little off the road and it suited Dave perfectly. He called it Dave's Bluff. He lived there for some years, but I only ever visited it once.

After he found the camp, things were good for Dave for a long while. He went quietly about his business and Chess was allowed to roam far and wide. Dave never troubled any of the locals and during those times came as close to peace as he ever had. Then suddenly, out of the blue, some of the neighbours got up a petition. Not far from Dave's camp, a group of very expensive homes had been built backing onto the forest. The occupants of these houses had got together and requested that the police and forestry department evict Dave. None of them had ever met or had any dealings with him, but they were all convinced he was not right for their neighbourhood.

A day was set for the eviction and Dave was duly informed. At daybreak on the appointed morning, a procession of police and forestry cars arrived at the campsite. I wasn't present, but the story of what unfolded soon got around the entire district. In fact, many of the officers who had been there were only too happy to retell the story to anyone who would lend an ear.

'Get out. Now,' an officer barked at Dave as he emerged from the back of the station wagon.

'No, I will not,' he replied hotly. 'I have a right to be here.'

'Oh no you don't,' the officer shouted back.

Apparently the conversation went back and forth along these lines for a while, with voices getting louder and words more descriptive. Inevitably the various parties eventually ran out of insults and swear words and a scuffle broke out. Fortunately cool heads prevailed, combatants were separated and things eventually calmed down.

'I can prove I have a right to be here,' Dave said defiantly as everyone was catching their breath. He then promptly dived into the back of his car and started throwing things around. Searching for a refrigerator would have been difficult in the back of that vehicle, so great was the mess, but after only a short period of time Dave emerged triumphantly clutching a piece of paper in his hand. The paper was then passed to the senior police officer who then handed it over for further scrutiny by members of the forestry department.

The tide of battle had been reversed at a stroke. Dave's piece of paper not only turned out to be a current miner's permit for that entire side of the mountain, but apparently, for the next five years, also covered the gardens and grounds of all the fancy houses that backed onto the forest.

The officers of the state stood around in shocked silence, then suddenly the senior forestry officer said, 'Miner's permits only stay valid if you are digging exploratory holes at least once every week.'

'But I am,' replied Dave, smiling at him through those awful teeth.

'Show us then,' they said, so he did.

Dave showed them the various holes he had dug around the camp area, used and then filled in.

'Those are not exploratory holes,' said the exasperated official.

'Oh yes they are,' said Dave with a cunning smile, 'but if I don't find gold, then I use 'em to shit in.'

There was nothing to say after that really. The boys in blue and beige got back into their vehicles and the sad procession of cars wound its way back down the hill and disappeared. Dave, on the other hand, stayed exactly where he was and continued to live at the camp until he died.

Funnily enough, in the end the petition worked out well for Dave. A week or so after the Battle of Dave's Bluff, as the incident came to be known, a forestry vehicle appeared unexpectedly and delivered a large rubbish container so that Dave could keep the camp tidy. Then a little while later a gate was installed across the path to stop spotlighters from troubling him at night.

Although Dave lived happily in the forest for most of the time, the winters became increasingly difficult for him. The cold and the damp started to affect him badly and each year his health deteriorated. Time and again I organised bricks and mortar accommodation for him during the winter months. But time and again he would stay for only a night or two and then head back to his beloved Bluff.

In the bad weather he would often appear at the surgery in threadbare sodden clothes, shivering with cold. I remember one occasion when he appeared for an appointment looking especially wretched.

'What on earth has happened to you this time?' I asked.

'Rats,' he said. 'I haven't slept a wink in a week. Rats have got into my mattress and I can feel them moving around all night.'

I am usually not stuck for a reply, but I sat for a while, thought about what he had said and decided that there are some things for which there is simply no answer.

After the vicar delivered Dave's eulogy, it was suddenly time for me to make my contribution. I was feeling a little emotional so I held tightly onto the lectern as I looked around the church. It was packed full of friends and well-wishers. I recognised many faces from our community, several members of the surgery staff and a few representatives of the local police force. I even caught sight of Peg from the newsagency. And standing in a wide semicircle three or four deep at the rear of the church were the members of Dave's old motorcycle club. They were silent and motionless as the coloured light from the stained-glass window fell across their leathers, bandanas and chains.

Betty, Dave's mum, was in the front pew, and sitting next to her was his brother George. Although I had occasionally spoken to them on the telephone, I had not met either of them before being introduced on the way into the church. I had not been sure what to expect but I was certainly taken a little by surprise. George turned out to be a respectably dressed bank manager and Betty looked for all the world like the sort of cuddly grey-haired woman you would feature on a wholemeal bread advertisement. They were lovely, both of them. How on earth had Dave become separated from this family? And why hadn't he ever wanted to become a part of it again?

I had somehow never got round to making any notes for my address. I justified this lack of preparation by saying to myself that I wanted the speech to be spontaneous. I looked around at the sea of faces for inspiration. I had no idea that so many would want to come and bid Dave farewell. I turned and looked over at the coffin with the flowers and the scarf and the photographs and I suddenly knew what I was going to say.

I told them the story about Angel. I took my time and I missed no details. It was wonderful to hear a church full of people laughing at a funeral. And then I told them how not long ago a group of final year medical students asked me if I would organise a practice final examination for them. They made a number of specific requests but particularly asked to be quizzed on X-rays. As part of the preparation for the day I spent a pleasant couple of hours or so going through many of the filed X-rays picking out interesting or illustrative films. Suddenly I came across the X-ray of Angel's leg. I sat and looked and smiled at it for a while. I was about to put it to one side when I changed my mind and, feeling in a naughty mood, slipped it into the pile of films for the examination.

The day was a great success. Everyone, including myself, learned a great deal and had a lot of fun. But I did wonder how the public would fare when these bright young people were released upon them as newly qualified doctors. For, when they were shown the films of Angel's leg, they all came up with many wonderful explanations. They went into detailed descriptions of the appearance and developed complex diagnoses to explain the unusual anatomy. What they did not do, however, not one of them, was to pick that the bones were not human.

When the service had ended, I helped carry Dave to the hearse waiting outside the church. When we had laid him gently down inside and the flowers, scarf and pictures of the dogs had been placed back on top, the rear door was closed and the vehicle drew slowly away. We stood and watched him depart in dignity, accompanied by two long lines of Harleys, riding in tandem ahead of him, helmets off.

George and I stood and watched the procession pass slowly up the street into the setting sun and around the corner. Even then we stood in the street for a little while before turning back to the church. The last thing I saw was the sun glinting on Angel's photograph as the car turned towards the crematorium.

Angel certainly filled Chess's shoes well. She was loyal and loving and she had Dave wrapped round her little finger.

'She's not as obedient as Chess, mind you,' Dave would say. 'She has a mind of her own.'

But she never left Dave's side until she was about a year old. Then one day she was suddenly gone. Dave never even saw her go. She was simply not there one morning. She was looked for, of course; Dave crisscrossed the entire district many times in his frantic search. Posters were pasted up and rewards were offered, but no trace of her was ever found. Maybe she was stolen or maybe she was run over. Maybe she was shot or maybe she simply went walkabout.

I don't think Dave ever recovered from the loss of Angel, especially never finding out what had happened to her. I never again saw him with a smile on his face. He had been very ill off and on for many years and her loss was just too much for him to bear.

Well, Dave was at peace now and didn't have to face another cold wet winter with rats in his mattress.

George and I turned back to the vestry where Betty was waiting for us.

'Thank you for all you did for him,' she said.

'It was my privilege,' I replied. 'But I don't know that it amounted to much in the end.'

'That's not true at all,' she said, shaking her head. 'I believe that in the last years Dave finally found a form of peace. It was a shame that it only came at the end, he was so talented.'

'We tried really hard to make contact after the family tiff,' she continued sadly. 'But he never replied.'

'I know, he told me,' I said. 'But I know that he thought about you a great deal. And maybe he did find peace,' I added, and I pulled from my pocket the note the policeman had given me that rainy night at the camp. 'This is for you,' I said.

Betty took the creased, smudged note and read it. She had held it together up to that point, but now the tears flooded down.

'What does it say?' asked George as he put his arm round his mother's shoulders.

Betty handed him the note. 'I can't,' she sobbed. 'You read it.'

So George read out loud Dave's last message to the universe.

'I love you Mum.
I love you George.
I love you Paul.
The rest of you bastards can just fuck off.'

2 Woongarra

I SAT ON THE patio in the warm afternoon sun, drinking tea, and knew that I was in love. The sky was unmarked by cloud and there was not a breath of wind. The cool country air tasted sweet and clean. It was that perfect type of autumn day that Victoria does so well.

Beyond the patio, the well-kept lawn fell gently away to an open wooded area of huge cypress trees between which one could glimpse the open paddocks and then beyond them again the hills and the forests. To the left the lawn led round to a picturesque lake set amongst a mixture of native and European trees. The slight fall of the land away from the patio and the pattern of the trees, planted thoughtfully so many years ago, combined to create a magical sense of distant horizons whilst preserving feelings of seclusion and privacy.

Although I could not see the creek beyond the lake, I could faintly hear it running over the weir and I could imagine the sunlight dancing on the water's rippling surface. I could see sheep lazily grazing in the distance, and somewhere a bull called repeatedly to his ladies. I can't remember now if there really were bees buzzing round the lavender by the patio, or whether the air really was full of the scent of honeysuckle, but if it was not like that, then it should have been.

Justin was chatting to someone on the telephone, so I sat back and drank it all in, every bit of it. This was the most beautiful place I had ever seen and I had fallen in love with it at first glance. It was just what the doctor had ordered. It had simply taken a while to find.

Ever since Linda and I had come out from England, and a long, long time before I met Dave, I had lived in inner Melbourne. Coming from London, Melbourne seemed to us little more than a large market town when we first arrived. We used to wonder where all the people were. In those days you could have fired a cannon down Collins Street on a Saturday afternoon without running the slightest risk of injuring anyone.

In just a few years, however, things moved on. So much so that Melbourne is now somewhere you can go shopping at midnight and sit at a pavement table drinking coffee whenever it takes your fancy.

Melbourne may not have a harbour but it has plenty else and Linda and I were very happy in those early years. At least it had seemed that way to me.

There was no difficulty getting jobs, and medical registration back then was simply a rubber stamp job whilst having a cup of tea with the Board. Within a week of our respective arrivals we were both working full-time. We decided to work in different practices to leave us with time together in the evenings and at weekends. It felt to me as if we were on an open-ended working holiday, as if we had finally escaped our troubles and left them half a world away.

As our stay in Melbourne stretched from months to years we continued in our respective practices, gradually getting busier and busier. From time to time I asked Linda about children, but she said she was not interested anymore, so we bought a liver-spotted English setter instead. In all truth, Polly was a bit of an idiot and she was certainly very hard on the garden, but she was affectionate and gave us an excuse to walk the local parks.

There was a particularly cold winter one year and the practice had been especially busy with chest infections and the like. As a result, I had been working so hard for so long that I hadn't noticed which way the wind was blowing.

I had finished a consultation with one of my regulars late one afternoon. He was on his way out of the door when he turned and said: 'You're not thinking of leaving the practice by any chance, are you?'

'Not at all,' I frowned in reply. 'What on earth made you ask that?'

'Oh nothing really, doc. I've probably got it all wrong. It's just that a friend of mine told me your wife has bought a house over in Brighton.'

'Well, there you go,' I said with a smile. 'First I've heard about it.'

That evening I noticed for the very first time that Linda seemed preoccupied. Like me she had had a busy day at work but, beyond that, I saw that she was drawn into herself. Over dinner, in an effort to cheer her up, I said: 'By the way, you'll never guess what some silly bugger said to me at work today.'

'And what would that be?' she replied without interest.

'He said you've bought a house in Brighton.'

Linda put her cutlery down and took a very slow sip from her wine. Then she looked up at me. 'Yes, I have,' she said quietly. 'Settlement's in six weeks. I'm leaving and I'm taking Polly with me. I was going to tell you tonight, I really was, and I'm very sorry that you had to hear it from someone else.'

I sat stunned. 'You're joking, aren't you?' I asked hopefully.

'No, Paul, I'm not,' she replied.

I digested the news in silence for a while and then asked: 'Is there someone else?'

'No, there isn't.'

'So why?'

'Because I need some space, Paul.'

'Is it to do with Amy?' I asked after a pause.

'Well, what do you think?' she said and burst into tears.

I tried to put my arms around her but she pushed me away. Then, still crying, she got up and went to bed, while I stayed behind and cleared the table. We did sleep in the same bed that night, but it was on opposite sides and I was very conscious of the huge gap between us.

And that was pretty much that. Of course I'd known that things hadn't been exactly passionate for quite a while, but it had never occurred to me that Linda and I had drifted to such different places. I was profoundly shocked by it all, the more so since I also felt powerless to change things. We had further discussions, of course, plenty of them, but they all came to naught. There was no acrimony, no screaming matches, no fighting over possessions. Nothing. Just under thirteen years after it started, our marriage simply fizzled out and came to an end.

Six weeks after that evening Linda told me she was moving to Brighton, and feeling just as bewildered as I had then, I sat at the table having dinner on my own.

The shock waves of Linda's decision continued for many months. For a long time I was paralysed, although life still went on, at least on a practical level. Not for the first time in my life I understood what it was to feel loss.

I grew irritable and everything seemed to take so much more effort. Traffic went out of its way to be more annoying, patients did their best to be more demanding and by the end of every day I felt exhausted. Inner-city living gradually transformed itself from an exciting experience to a grey and grimy drudge. I leaned on my friends, and my parents too, who by this time had also made the move to Melbourne; they were all very loyal and supportive, but they had no solutions either.

I did see Linda on several occasions. Once we had coffee together and once she came over for a curry which I got from a local take-away. After dinner I asked her if she would like to stay the night. I had really hoped she would say yes but she didn't.

For many months I was very lost indeed.

Then, one cold wet night, on my way to have dinner with friends, I got stuck in traffic. There had been an accident at the lights ahead. I had already been running tight for time and now realised I was going to be hopelessly late for dinner. I couldn't even let my friends know as I had left my mobile back at the surgery. There was nothing whatever that I could do about the situation. I just had to sit there and accept it. I slumped back in my seat in resignation and gazed out at the rain-distorted lights of the emergency vehicles.

And as I sat there in the dark and the wet, I glanced across the road. There, on a noticeboard outside a rundown weatherboard church, and thoughtfully lit up for the late traveller, was a message.

Unless you change direction you will end up where you are going.

'It's a sign,' I said, 'Ha! Ha!' but I had already taken the message to heart. In that instant I knew that I didn't want to end up where I was currently going.

So I came to a decision. Sometime between getting stuck in the traffic and the last ambulance departing the scene, I decided that something had to change.

Although quite excited by the concept, at first I wasn't sure what kind of change I meant. Over the next few days, I thought of small changes such as going on a walking holiday, buying a new wardrobe of clothes, or going on a cooking tour. All of these are nice things to do, of course, but I knew that they were not really what I was looking for. After all, I had already tried a few similar things and here I was, still stuck.

Gradually it came to me that what I needed was a big change. In fact, what I needed was a really big change, a change that would keep me busy and challenged forever.

At first I considered sailing single-handed round the world and even told a few friends that this was what I was going to do.

'Have you sailed before?' they asked.

'Er, no,' I replied.

'Ever owned a boat?'

'Er, no.'

'Know anything about navigation?'

'No.'

'Thought you said you got hopelessly seasick just looking at boats.'

'Well, as a matter of fact, I do.'

'Ah,' they said, nodding their heads. 'Sounds like a great idea then.'

I also dreamed of changing careers. For as long as I can remember I have wanted to conduct orchestras, be a world famous tenor, open the batting in a test match, drum a number-one hit for a rock band and fly with the Roulettes.

In the end I decided against these ideas too. Not that I thought any of them would be impossible, I hasten to add. In fact I still see them as all perfectly do-able. I have an unshakeable belief in my own talents and am very dogged in my determination. It was just that most of them would require long lead times and therefore be unsuitable to fill my immediate needs.

I came up with all sorts of ideas, but none of them seemed to fit. I knew that I wanted to stay in Australia. That was a given. I was not going back to England. From the very moment I stepped off the plane some eight years before, I had loved every bit of Australia. I remember that first day so clearly: flowering trees, birds that I had only previously seen in cages, and space. Lots and lots of space.

I had come to Australia on a university exchange programme, which had been arranged at the last moment when somebody else had backed out. I arrived on my own, and Linda, for reasons relating to her work in England, arrived a couple of months later. Linda had already been issued with a permanent resident's visa in London but, because of the rushed nature of my arrangements, it had only been possible to issue me with a temporary one.

Although she hadn't been overly keen to come initially, Linda loved Australia just as much as I did and we decided to stay on after my exchange came to an end. In the excitement of the move across the world, selling the house in London and creating a new life in Melbourne, the limited nature of my visa was quite forgotten.

Time flew by and, before we knew it, we had been in Australia for a little over two years. At about this time, Linda got word that her mother wasn't too well. She therefore planned a trip back to England and was rummaging through the deed box for her passport. Suddenly she stopped and held up mine.

'Do you realise your visa expired eighteen months ago?' she asked.

'Blimey,' I replied. 'I had forgotten all about that. First thing tomorrow, I'll phone up the authorities.'

'Do you think you'll be clapped in irons and put in a hulk,' she laughed. Then she stopped and frowned, 'Do you think you could be sent back home?'

'Hope not,' I replied quietly. 'This *is* my home.'

I made the call the next morning and two or three days later I was sitting in an office in the department of whatever it was called then, being interviewed by a rather dour man in a grey suit and no sense of humour whatsoever. I was feeling more than a little nervous and my hands were clammy.

'If I have got it right,' the officer said looking down at my passport, 'it has just come to your notice that your visa expired some eighteen months ago?'

'Yes,' I said, trying to keep the nervousness out of my voice.

'You do realise that this makes you an illegal immigrant?'

'Well, yes, I suppose it would,' I agreed.

The officer looked up at me for the first time. 'Do you have a job?'

'Yes, I do. I'm a GP.'

'And do you pay income tax?'

'Well, yes I do, quite a lot of it actually. Any ideas?' I asked in a weak attempt at humour, but the officer neither smiled nor offered advice on tax evasion.

'This sort of thing cannot be tolerated,' he said, and then launched into a lecture about respect for his department, respect for due process and, not least of all, respect for Australia.

When he had finished he added: 'I want you to realise that this is a very serious matter. There has been a major breach of protocol and the matter must be resolved immediately.'

I sat nervously wondering what he was going to do. I thought I was about to be ushered to the airport to catch the next flight back to the UK, when he opened a drawer, pulled out a stamp and imprinted my passport with a loud bang. He then handed my passport back to me and told me I could go.

I met Linda in the foyer.

'How did it go?' she asked.

'You are looking at Australia's most recent permanent resident,' I said with a smile.

'What!' she said incredulously and grabbed my passport to check for herself.

And it was true. That was all there was to it. I'm sure it wouldn't happen like that now. These days I would probably be put in a detention centre whilst awaiting deportation. But, in those days, Australia was a very different place indeed.

I was getting more than a little frustrated with my search for a sea change. Then, one day, when I was not even thinking about it, the answer was handed to me on a plate.

I had an appointment with a chronically depressed woman I had been seeing on a regular basis for quite some time. On this occasion, however, she almost bounced into my room and, to my surprise, smiled at me for the very first time.

'Good afternoon, Paul,' she said brightly. 'I've come to say goodbye and to thank you for all your help. I won't need any more of your pills from now on. I've found something much better.'

'That's great, Virginia,' I replied. 'What's the secret?'

'Norman and I are moving to the country,' she said. 'We've bought a farm and we're leaving the rat race behind us. You can have all your rush and stress and noise. I can't believe how good I feel about it all already. We should have done it years ago.'

I was very impressed. The family hadn't yet moved and already Virginia looked years younger. Her new-found enthusiasm for life made a big impression on me and I ran even later than usual as I listened to her chatter on excitedly about their new property.

I don't know whether I decided right there and then in the surgery or whether it was a little later, but certainly by that evening I had decided that, like Virginia and Norman, this would be my solution too. I would move to the country.

It felt so right that I wondered why I hadn't thought of it before. After all, my mother had often told me that it was impossible to prise me from the seat of the toy tractor I was given when I turned four.

This was undoubtedly the change I had been looking for. I would exchange inner suburbia for fresh air. I would give away rushing and congestion for wide open spaces. I would live a healthy and peaceful lifestyle and I would live it on my own patch of dirt. Like yachting, I had never done it before but I was sure I could learn and was pleased to reflect it also had the advantage that, unlike yachting, I probably wouldn't drown if I got it wrong the first time.

As I tend to do with all things, I became more than a little obsessed with the whole matter and took on my relocation as a serious academic exercise. I studied maps, looked at rainfall charts and found out about soil types. I looked at balance sheets of different farming ventures and studied access routes to the big smoke. I speculated about the future appreciation of property values, pored over likely patterns of urban sprawl and bored pretty much all of my friends rigid by talking endlessly about the entire thing.

Within a few weeks I reckon I would have made a good minister for primary industry. There was nothing rural on which I was not an expert and friends started avoiding me.

Despite this, however, I was still not completely clear about what sort of property I wanted. For all of my research all I could say to anyone who asked was: 'I will know it when I see it.'

Nevertheless, there came a time when I felt ready to take the next step. I purchased a copy of the *Weekly Times*, spent a pleasant evening extracting names and numbers and, in the morning, contacted a handful of the most prominent rural real estate agents.

Those calls marked a point of no return. I had crossed the Rubicon. From that moment on, exactly as the song says, my serenity was through. The phone rang hot twenty-four hours a day. Not anticipating the scale of the response, I had, perhaps irresponsibly, handed out the surgery phone number to all and sundry. The poor reception staff went almost insane with the sheer volume of messages that were left for me.

The real estate camp was certainly in a state of excitement. On the horizon had appeared a city slicker whose apparent sole intent was to make their fortune. And not only that but a city slicker with 'Dr' in front of his name, and everyone knows how rich they are.

The upshot of all this was that I was presented with many properties dotted across the state. Over the next few months, I visited most parts of Victoria under the guidance of a variety of delightful and enthusiastic people. I looked at a couple of properties most weekends. Many of them were very nice and some were even beautiful. Sadly for the agents, they all had one thing in common: none of them was what I was looking for. Sadly also, many fruitless miles were travelled and many frustrating weekends wasted visiting places that were not a bit like their brochures.

In their keenness, agents ignored my wish list and simply showed me whatever they had.

'I wish for trees,' I said, and was shown wheatland.

'I wish for running water,' I said, and was shown mallee.

'I wish for character,' I said, and was shown cream brick veneer.

'I wish for hills,' I said, and was taken to irrigation paddocks.

'I wish for something not too far from Melbourne,' I said, and was taken in a plane.

Somewhere in all of this I gradually became a bit cynical and even a little annoyed.

'You will have to compromise,' they said.

'No I won't,' I replied. 'This is my new life. Why on earth would I compromise?'

'OK, OK,' they would reply. 'But we still think that you'll have to compromise.'

'Well, we'll just have to see about that,' I would reply through my Dirty Harry face.

And so the search continued. Weekend after weekend spent travelling far and wide, tramping up and down hills, driving round properties, looking through houses. By the end I knew my home state like the back of my hand. I had seen many lovely places, but none of them sang to me.

There wasn't a dramatic drawing of a line on a page. There was no definable watershed. It was just that over a period of several months the number of calls from agents gradually dwindled and the number of messages left at the surgery fell to a point where it stopped annoying the reception staff. One by one, the agents fell by the wayside and gave up on me as too hard, too awkward, too fussy, too Pommy.

The faint-hearted ones were the first to go, but eventually even the more hard-bitten agents pulled out of the race. Justin was the last of them. He had hung in there for a lot longer than the others, but even the weekend trips with him dried up. Eventually the phone stopped ringing altogether.

Perhaps the agents were right. Perhaps it was all too hard. Perhaps I was being too fussy. Perhaps I would need to compromise.

'Found your dream yet?' everyone kept asking.

'No, not yet,' I would reply.

'Still looking?' they would persist.

'Yes, yes of course,' I would say, though the truth was that I wasn't. Although I thought about it from time to time, the reality was I had given up looking, on the excuse that I was too busy running on my treadmill again.

So it meant nothing to me when, some weeks later, my receptionist asked if I would take a call. It had been a busy morning, of course, and I was running way behind time, as usual. The poor man with whom I was trying to consult had already had proceedings interrupted several times by other matters and I did not want to take another call.

'Who is it?' I asked tersely.

'Some bloke who says it's personal.'

'Yeah right,' I replied. 'Probably selling insurance. Just take a message and I'll sort it out later.'

When a morning clinic finished it was my habit to sit at my desk for what passed as a lunch break and deal with the inevitable mountain of paperwork and messages. I had pretty well sorted everything out when I came across a message asking me to call Justin. I dialled the number and found my last remaining real estate agent on the other end of the line.

'Paul, your staff are tops. You're a bugger to get through to,' Justin said.

'Yes, I know. I pay them well to block people like you,' I laughed. 'So what can I do for you?'

'It's not what you can do for me, old son,' he said. 'It's more a matter of what I can do for you.' There was a pause and then he added in a rather conspiratorial and melodramatic voice: 'I have found it.'

'Found what?' I asked.

'*It*, Paul. You know: *the one*,' he said. 'The one with no compromise.'

'Justin, we've been through this before. No compromise means no compromise.'

'Shall I pick you up at your place? Eight am, Saturday, say?'

'We're not going to be wasting our time are we?'

'Paul, listen to me. This is the one,' is all he said.

'So it's worth putting off a trip to the supermarket and the laundromat?' I asked facetiously.

'Saturday, eight am,' he replied, 'and if you think it's been a waste of time then I'll get your groceries and wash your socks for you when we get back.'

'That's certainly the best offer I've had all day,' I replied.

And that is how it happened. The following Saturday I responded to a toot on a horn outside my house at five to eight. I grabbed my camera and notepads, locked the house and climbed into Justin's car for the umpteenth time.

I handed him a sheet of paper.

'What's this?' he asked, glancing down at it.

'It's the shopping list for when we get back.'

He looked at me, and shook his head. 'Very funny,' he said. 'So exactly which bit of "this is the one" didn't you understand?'

We pulled away from the kerb and headed across the city.

'Are we going by plane again?' I asked, catching sight of a sign to the airport.

'Patience, ye of little faith,' Justin said.

The suburbs gradually slid behind us and at the northern ring-road Justin took the turning that headed off to the Great Divide.

'Well this is certainly an area we haven't explored before,' I said. There was no special reason why. It just hadn't happened.

We didn't speak much on the journey. We simply enjoyed watching the suburbs and then the countryside slide away beside us while Stephen Hough entertained us with some Hummel.

About an hour out of Melbourne, Justin turned left onto a pretty side road which wound its way through rich-looking countryside. Just a few minutes later we rolled into Stoney Creek where we stopped outside the bakery to stretch our legs and water the horses.

Stoney Creek is a nice little town with a quaint village feeling to it. I had not been here before and rather liked the look of it. The tea, served by a young lady with spiked blonde hair and a tongue ring, really hit the spot.

We were about to get back into the car when I looked at Justin across the car roof.

'No compromise means no compromise,' I said, fixing him with what I hoped would pass for a steely glare.

'What do you take me for?' he replied in a mock hurt voice.

'What I take you for is a bloody real estate agent,' I said and we both chuckled as we got back in the car and headed off.

Only ten minutes or so out of Stoney Creek we turned left off the main road onto a country lane and entered a different world. A world where everything was pleasing, where nothing jarred the eye. A world the rush of progress had passed by, or at least forgotten to ruin.

We followed the winding road down a hill and crossed a small willow-lined creek that meandered under the road. Before us the horizon was an endless range of forested hills.

Justin stopped the car on the next rise and gestured with his hand at the scenery. 'So how about this?' he said.

I deliberately refused to be appear excited. There had been many a slip twixt cup and lip and I wasn't going to get my hopes up just yet.

'It's OK,' I said grudgingly.

Justin laughed and shook his head as he got back in the car. 'Jeez,' he said with a smile.

We headed off again and a few minutes later, without warning, Justin turned off the lane into the driveway of a property and skidded to a halt on the loose gravel. There was a row of poplars either side of some white post-and-rail fencing. The driveway itself gradually wound its way out of sight through what appeared to be the sort of open-treed parkland that Capability Brown would have been proud of.

Justin started slowly up the driveway and, as we crested a small rise, we had a clear view of a creek in the shallow valley to our right. After crossing the park we came to a seemingly endless tunnel of trees which wound up the hill. Then to our left there was a lake and, on the right, a low brick house which seemed to ramble on forever, nestled like an island in a sea of colourful profusion.

Justin parked on the gravel at the front of the house. He told me that the owner hadn't been able to meet us but, on the plus side, we would have the place to ourselves.

I got out, stretched and looked around. There were trees, there was running water, there was character, there were hills and there was even, just visible on the far horizon, Melbourne. I gradually turned on my heel and looked at every point of the compass. I had no need for camera or notepad. The whole place sang to me.

I stood silently hoping that this wasn't just a dream.

'Well?' Justin asked.

'Well, I haven't even seen inside the house or walked the boundaries. I haven't looked at the pastures or checked out the sheds. But Justin, there is one thing I already know.'

'And what might that be?' he said with a knowing smile.

'This is the one.'

3 Locals

AS SOON AS THE removal truck disappeared down the driveway we stood on the back patio in the warm late afternoon sun and popped a bottle of bubbly.

'I give you a toast,' I said as the three of us raised our glasses.

'To Woongarra,' we said and clinked.

'Do you know how to look after a farm?' my father asked, looking around.

'Course I do.'

'It's just that there seems to be a fair bit of it,' he added.

It had been the better part of a year since I had first sat on this patio and fallen in love. For someone not known for his patience, it had been an annoying year of problems and delays, but now that was all in the past.

I looked beyond the lawn to the forest and hills and then over to the lake with the valley beyond. It was stunning and I could still hardly believe my luck. It seemed even more beautiful than I had dared to remember.

'Well, we'd better make a start on the unpacking,' said my mother, interrupting my reverie.

'You,' I replied firmly, 'are not helping with my unpacking.'

'Oh yes I am,' she said. 'Just try and stop me.'

So I did, and completely failed until she and my father went back to town that night.

I had always known that I would probably not be able to make my living out of Woongarra. Not only did I know nothing whatever about farming but, since this was a very special property and the number of beans in the Carter jar had recently been divided into two, the bank had more than a passing interest in proceedings. Consequently, I would have to do what Bertie Wooster and his friends always avoided like the plague: I would have to get a job. And since I have only ever done one job in my life, then that's the one it would have to be.

I had made a deliberate decision to do nothing about finding a job before the move. Wrapping up the old practice and organising shifting had been time-consuming enough, but the main reason was that I didn't want to fall back into the same old lifestyle before even getting to the farm. I would simply knock on a few doors and see what happened after I had settled in.

The Monday morning after I shifted also marked the beginning of my fitness programme. I was going to take the opportunity of moving to the country to get myself fit again. I had boxed at university and it had all been downhill since then. Who needed a gym subscription when you lived on a farm, I thought, and decided I would go for a run first thing each morning before getting on with the day. Consequently I hopped out of bed as soon as I woke, threw on some gear and jogged off down the driveway.

When I returned I had a quick shower and then jumped in the car to get some shopping and do a bit of exploring. I had intended going into Stoney Creek but when I got to the end of the driveway, on the spur of the moment, I turned northwards instead and decided to give Dixon's Bridge the benefit of my trade. It's a nice little town and has a lovely tree-lined main street. I grabbed a coffee when I had completed my purchases and then headed back home.

As I was leaving the town my eye was caught by a huge and beautifully manicured hedge. I glanced across at it admiringly and realised that in front of it stood a small faded sign which stated that Dr F Turnbull MB, BS was not only a physician but a surgeon as well.

On a whim I turned the car around and decided to pay him a visit.

It was a stinking hot day. I parked under a peppercorn and followed the path past the sign. Behind the hedge, surrounded by its own small but colourful garden, I found a tiny Swiss cottage, complete with high-pitched shingle roof and brightly painted shutters. A sign on the door told me I had found the surgery.

'Gracious,' I thought. 'I'll be bumping into Hansel and Gretel if I hang around here for too long.'

I was still standing on the path admiring the cottage when I suddenly realised that I was being watched. I turned round and nearly jumped out of my skin. Through a gap in the hedge, not a metre away from where I was standing, was the disembodied head of an attractive, well-preserved woman in late middle age. Her face was framed by a profusion of foxgloves and hollyhocks and she smiled at me from under a wide-brimmed straw hat.

'Hello,' she said in a friendly voice. 'Are you new?'

'Well I'm quite old really,' I replied, 'but I guess I'm new to the district.'

'Right, well I'd better come round and introduce myself,' she said and disappeared behind the annuals and perennials.

'Right,' I repeated to myself and entered the cottage.

It was lovely and cool inside. The waiting room had the genteel air of a private club gone to seed. The scattered patrons looked engrossed in their magazines and the only sound was the second movement of Wolfie's third violin concerto.

I approached the woman at the reception counter who had her head buried in some paperwork. I coughed discreetly and she took not the slightest notice of me. I coughed again, a little louder.

'Now I've lost my place,' she said, looking up at me with irritation.

'I was wondering if I could speak with Dr Turnbull?'

'No,' she said and went back to her figures.

'Is there a reason why I can't speak to him?' I asked, a little surprised.

'Yes,' she said and started counting again.

'Would you like to share it with me?'

'He's not here and there are no appointments left.'

I was about to explain that I didn't require an appointment when the lady from the herbaceous border, complete, I was relieved to see, with arms and legs, came to my rescue.

Delphine was as friendly as the receptionist was not. Within a few minutes of presenting my credentials I was whisked off into the house for a cup of tea to wait for Felix who was apparently out on a house call.

'Did I upset her in some way?' I asked, referring to the receptionist.

'Oh, don't worry about Madge,' said Delphine. 'She's like that with everyone.'

'Is that good for business?'

'Oh, definitely,' said Delphine. 'The patients all love being insulted by her. It gives them something to talk about.'

I sat for a while with an expression of thoughtful surprise on my face and was just about to ask if I could have a second cup of tea when there was a scrunching of tyres from the backyard. A well-groomed man, who must have played in the second row in years gone by, burst into the room. He gave Delphine a peck on the cheek, told her he had to dash, and then caught sight of me and stopped.

'Hello,' he said with a big smile whilst holding out an even bigger hand.

'This is Paul,' said Delphine. 'He trained in London.'

'Wonderful to have you aboard,' he said as he shook my hand.

'What do you mean?'

'The job's yours.'

'But I didn't even know there was a job.'

'Well there is and it's yours,' he replied.

'But I'm not even sure I'm looking for a job,' I protested.

'Course you are,' he continued. 'You wouldn't be here if you weren't.'

'But you don't know anything about me.'

'I know this much,' he said, still smiling, 'you must be a good bloke or else Dellie wouldn't have given you a cup of tea,' he added, tapping his nose as he disappeared out of the room.

I was still sitting there, rather stunned, when the door opened again and Felix stuck his head in once more.

'Monday morning, eight-thirty sharp, if that's OK with you? We won't be here for the first week, of course, as we're going to Sydney, but that'll simply give you a chance to settle in. Madge will show you the ropes, I think you've already met her. This has really made my day,' he said. Then, looking for all the world like the Cheshire cat, he disappeared for the second time.

'Well that's that then,' said Delphine with a smile. 'Welcome aboard,' she added as she shook my hand.

'But shouldn't we be talking conditions? Isn't there paperwork to fill in?' I spluttered.

'Later, later,' Delphine replied with a shake of her head. 'Now would you like another cup and a piece of cake?'

Half an hour later I was in my car on the way back to the farm, feeling like a rabbit that had got caught in Felix's headlights.

It had taken two years to find and move into a property. At some level, I had been looking forward to similarly agonising over a job as well. I'd imagined myself visiting every one of the local practices, submitting CVs, discussing conditions, analysing future population trends, organising provider numbers, and spending until Christmas ear-bashing my friends before making a decision.

But the entire thing had been done in an instant and I wasn't even sure I had been part of the process.

And somewhere along the line, I remembered as I drove home, I had somehow agreed to look after the practice the following week.

I also remembered that I had to arrange my mail. Fortunately the post was organised through the general store at Warraweet, which was on my way home, so I decided to stop off and sort it out right there and then.

Warraweet isn't much of a place even now and there was even less of it back then. Travelling along the main road at a hundred kilometres per hour, one could easily miss it altogether. Set back behind a row of cypress trees, it comprises nothing more than an old sawmill and a few tired-looking houses clustered around a dilapidated general store.

I pulled off the highway in a flurry of dust and parked in the shade of the trees by the store. A bell on a large curly spring announced my arrival and two very dirty naked children appeared out of nowhere and offered to sell me the cakes and scones they were holding.

'Get out you, little buggers,' yelled a big woman with a huge bosom as she struggled up the steps at the back of the store. She wore a grubby pink towelling dress and, as she climbed, it was obvious she had decided that today, at least, she would be a liberated woman.

When the store owner had got herself organised behind the hopelessly overcrowded counter she smiled at me with her whole face.

'Mind you, they're very nice,' she laughed, catching her breath. 'The scones that is, not the children. And they're home-made, too.' She giggled and added: 'But then I suppose the children were as well.'

'Oohh, I bet you're the new doctor,' she suddenly said with an even broader smile and I reeled a little at my first encounter with the local bush telegraph. 'I'm Ros. Geoff and I run the store and the post. We occasionally deliver, but Geoff is usually too busy doing other things. It's best if you pick it up. I can give you one of these pigeonholes. All to yourself, of course. What most people do is to phone in and ask what post they have. If it's bills they generally leave it, but if it's cheques they'll usually come in straight away.'

'Thanks,' I said, a little alarmed at the prospect of having Ros as my secretary. 'Maybe I'll just pop in each day on my way past.'

'Not a problem,' she said with a big smile, 'and perhaps I'll come and see you next week too, I'm overdue for a pap smear anyway.'

'I wonder if you could put an ad up for me?' I asked, pointing at the community board and keen to change the subject.

Of course,' Ros replied.

I wrote on the slightly grubby, dog-eared card she gave me and handed it back to her.

'*Four-wheel drive suitable for heavy farm work*,' she read slowly back to me and then pinned the card up between all the others. 'I'm sure someone will get back to you on that one.'

My head was still in a spin when I got home. I put the car in the carport and was about to open the back door when for the second time that day I knew I was being watched. I turned to find myself looking straight into the eyes of a grey cat, missing a tail, who was sitting on the end of the wall by the carport.

'Hello, cat,' I said, expecting suburban friendliness. But none was forthcoming. All I got was an arch of the back and a hissy fit. I didn't even get a chance to introduce myself before he'd disappeared from sight.

I shrugged my shoulders and went inside to call my old practice in Melbourne and get them to send Delphine all the necessary paperwork. I was just getting myself some lunch when the phone rang. It was Felix.

'Hello, Paul,' he said. 'I've just been subpoenaed to a case in Melbourne this afternoon. I've managed to wrap everything up from this morning but there's a house call still outstanding that really should be done today. Her name is Heather. I know you haven't officially started yet but I'm assuming you're insured and haven't been struck off, so I wonder if you wouldn't mind helping out.'

And, before I could make any protest, he had rung off, leaving me holding a piece of paper on which I had written a name and address. I felt a bit put-upon at first but soon got over that, had a bite of lunch, found my bag from under a pile of books and sallied forth.

Heather, together with Rob and her two impressively misbehaved fur-children, lived in Dixon's Bridge, just two streets back from the main road. She was sitting on the couch in her sunroom hooked up to an oxygen line and looking very blue indeed. I understood from the details Felix had given me that she was waiting for some new lungs.

'Hello,' I said as we shook hands. 'I'm Paul.'

'And I'm Heather,' she gasped. 'Nice to meet you,' she continued in an accent which unmistakably placed her origins as north of the Scottish border.

I checked her over, made some changes to her medication and wrote her out some prescriptions. She and Rob were both lovely and I stayed a while and had some tea with them before leaving.

On my return I found three people waiting for me. The first two were Trevor and Bill who had come to drench the flock. Apparently the previous owner had organised it before he left. 'We'll just get started,' they said. 'Join us later if you get a chance,' they added as they headed off for the yards.

The other man was Arnold who was, and indeed still is, the dirtiest man I have ever met, including Dave. His hair was dirty, his face was dirty, his clothes were dirty and his hands were black. Next to him stood Lilly, the world's ugliest dog. Not only was Lilly a collection of the least attractive bits of every breed ever created but, at some stage, Arnold had treated her skin cancers by cutting off her ears. Apparently Arnold and Lilly were delivering the four-wheel drive.

'What do you mean, delivering the four-wheel drive?' I asked, rather confused.

'The one you advertised for,' he replied. 'Ros gave me a call.'

'What . . .'

'It's a Subaru four-wheel drive and it's exactly what you're looking for,' he continued, just to make things clearer.

We walked through to the farmyard where Arnold had parked, and there it was. Up to that precise moment, the term 'Subaru four-wheel drive' had always tended, in my mind at least, to conjure up an image of a Subaru four-wheel drive. What sat on the trailer behind Arnold's battered blue panel van was something else altogether. I could see that it had once been a car but there were no doors and the windscreen was also conspicuous by its absence. There was, however, an extremely impressive array of bull-bars, side bars and roll bars. A tip tray had been welded onto the back. It looked like something out of *Mad Max*.

'Which bit is the Subaru?' I asked after a few moment's silence.

'The bit before the crash,' Arnold explained seriously. 'When I repaired it after the accident I decided to add some modifications.'

'I can see that,' I said, 'but why fluorescent yellow?'

'Oh, that,' he said a little dismissively. 'I happened to have a tin of it.'

'Has it got a roadworthy?'

He laughed and shook his head. 'What do you reckon?'

I loved it. It was completely bizarre. It would glow in the dark and I wanted it. Arnold and I went inside to discuss finances over a cool glass of water and within half an hour 'the Flying Banana', as it came to be known, had changed hands.

We were just finishing our tea when Arnold said: 'Whilst I'm here . . .'

'Yes?' I replied a little cautiously.

' . . . I would like to seek your advice on something.'

'Fire away,' I replied as enthusiastically as I could manage.

'Well, just before Christmas a cousin of mine said that a friend of hers was coming over from New Zealand and had nowhere to stay. Could I put him up over the holiday break? I reluctantly said yes but now I can't get rid of him. He just doesn't seem to want to go.'

'Goodness,' I said. 'That's a long time. It's been over two months since Christmas.'

'No, you don't understand,' said Arnold. 'It wasn't last Christmas.'

'When on earth was it then?' I asked.

'Eighteen years ago,' he said.

I told Arnold I would certainly think about it but couldn't come up with a solution off the top of my head.

When the Flying Banana had been unloaded and Arnold and Lilly had departed, I headed off to the yards to give a hand.

Trevor and Bill and a truckload of dogs were in full swing. We got through the introductions and I was put straight to work.

By late in the day the job had been done. The flock was back in the paddock and the noise, dust and excitement had come to an end. I was a much wiser man than when we had started. I had learned how to get sheep through gateways and races, how to swear at the dogs so that they actually listened to what I was saying, and how to drench sheep. I had also learned the pleasure of working with blokes who knew exactly what they were doing.

I passed round some cold beers I had brought from the house and, surrounded by a forest of waving tails, we all sat on the back of the Flying Banana, enjoying the feeling of honest tiredness.

'Where did you get this thing?' asked Trevor, banging the side of the tip tray.

'Oh, just locally,' I said a little defensively, expecting him to pour scorn. I shouldn't have worried, I wasn't in the city any more.

'It's great, isn't it,' he said. 'This'll get the job done real well. You'll get a lot of use out of this I would think.'

There was a pause for a few moments while we drank our beer and then suddenly Bill asked: 'Is that a cat I can see over there?'

I looked up. At the far end of the yard the grey cat was sitting in the setting sun cleaning himself.

'Yes. Came with the property. Why do you ask?'

'Because this pack of mongrels are cat killers. They hate them,' he said. 'If they see that cat they'll rip it to pieces. Don't say I didn't warn you.'

But the dogs had already seen the cat and they tackled the matter with that simplicity of approach which so endears their species to humans. They neither agonised nor spent time in self-doubt. They simply lowered their heads and charged.

Six black and tan kelpies charging at full speed across the farmyard was certainly an impressive sight, but not as impressive as a lone grey cat looking up at them for a moment and then going back to cleaning himself again.

Bill told me later that the dogs had not previously come across a cat which didn't run away, and he reckoned that this was what confused them. As the dogs all skidded to a halt, the cat finally responded. He arched his back, lifted every strand of his fur completely vertical and spat at them.

'One step closer,' he hissed, 'and I'll rip your fucking eyes out.'

The dogs, who all recognised the importance of sight in their line of business, hesitated.

'I fucking well mean it,' the cat repeated even louder as he advanced towards them.

It was all too much for the pack. Like the blue and khaki line on the slopes of Dave's Bluff many years later, they broke ranks and fled.

'Now that,' said Trevor when all the excitement had died down, 'is one impressive cat.'

I was glad to put my head on the pillow that night. 'Good job I didn't come up here for a rest cure,' I smiled sleepily. 'I haven't even unpacked,' I added, 'but I've already met lots of the locals.

'They seem a good crowd, too,' I murmured as I drifted off to sleep.

The following morning I jumped out of bed at first light again, only to feel that my legs were a bit sore from all the sheep work. I walked about for a minute or two and did some stretching but it didn't help. I was wondering what to do when I suddenly remembered that interval training was thought to be even more effective than training on a daily basis. 'That's what I'll do,' I said with relief, 'I'll do interval training. I'll take a break today and then run again tomorrow.' So, with nothing planned, I had a nice leisurely day settling in.

I couldn't be bothered going out so I phoned Ros to see if I had any mail.

'Just a couple of bills,' she answered, so I told her I'd pick them up later in the week.

At breakfast the next morning my legs were fine but I decided I had to get on with the unpacking. 'Running twice a week would surely be enough to keep me in good trim,' I argued to myself. 'Yes, twice a week would be plenty,' I agreed.

Thursday I forgot to go jogging, Friday I was too busy moving furniture around and Saturday I had to get the house tidy for my parents who were coming up for another visit.

'What's that in the shed?' my father asked as we were strolling round.

'A Subaru,' I replied.

'I don't think I know that model,' he said, and we both laughed.

'So what have you been up to this week?' asked my mother as we sat down to lunch. 'Just mucking about I suppose.'

'Well as a matter of fact—' and I was about to tell her about Felix and Delphine and Ros and Heather and Rob and Arnold and Lilly and Trevor and Bill, but she interrupted me before I even got started.

'Before I forget,' she continued, 'I'm having a luncheon next week and would like you to come. Everyone wants to meet Farmer Paul. They all think it's very amusing.'

'I'm afraid I can't,' I said, relieved to have an excuse. 'I'll be working.'

'Oh,' she said, obviously a bit put out. 'I didn't know you had a job.'

'Nor did I until last Monday.'

'And how's the jogging going?' she added after a short pause.

'Really well,' I lied.

'And are you doing it every day, just like you said you were going to?' she persisted.

'Of course I am,' I lied again, 'and sometimes twice.'

4 Es

FELIX TOOK THE OPPORTUNITY of my joining the practice to take some time off just a month or so after I started. He and Delphine hadn't had a break for quite some time and were both thoroughly looking forward to it. They planned to visit their various and scattered children and catch up with their growing number of grandchildren.

'You're sure you'll be OK?' Felix asked as they were leaving.

'Of course I will,' I replied. 'I coped perfectly well that week on my own, didn't I? Don't be silly. Off you go.'

'And you're sure that you're happy to look after my regulars?' he asked as he got into the car.

'No problemo,' I said to him through the car window as I closed the door.

Twice a week Felix spent the afternoon looking after his regulars. They had all been seeing him for many years and on those two afternoons he visited them in rotation.

It seemed that there were a number of different ways of becoming one of Felix's regulars. Some folk had got there on grounds which were strictly clinical, and others had got there on grounds which were purely social. Then there was a third group whose reasons for inclusion on the list had simply been lost in the mists of time.

Felix would reappear at the end of these afternoons looking completely whacked.

'Blimey, you look all done in, Felix,' I would say. 'Had a big afternoon?'

'Sure have,' he would sigh as he sipped his tea. 'I managed to get round four of them today.'

'Goodness,' I would say, nodding my head in sympathy as I thought of the packed waiting room that had characterised the afternoon surgery.

Within a week of Felix leaving it was time for an afternoon of visiting.

'Here's your list,' Madge said, handing me some history cards.

'Is that all?' I asked, looking at the thin pile.

'Yes, four, as usual,' she replied.

'Come on,' I smiled at her. 'Give us a few more. These won't keep me busy for long.'

'Really?' she asked.

'Of course,' I replied. So she pulled out four more.

The first call on my list was Es who lived on a small farm on the Rushby road. Felix visited her every few weeks to give her a vitamin shot and the injection was due once more.

I glanced at Es's notes. 'Good, a quick one to start with,' I said to myself. 'Shouldn't take too long at all.' I loaded all my bits and pieces into the car and headed off into the rain.

It had been raining heavily off and on for most of the previous week and as I set out on my calls the heavens reopened once more.

I knew that I would have no difficulty finding Es's place for I had driven past it many times. It was right on the bend opposite the cemetery just a kilometre or so out of the township. It was easy to pick out anyway because of the vegetables for sale piled high in crates either side of the entrance.

The farm, which gently sloped up to the hills behind, was obviously well cared for, but the farmhouse and buildings were a different matter altogether. Set back from the road at the end of a rutted, potholed driveway, the house looked as though it was about to collapse at any minute, whilst all the surrounding sheds looked as though they already had. A jumbled sea of ancient and rusting equipment encircled the buildings, and a row of old Holdens, in various stages of disassembly, were quietly disintegrating into what might once have been a front lawn.

Unfortunately for my timetable, the driveway to the house also served as the farmyard. Driving on the rain-softened surface, tractors and trucks had further damaged the already deeply scarred causeway, and under the influence of the recent rain the entire area had become a complex system of interconnecting lakes. As best as I could, I tried to keep the car on higher, drier ground, but it was just not possible.

I had gone barely twenty metres from the road when I lost traction and skewed sideways into what looked, for all the world, like a large and muddy inland sea. The more I tried to extricate myself, the deeper in I went. At first I was calm and gentle in my attempts to free myself, but when that got me nowhere, I lost my temper and floored the accelerator. The result was spectacular. Mud and water flew everywhere and the car skewed suddenly sideways and then tilted over a little. Water started to come in under the driver's door. In just a few seconds I was stuck like glue.

I had been in a really cheerful mood when I left the surgery and had been looking forward to the afternoon. As I sat in the car watching the water seep across the carpet my cheerfulness evaporated. I cursed and I cursed and I cursed. I cursed long and I cursed loudly. I cursed the rain, I cursed the car, I cursed Felix for going on holiday and, most of all, I cursed Es and her driveway.

After a while I ran out of things to curse. None of it had shifted the car one inch, of course, but I definitely felt a lot better in myself.

I took three slow deep breaths, grabbed Es's notes and my bag, opened the car door and waded to shore. The water may have only come a few inches up my trousers but the mud on my shoes was impressive indeed.

Through the angled rain, I hurriedly splashed my way up to the house, slipping occasionally but thankfully avoiding going base over apex.

By the time I reached the safety of the front step I was soaked through. There being no bell or knocker, I banged loudly on the peeling paint. Receiving no reply, I simply pushed the door open and went inside to find that it opened directly onto the kitchen.

And as I stepped through the door I stepped back in time. Beyond the front step was a different world. Apparently the house dated from when the road to Rushby had been the main route to the goldfields, and though that was now a long time ago, it looked as if nothing, including housework, had been done to it since then.

The entire room, apart from a network of narrow interlacing walkways, was piled waist-high with a chaotic collection of clothes, abandoned household appliances, boxes full of gawd knows what, pieces of agricultural equipment and newspapers. Millions of newspapers.

In the middle of the room, spilling off the kitchen table, were the remnants of last week's grocery shopping, a huge mound of dirty washing, a really old-looking bowl of porridge and some cardboard boxes full of yet more newspapers.

At the far end of the kitchen was a large open fireplace which crackled with a warm and inviting fire. Above the flames a hissing kettle hung from a hook. On the mantelpiece above the fire a row of wilting birthday cards, just barely visible through their coatings of cobwebs, propped one another up.

In the dim light I initially thought I was alone but as my eyes accustomed to the gloom I realised that an elderly lady in a rocking chair sat by the fire. She lifted her lined face to me and smiled toothlessly.

'Good drop of rain,' she said in greeting. 'Nice to meet you, young man,' she added. 'I was told that a youngster was coming to give me my needle.'

I regained my good humour as we shook hands.

'Nice to meet you,' I said. 'But before we get started, is there anywhere I can get cleaned up, I got in a bit of a mess on my way here.'

'You certainly have,' Es said as she looked me up and down. 'It's obviously been a very good drop of rain indeed. Use the lavatory on the back verandah, there's a basin in there.'

'Thanks,' I said and found my way to the back door through a hundred years of serious hoarding.

I was careful to step on only the soundest-looking boards as I made my way across the verandah. I found the loo without any bother, but although the door was ajar, it steadfastly refused to budge in response to my pushes.

'The door might be a bit stiff, what with all the rain,' called Es from inside. 'Just give it a good kick at the bottom,' she added, so I did.

At my first attempt, the door flew inwards, bounced off the far wall and knocked me off my feet on the rebound. Before I could get up, a motley-looking flock of chickens burst out from behind it. They swore at me loudly and vigorously for disturbing their siesta, making my earlier efforts in the driveway seem amateur by comparison.

Having evicted the tenants, I now had the place to myself. Es was right that there was a hand basin, but had declined to inform me that it had no water supply and must have been used exclusively as a nesting box for quite some time.

It was obvious that the night soil hadn't been emptied for a while either, so I decided to wait until I got back to the surgery to clean myself up and carefully tiptoed back past the holes in the verandah to the kitchen.

'Find it OK?' said Es when I came in. 'Good,' she added to my nod. 'Any eggs?'

I handed her my finds and sat next to her by the fire.

I hadn't met Es before so I decided to give her a quick onceover. After all, that was what all my old professors had taught me to do.

Apparently, even as a little girl, Es had always felt the cold, and in her latter years she protected herself against it with an amazingly complex system of clothing. To accommodate my stethoscope, she removed coats, jumpers, cardigans, spencers, singlets, thermals and several garments I had never seen before and still could not name to this day.

It was a complicated manoeuvre and it took a great deal of time. It also reminded me of the children's game of pass the parcel, so I was not surprised to eventually find that underneath it all she was really quite petite.

'Quick, quick, I'll die of cold!' she said as she moved closer to the fire. 'Do you really need to do this? Dr Turnbull simply listens through my clothes.'

Maybe not the recommended practice, I thought to myself, but I could certainly understand why he did it.

I completed the examination as quickly as possible, vowed quietly not to get involved in disrobing Es again, and indicated to her that she could get dressed.

'Thank gawd for that,' she said. 'I thought for a while there that I was going to freeze to death.'

She carefully restored all the various layers and when she had finally done so she turned to me and said: 'I need some scripts.'

It was at about this point that I realised that my rather nice pen was somewhere outside in the mud of the driveway.

'Could I borrow a pen, please?' I asked with a slightly forced smile.

'Of course,' she replied. 'Take one out of Max's coat, over there.' She pointed across the room.

On the back of the kitchen door there hung a large assortment of coats of all kinds. I tried a few and then found Max's. There were at least a dozen pens in the outside pocket and many more inside. I took one out and then, when I had finished the script, went to put it back.

'No. You keep it,' Es said.

'Are you sure Max won't mind?' I asked.

'I am sure he won't,' Es chuckled. 'He's been dead for, let me see, it must be all of ten years by now.'

Oh, I'm sorry,' I replied. 'So who was Max?'

'My fourth husband,' she replied. 'He was a good bloke, he was. Treated me real nice. Mind you, they all did. Farmers, every one of them. Yes, they all treated me nice, but Max was my favourite.'

I looked at Es silhouetted by the light of the fire. Four men, at least, had fallen in love with her. I imagined her as they must have seen her: lively, funny, pretty and passionate. Perhaps it was still all there, only hidden behind a million wrinkles and twenty layers of clothing.

'I hope you don't mind me asking,' I said, 'but why is his coat still hanging on the door?'

'Well, that's easy,' she said, 'Max was always good with pens. Always had plenty of them on him. It was a thing of his. There were loads of them in his coat when he died and we've just never found a better place to keep them.'

I nodded my head thoughtfully, packed my things and stood up to go.

'Did you notice my cards?' Es asked, pointing to the mantelpiece.

I said that I had.

'That was my sixtieth, you know. Back a while now of course. It was lovely. Henry took me over to Heddington for tea. It was my best birthday ever.'

I had got as far as the back door when Es suddenly called out: 'But what about my injection?'

I had forgotten all about it. In all the to-ing and fro-ing it had completely slipped my mind. Muttering an apology I returned to the fire and got out my things once more. I gave Es her jab, repacked my bits and pieces, bade her farewell and was outside before I realised that I had also forgotten about my amphibious car.

I was about to turn back, this time to telephone for help, when I saw that the job had already been done. To my amazement, my car was standing high and dry, facing the road and simply waiting for me.

'Hallelujah,' I said in quiet prayer. 'There is a god, after all.'

The rain had eased off by now and I picked my way to the car much more easily than on the way in. Opening onto the driveway opposite where the car stood was a shed which rested at an odd angle. In the opening a small weather-beaten man was leaning against the door post watching my progress. He had a yellow sou'wester pulled down hard over his head and was wearing a jumper more full of holes than wool.

Assuming him to be my rescuer, I went across to thank him for pulling my car out.

'Pretty interesting, being a doctor, is it?' he said before I could speak.

'Yes it is,' I replied, taken a little by surprise.

'Still, I expect you have to do a powerful lot of study,' he continued, nodding his head in agreement with himself.

'Yes, you do,' I confirmed.

'I'm fifty,' he added after a short pause.

'Right. Well you look pretty good for fifty,' I replied cheerily.

'Keep myself in good shape.'

'Yes, I can see that, oh and thanks a million for pulling the car out.'

'Any time, any time at all, doc,' he called. 'And how's Mum?'

'Fine,' I called back.

'Well we're all fine then,' he replied.

I got into my car and closed the door. My pen was on the passenger seat. There were still traces of mud but someone had had a good go at cleaning it for me.

'Right, where's the next visit?' I asked myself, glancing at my watch. 'What!' I groaned out loud. 'It can't be that late.' But it was, so I decided to head back to the surgery.

'Goodness, what happened to you?' asked Madge when I got back.

'I've taken up mud wrestling,' I replied.

'Well, that's certainly what it looks like,' she agreed.

'So who did you see, so that I can note them in the book?'

'Es.'

'Yep, got that one,' she said. 'Who else?'

'That's it actually,' I said quietly. 'Just Es.'

'Right,' she said as she slightly raised that eyebrow of hers. 'So just the one then?'

'Yes.'

'No others?'

'No.'

'Well, I'll put her in the book then.'

As she turned away, I realised that although there may be times when Madge can hide her smile, there are some times when she can't.

I started to see Es on a regular basis, even after Felix returned from holiday. I enjoyed going to see her and he was pleased to offload some of his home visits. The driveway never improved but my driving skills did and I never got bogged again.

I often wondered why Es lived the way she did, whether she liked it that way or simply did not see it. Then one day it occurred to me that perhaps she really could not see the mess she lived in. I organised for her to have an eye check and it turned out that she had cataracts not just in one but in both eyes.

When told about the treatment, Es was initially very resistant to the whole idea of leaving the farm, let alone going into hospital, let alone having surgery. Eventually, however, she was persuaded to have something done and the cataracts were removed without any complications at all.

I visited Es on her return home a short time after the operation.

'It's really nice to see properly again,' she said, 'but there is a problem.'

'And what might that be?' I enquired.

'Well, now that I can see clearly, I can see that this room is a bit dusty.'

'A bit dusty?' I exploded. 'This room is . . .' and then I stopped, for, after all, what the room was like was none of my business. None of my business whatsoever.

I did feel like writing the quote down with a view to submitting it to the *Guinness Book of Records* as the understatement of the millennium, but I didn't. I just smiled at her and said: 'But isn't it great to be able to say that.'

Although I almost always saw Es at the farm, she did occasionally present herself to the surgery. There was an occasion late one autumn when she had got herself tangled up with a farm gate and broken her forearm. Henry brought her to the surgery. The arm was X-rayed and we decided that we could fix it locally rather than have to send her to town.

Es was clad in her usual complexity of layers, which would clearly not fit over any plaster. Consequently, Lesley, the nurse who was getting things ready for the plastering, asked her to remove her clothing.

'Is that his request?' she asked, referring to me. 'He's a devil for wanting to get women's clothes off is that one.'

When I arrived to make the cast, I found that Lesley's request had been turned down.

'It's too cold to take any clothes off,' Es complained.

'But they won't fit over the plaster,' I protested.

'I tried to tell her that,' Lesley added.

'Well, I'm not taking them off,' said Es. 'Anyhow, how long is the plaster going to be on for?'

'About six weeks,' I replied.

'There's no problem then. These clothes are on until springtime anyway, and the plaster will be long gone by then.'

Es had dug her heels in and her mathematics were faultless, so that's what we did. Lesley and I just pushed the clothes up as far as we could and put the plaster on below them.

Then, six weeks later, we took it off again.

'See,' said Es with that wonderful toothless grin of hers. 'Good as new,' she added as she pulled her sleeves down and waved her arm about. 'Don't know what all the fuss was about.'

When Es had gone, Lesley turned to me: 'Do you think a squirt or two of air freshener would be a good idea?'

'That's exactly what I was thinking,' I replied.

Over the years I have visited Es's house on many, many occasions and every time Henry comes in from the fields when he sees my car. And every time he stops me on the way out.

'Pretty interesting, being a doctor is it?' he says.

'Yes, it is,' I reply.

'Still, I expect you have to do a powerful lot of study,' he continues, nodding his head in agreement with himself.

'Yes, you do.'

He then tells me his age and informs me that he keeps himself in good condition.

Just last September, Henry was settling down to watch the AFL Grand Final when, an hour before play was due to start, he suddenly decided he would like to see the game live. He pulled on his hat and jumper, walked to the end of his driveway and stuck out his finger. Within seconds a motorist had pulled over and with just minutes to go before the kick off he found himself standing outside the turnstiles at the MCG. Henry hadn't realised he would need a ticket to get into the game and was being turned away by the officials at the gates when a ticket tout came up to him and handed him a ticket.

'Your lucky day,' he said to Henry. 'I've done well today, mate, and I've got just one left. This one's on me.'

So Henry watched the entire game from a box and then hitchhiked home again in time for tea.

Henry might struggle in some ways, but I bet I wouldn't have finished up watching the Grand Final from a box if I had walked down my driveway with just an hour or so to go before kick-off and stuck out my finger.

He lives at the farm on his own these days. Es continued to live there for many years after the day I first disturbed the chooks, but she gradually became very frail and eventually had to be looked after somewhere else.

In all that time, even with her new eyesight, nothing ever changed. I never had to worry whether or not I had a pen on me and the house always looked exactly as it had that very first time. Nothing ever got tidied, nothing was ever modernised, no housework was ever done and the bowl of porridge never moved either.

5 Digby

IT WAS DIFFICULT TO get into the chook pen because the gate was tightly closed with bits of wire and string, and the inmates were keen to get out while the dogs were keen to get in. After a bit of a struggle, however, I eventually worked it out, and, bag in hand, stepped inside. I even managed, with some footwork of which Pele would have been proud, to dissuade both the feathered and the furred from achieving their respective ambitions.

The instructions had been quite clear: go down the side of the house, follow the path past the vegetables and the chook pen is on the right.

'Are you sure?' I asked Meaghan, who had recently joined the practice as Madge's assistant. 'It seems a trifle odd to say the least.'

'Well, that's what he told me,' said Meaghan with a smile. 'I thought it was odd too, so I double-checked with his wife but she just said exactly the same.'

'That must be it then,' I replied. But it still seemed a trifle odd.

I stood there in the heat and the dust, seemingly all on my own apart from the chooks who came up to check whether I had any food for them.

It was, or at least had been once, quite a grand enclosure. It comprised a central rectangular compound, full of holes where the inhabitants had scratched out dust baths, and a collection of non-matching sheds and covered areas which ranged from the dilapidated to the extremely dilapidated. It had all clearly been standing there for a very long time, but it wasn't at all clear to the casual observer whether the buildings were holding up the wire, or vice versa.

'This is ridiculous,' I said to myself as I shielded my eyes from the glare. 'But I guess I'm here now.'

'Digby!' I called out loudly.

There was no answer so I called out again. I had just decided that I was on a wild-goose chase when, to my immense surprise, I got a reply.

'Over here,' came a cultured, if slightly slurred, voice from the henhouse in the far corner.

I walked over, carefully avoiding the dust bowls, and stuck my head through the door at the top of the ramp. There, against the far wall, a very small, well-dressed man was sitting on a bed.

He had a glass of wine in his hand.

'Hello,' I said. 'I'm Paul. You asked for a home visit.'

'I did indeed,' he replied in a whistling sort of way. 'And how frightfully nice of you to come, sir. You know,' he continued after sipping his wine, 'I always feel privileged when a professional man like yourself manages to find the time to attend to the needs of a humble man such as myself. Do please come in.'

I climbed up the small wooden ramp, ducked through the door, avoided the hanging feeders and managed to sit on the bed beside him without once banging my head on the roof. He smiled at me with eyes twinkling out of a very weather-beaten face.

I looked around at the wardrobe, the bedside table complete with lamp and regimental photograph, and the coffee table that boasted a television set and a wine cask.

'You seem to be very nicely set up here,' I said.

'Well, the floor's off the ground and the roof doesn't leak,' he nodded in agreement, 'and besides that, a man does have standards to keep. You would understand that, for, unless I'm very much mistaken, you are, sir, like myself, an Englishman. And I would just like to add that if there is one thing I like more than a professional man, then it is a professional *Englishman*,' he smiled at me.

'Thank you. Yes, you're right,' I agreed. 'I am English. But tell me, why on earth do you live out here?'

'Because I like it,' he said with an expansive gesture of his arms. 'It might be humble, but it satisfies all of my needs.' There was a short pause. 'And also because Brunhilde won't let me into the house. Not for many years. Not that I mind, I hasten to add, except in winter. After all, we had to put up with much more than this when we were holed up in Tobruk.' He pointed at the photograph.

'Yes,' I said, 'I dare say.'

'But if the opportunity of moving back did arise, then I don't deny that I would embrace it with open arms. Speaking of which, should you see your way clear to having a word with Brunhilde about reinstating me, then it might carry considerable weight seeing that you have, I imagine, qualifications. Qualifications have always carried a lot of weight with Brunhilde.'

I promised that I would raise the matter at the first available opportunity and then got down to the reason for the visit. I questioned Digby about his emphysema, listened carefully to his chest, checked all his medicines and wrote him some scripts, which I said I would drop into the chemist for him when I got back to town.

I was putting everything back in my bag when Digby said rather grandly: 'Before you go, sir, there is something I would like to show you.'

'Of course,' I said.

'I would like,' said Digby with pride, 'to show you my collection,' and with a great deal of ceremony he opened the wardrobe door.

I am not sure what I was expecting but I was definitely taken by surprise. The entire wardrobe, from top to bottom, was filled with ties. There were hundreds and hundreds of them. They were in all shapes and sizes and they were all neatly arranged according to colour and pattern on racks fitted especially for the purpose.

'My tie collection,' he said, gesturing toward them with his hands.

'As you can see,' he continued proudly, 'I have been collecting for many years. This may well be the largest collection in the southern hemisphere, although there could of course be larger ones in Europe or America.'

For a few minutes I poked and prodded the collection, indicating how impressed I was.

Then abruptly Digby said: 'But I must not keep you, doubtless you are a busy man with many calls upon your time.'

I muttered that I did indeed have other calls to attend to and, after saying goodbye, took my leave. I managed the gate much better this time but still had to do an impression of David Beckham to keep the dogs from the birds and the birds from the vegetables.

The house in front of the chook pen was a small weatherboard cottage built way back in the gold rush days. It had not seen paint in many a long year and, at the corner furthest from the path, it was a long way off true.

In the front garden there was a woman on her hands and knees tidying a flowerbed. As I walked back up the path, she got up slowly with the stiffness of arthritis. She was a tall woman with a large handsome face and a mop of steel-grey hair. She was a little bowed over at the shoulders but still looked down at me. One of the lenses in her glasses was broken.

'Autumn crocuses,' she said.

'I beg your pardon?' I replied.

'Autumn crocuses,' she repeated.

It still made no sense to me. I was going to enquire further but fortunately the woman clarified things for me.

'I have been tidying the autumn crocuses,' she shouted as if I was deaf.

'Ah,' I said, enlightened.

'I guess you have been to see Digby. Come on in and have a cup of tea. Brunhilde's the name. I won't shake hands,' she said, displaying massive, soil-stained hands to me.

'Thanks very much,' I said brightly, 'but I've got a fair bit to do and I'm behind schedule, so I think I'll just keep moving.'

'You *will* have tea with me,' she said, looking at me keenly through her broken glasses.

'Not a problem,' I said. 'Love to.' So I put my car keys back in my pocket and meekly followed her into the house.

Brunhilde rinsed her hands, put the kettle on and then turned to me and said: 'Before you say anything, yes, my father was an ardent admirer of Mr Wagner. I imagine you are aware of his works. And before you say anything else, since I can well imagine that Digby has already spoken to you, no, I will not have him in the house until he has divorced himself from the devil.'

'What?' I asked.

'The devil,' Brunhilde repeated. 'The devil in the bottle. Drink, Dr Carter, not only destroys the individual but has been the ruination of mankind and the destroyer of civilisations. No. I will not let that abomination into my house.'

I sat very quietly sipping my tea.

The sunlight caught on the broken lens as Brunhilde turned towards me once more. 'Digby drinks, Dr Carter. He associates with the devil. I smell it on his breath. Every Thursday he sneaks down to that den of iniquity on the corner of the High Street where he meets those other sad and broken men. Together they join in sin and as the evening wears on they make fools of themselves with loud talk and inane laughter.' She paused for a while and then continued: 'I have even suspected that he might smuggle alcohol into his current accommodation but I have never lowered myself to go and check, even when collecting the eggs. No, Dr Carter, until Digby takes the pledge, the chook house is where he will stay.'

I sat silently for a while and then came to a decision. I decided to break my promise with Digby and not argue his case for reinstatement. Not today at least. Perhaps when I knew her better. Whoever first discovered that discretion is the better part of valour, I thought to myself, definitely knew their onions.

'Do you drink?' Brunhilde asked suddenly.

'Good Lord, no,' I said, shaking my head vigorously. 'Can't stand the stuff.'

'But you blaspheme,' she said.

'Sorry, what I meant to say was: no, no, never touched a drop.'

'It is so refreshing,' said Brunhilde wistfully, 'to know that there is at least one civilised man in this district. Would you like another cup of tea?'

'Love to, but really must get going this time.' I looked at my watch. 'How times flies!' I said, and escaped as quickly as possible.

Not far from Digby and Brunhilde's small farm, Bert was living out his evening years with his daughter and son-in-law. Bert was my next port of call. He was a wonderful man with a razor-sharp intellect and eighty-five years of country yarns inside him. He had a kindly face and an unhurried manner which often caused me to run late. Like Digby, Bert loved nothing better than yarning.

On the mantelpiece in his daughter's sitting room, there stood a creased and faded photograph of Bert and his three brothers standing in front of thirty-two harnessed horses, all ready for a hard day's work dragging irrigation and drainage channels. Bert would often hand me this picture and point to one or other of his brothers while telling his stories. I loved the picture and I told him so.

Since tea with Brunhilde had put me hopelessly behind schedule, I screeched to a halt in Bert's driveway, charged into the house, attended to his needs in record time and was almost out of the door again when he called me back.

'You seem a bit wound up today, lad,' he said in that big slow voice of his. 'Whatever you've got on will wait for a while. Why not stop and catch your breath with us?'

'Really I shouldn't,' I protested.

'Well, I'm pretty clear that you should,' he replied.

'OK then,' I said, and sat down again.

Bert's daughter brought in a tray of tea and Tim Tams and we peacefully nibbled and sipped as Bert chatted on about this and that.

'Feeling better, lad?' he asked when the tray was empty.

'Much, thank you.'

'Good,' he said, and poured me another cup.

'As you know,' he continued in his leisurely manner, 'I haven't always lived round here. For many years I farmed up in the Mallee. That was real farming, that was. We had to do everything. Once you got your block after the war, the first thing you had to do was clear the scrub with a great ball and chain between two teams of oxen. Buggers of things some of them were too,' he said with a chuckle.

'Of course we had no idea what we were doing really and great tracts of land got cleared that should never have been touched. The soil was too light, you see, and as soon as you took the scrub off it the wind would just blow it away. Mind you, sometimes it could work out in your favour.

'I got my first farm just after getting married and, with the help of some friends, cleared four hundred acres for cropping. But just as we were due to seed we were hit by a terrible storm. I think the weather might have got easier in recent years but we certainly got some good'uns back then.

'That night the windstorm took the topsoil clean off of all the cleared area. Every square inch of it. Not so much as a handful left. We thought we were ruined but you'll never believe what happened. A week later another windstorm came in, even worse than the first. And when we got up in the morning we found that the storm had covered the entire farm with topsoil again. Right to the top of the fence posts.

'But the best part was,' continued Bert confidentially, 'it was much better soil than we'd lost the week before.'

When he had finished, I looked at him sideways. I could never tell if he was pulling my leg or not, but with Bert's story and his daughter's tea and Tim Tams inside me, I certainly relaxed for the rest of the afternoon.

Because of the deteriorating state of his chest I began to visit Digby on a regular basis. I became quite an expert at opening the gate and never once let either the chooks out or the dogs in. At Christmas and birthdays it became my habit to take ties, which were always well received, and in winter I always remembered to wear a thickly padded jacket.

At each visit Digby, after we had finished the medical part, would take a long sip from his wineglass and then give me the next episode in his life's story.

Like Bert, Digby was an entertaining storyteller and I came to look forward to these afternoons with great anticipation, even learning to allow plenty of extra time for all the yarns as well as the inevitable tea with Brunhilde.

On one occasion I heard how, when he was twelve, Digby's family decided that they could no longer afford to keep him because of the Great Depression. Accordingly, his uncle took him by horse and cart down to the docks at Liverpool where he was put on a ship to work his passage to Australia with only the clothes he stood up in and twelve and sixpence in his pocket.

When he had arrived in Sydney he landed a job loading wool bales before he had even left the docks.

'They can't have been very big wool bales,' I joked, looking at the size of him.

'They were the normal size, sir, I can assure you,' he replied very seriously. 'And that very same day I joined the Scouts as well. If you turn round, on the wall behind your head is the certificate I received when I became a King's Scout,' he added proudly.

What Digby liked most was telling stories about Tobruk, for he had been one of the rats who had held on there against seemingly overwhelming odds. He told me of the hardships of the siege, of the friendships that had endured even up to the present time, of the death and of the glory. He told me how he was reported for refusing to shoot unarmed prisoners and he showed me his DSO which sat behind a pane of fly-spotted glass in a small wooden frame above the nesting boxes.

Before the war, Digby had taken himself to night school to further his knowledge and to dancing classes to improve his social chances. At night school Digby had found education and at dancing class he had found Brunhilde. Although he barely reached up to her shoulder, the teacher had paired them off together and for Digby it had been love at first sight. Only a year or so later they were married, after which Digby joined Brunhilde on her small farm outside Rushby, exactly where I visited him all those years later.

Brunhilde proved to be a strict housekeeper, a strict wife and a strict mother to the children who started to appear. Nevertheless, I understand that it was a harmonious, if not particularly joyous, home. At least until the war came.

When war was declared, Digby signed up at the first possible opportunity and, after completing his basic training, was posted to North Africa where he came across alcohol for the very first time. Egged on by other members of his company, Digby found that he rather liked the taste of it and on his return to Australia Digby saw no need to stop his indulgence.

There were few things Brunhilde despised more than alcohol. Digby's lack of sobriety caused a huge rift between them and apparently things were never the same again. It wasn't long before Digby started inhabiting the chook house. The move from the marital bed clearly wasn't completely cut and dried, however, since they did manage to produce three more offspring in the years following the start of hostilities.

Although I admit to dragging feet, I always had tea with Brunhilde after each visit with Digby. She was perfectly pleasant to me, but I did feel a bit intimidated by her and, when questioned, often lied to her about my sobriety. I am also ashamed to admit that I even took sides. Whilst on the one hand I really liked Digby, I didn't feel the same about Brunhilde.

Still, no matter how tense I felt coming away from teatime with Brunhilde, I always knew that the next port of call was Bert.

'I hear you've been visiting Digby,' he said one day.

'Yes, I have,' I replied. 'In fact, I've just come on from there.'

'Still in the chook house is he?' Bert smiled. 'Don't worry, I don't expect an answer, I know you can't discuss your patients. I bet you've heard a few stories from Digby, though, and I also bet that you've not heard any from her.'

I nodded silently in agreement.

'Does he call you "sir"?' he chuckled. 'Silly bugger thinks he's still fighting the Germans.

'And does she insist you have tea with her?' he continued. 'And have you lied to her about whether or not you drink alcohol?'

I nodded again a little ashamedly.

'Good. It seems that nothing changes then,' he laughed.

'Now although you can't tell me stories, there is nothing whatsoever that stops me from telling stories to you. So if you've got a few moments and you're interested,' he said settling into his chair, 'I'll tell you a story about Brunhilde.'

'Go right ahead,' I said, and settled back as well.

And just for once, Bert put aside his wonderfully inventive nature and stuck to the straight and narrow of plain historical fact.

'Brunhilde was the only child of an elderly couple who lived on that very same small dairy farm in Prospect Hill Lane you've just come from. They were terribly straight-laced people whose only excitement of the week was attending chapel. Everything was a sin: smoking, drinking, gambling, laughing, even just enjoying yourself.

'Dancing, apparently, was an especial sin, probably worse than drinking. It was a matter of debate round the district for many years as to how Brunhilde was conceived in the first place. But conceived she was.

'Poor Brunhilde had a horrid childhood. She was only ever dressed in plain black or grey and was never allowed any toys or friends. She never had a birthday party and would never have been given a present. Christmas was for chapel and nothing else.

'When she was fourteen she left school and got a job at the glove factory that used to be in that big two-storey building on the corner of the main road. Although she was very shy she liked it well enough and over time made a few friends. She never went out with them of course, always going straight home to help with the dairy. When she had been at the glove factory for a couple of years or so, one of the fellows who worked there took a bit of a shine to her and asked her out to a ball. She was fairly taken with this fellow too, so she agreed.

'They both knew it would be completely useless asking Brunhilde's parents' permission for her to go to the dance, so they decided to do it in secret. The first naughty thing Brunhilde had ever done in her life. The fellow quietly came round to the back of the house and held a ladder up against Brunhilde's window. Once clear of the house, they got into his sulky and away they went. She looked really nice that night and spent the entire evening dancing and laughing. I don't believe she had ever been so happy in her life. The ball went through until around three o'clock. Then, along with everyone else, it was time for her to go and her partner carefully and quietly delivered her home again. Just before she started back up the ladder he gave her a kiss. The first kiss she had ever been given.

'Brunhilde's return went without a hitch and all was quiet for a week or so, but then it all came out. Some gossipy big-mouth let it slip to Brunhilde's father that Brunhilde had been at the ball.

'Apparently he turned purple with fury and went straight to the chapel to seek God's advice on the matter. Then, being the good, kind, pious, Christian man that he had always held himself up to be, he beat Brunhilde with a stick so badly that she couldn't walk for weeks and forbade her mother from bathing the wounds or comforting her in any way.

'When Brunhilde was well enough to stand again, her father summoned her. "I have prayed to God for advice on what punishment He wishes me to administer for your sins," he roared at her. "And in His infinite wisdom He has seen fit to answer my prayers. From this day forth, the old mare shall be sold and you shall do her work around the farm."

'And, unbelievably, that is exactly what happened.

'Word of this spread round the district like wildfire. When I was told the story I just couldn't believe it, but I made an excuse to go up Prospect Hill Lane one day and there, to my amazement, was Brunhilde, bent over, pulling a small plough in the front paddock.

'Her father couldn't sell the horse locally of course, everyone was so disgusted, and I understand that he had to go as far as Lockridge before he could find anyone to take it off his hands.

'And Brunhilde pushed and pulled and heaved and lifted for years until eventually her mother died, followed, mercifully shortly afterwards, by her father.

'It was only after her parents had died that she started going to dancing lessons. She had had such a wonderful time that night at the ball that she was determined to recreate the experience. And it was at the dancing classes, of course, that she met Digby.'

I sat quietly for a while. 'Thanks for that, Bert.' I said, quietly deciding I would try very hard not to put Brunhilde in the wrong again.

Then a thought occurred to me. 'Bert,' I said, 'just how do you know the story in so much detail?'

There was a long pause, then Bert looked up at me. 'Well, who do you think was the bloke with the ladder?'

'That day I saw her in the front paddock, I went over and asked her to come away with me,' he said quietly, 'but she wouldn't even speak to me. I've really had no contact since.'

Three weeks later, on my next visit to Digby, I stopped in the driveway next to the front paddock and tried to imagine a young woman being forced to pull a plough in atonement for her sins. I could barely imagine it happening in the Middle Ages, let alone just fifty-odd years ago.

Digby and Brunhilde are both in heaven now and their eldest daughter lives on the farm these days. She is a healthy woman so I have no reason to go there anymore, but I have often wondered what happened to the tie collection.

The ladder man has gone to the next world too. There was a good turnout to his farewell, of course, and all his old mates had a story to tell about him.

Accompanying Bert on his last journey was a small enamelled badge which said *Welcome to Minyip*. Some years before, on a trip from Lord knows where to somewhere else, I had found myself in Bert's home town and had acquired it for him as a memento of his Mallee days. I had quite forgotten about it until I saw it pinned to his lapel that day.

A week or so after the funeral, unexpectedly, a parcel came addressed to me at the surgery. Inside there was a card which said, *Many thanks for looking after Dad.*

How nice, I thought, then I undid the wrapping and found myself looking at a creased and faded photograph of four young men and thirty-two horses.

6 Hardy

I HAVE BEEN A card-carrying member of the dog fan club all my life. I can't remember the exact moment when I decided to move from membership to ownership but it was probably when I had been at Woongarra for around six months or so.

I had owned dogs before but they had never meant that much to me. My parents had kept a succession of small snappy, yappy, fluffy things during my childhood with which I had completely failed to bond, and Linda and I had had an English setter called Polly. Polly was affectionate but she was also silly and destructive. I enjoyed walking her in the park at the end of the day, but never became really fond of her. I guess she was only ever a child substitute. This may have worked for Linda, but it had never really helped me. The dog's antics certainly didn't help our relationship any either, and when Linda left I was not upset that Polly went with her.

I had thought hard about getting a dog when I first became single, but somehow I hadn't got around to it. But now my life was largely back on an even keel, and I had plenty of space as well.

The time was right. But this was not to be just any dog but a proper farm dog, a real man's dog. Not a bit like my parents' fluffballs. Not a bit like Polly. Maybe a border collie or a kelpie or a heeler.

As soon as I mentioned my thoughts about dog ownership, it seemed to become a kind of community quest to satisfy my needs. I was shown every crossbred litter and stray in the district on the one hand and constantly regaled with dog disaster stories on the other.

Trevor was particularly keen to share his experience regarding a young kelpie he had recently bought. Trevor had made it known locally that he wanted a new working dog for his flock, and a breeder from Heddington phoned shortly after and said that he had exactly what Trevor was looking for. A few days later the dog was duly brought over for a trial. Trevor, very reasonably, asked the breeder to demonstrate the dog's ability by getting her to bring a mob of sheep in from a paddock. The breeder had apparently started proceedings with the traditional 'Way back' and the dog had headed off at high speed.

'Now I'll show you something really special,' the breeder had said to Trevor, and then shouted out: 'I've changed my mind, dog. Split the mob in two!'

The dog had gone straight through the middle of the flock and had split the sheep neatly into two groups. It had all been very impressive and Trevor had bought the dog on the spot. It was only some days later, long after the breeder had disappeared, cheque in hand, that Trevor found out that this was all the dog ever did. Whatever command he gave the dog, he always finished up with two groups of sheep.

'Useless,' said Trevor. 'The dog was completely bloody useless.'

'How much did you pay for her?' I asked.

'A thousand dollars,' he replied.

'Gawd almighty!' I replied, 'That's a lot of money. How come you don't look more upset?'

'Well, there's a very good reason for that,' said Trevor with a chuckle.

'And what might that be?'

'The cheque was as useless as the dog,' he replied and then doubled over with laughter. 'You can have her for nothing if you want. A real bargain,' and he started laughing again.

Undaunted by such tales, I phoned around all the local border collie, kelpie and heeler breeders but there was nothing available, not even a single pup. Apparently it was not the right season. I was offered plenty of other dogs but I decided to stay my hand a little longer. Poodles, Maltesers and even Labradors were not what I was looking for.

Broadening my search, I visited the pound, the local animal welfare kennels and even, one Saturday, a dog refuge in Melbourne. I must have said hello to, patted and stroked fifty to a hundred creatures. Knowing they were all on death row, my heart went out to them all, but I never felt any real chemistry and I never took any of them home with me.

I wasn't sure where to turn next and I was getting rather disheartened, so I put the whole idea on the back burner for a few weeks.

I hadn't thought about the matter for quite some time when I took a call from the welfare kennels during an afternoon surgery.

'Is that Dr Carter?' a voice said.

'It is,' I replied.

'Oh good. Did you get yourself a dog?'

'No, I didn't.'

'Are you still looking for one?'

'Well, yes, as a matter of fact, I am,' I said.

'In that case I may have something of interest to you. There is a young dog over at Stoney Creek who belongs to a couple who are separating. In all the nastiness of their split the dog has been badly neglected. In fact, so badly neglected that the neighbours have contacted the RSPCA. The RSPCA have been out to the property and seen the animal and have said they will prosecute unless a new home is found for the dog immediately. Apparently the couple have agreed. Would you like the telephone number?'

'I would, thanks,' I said and jotted it down.

I put the phone down and turned round to continue the consultation with the pleasant middle-aged woman whose blood pressure I had been taking prior to the call.

'That's a terrific idea,' she said.

'What is?' I asked.

'Getting a dog. Sorry. Couldn't help overhearing the conversation. Yes, we were only discussing you at the CWA meeting the other day and saying how lonely you must be out at the farm. I think it was Mrs Pearson who said you should have a dog. We all thought it was a very good idea. I'll let them know you're getting one. It will put all their minds at rest.'

'Thank you for your concern,' I replied, a little alarmed that my domestic arrangements were the lunchtime topic of conversation at the Country Women's Association.

'What breed and what age?' she asked as she stood to leave.

'Now you come to mention it, I forgot to ask,' I replied.

'It's just that the girls would like to know,' she said. 'Oh well, I guess we'll find out soon enough.'

'I've no doubt whatsoever,' I muttered. 'And probably before I do.'

That night I phoned the number I had been given and, after a long wait, found myself speaking to a most disagreeable-sounding woman with whom I arranged to meet the following day as I had the afternoon off.

I drove over as soon as surgery finished and found the address I had been given. It was a very run-down place. The garden was halfway back to jungle and the front verandah was piled high with boxes and broken gym equipment. I knocked on the door. There was no answer and I was just beginning to think that the trip had been wasted when the next-door neighbour stuck her head over the fence.

'Are you the fellow come about the dog?' she asked.

'I certainly am,' I replied.

'Good. They're not at home, thank the Lord. The dog's round the back, in the shed. I understand that his papers are in an envelope tucked in the door. Poor little bugger. They said you can take him now if you want. I hope you do.'

I drove round to the back of the house and parked next to a very tumbledown excuse for a shed. I got out, picked up the envelope which had fallen on the ground and opened the door.

A wall of stench hit me. In the dim light of the shed I could see a black and white dog chained to the wall. He was missing most of his hair and there were open welts on his back. His front legs were badly bowed and he held his head as if he was listening to me rather than seeing me. The floor was a disgusting mess of excreta and there were flies buzzing everywhere.

Suddenly the dog strained towards me as far as his chain would reach, wagged his tail furiously and, in a very excited way, said, 'Hello.'

My heart melted instantly. 'My dear friend,' I said as I bent forward. 'If you can endure this sort of treatment and still be pleased to see someone, then you are definitely the dog for me.'

I released the chain and helped him onto the front passenger seat of the ute after first covering it with an old wool sack. I jumped in the driver's side, turned to him and said, 'Friendly dog, you have just won first prize in the Woongarra lotto.'

I was so angry, I didn't even bother to go back to the house to leave a message. I just opened the car windows and drove off.

The dog turned to me as if to say: 'Why did you do that?'

'Well, without putting too fine an edge on it, and no offence intended,' I told him, 'you are a bit on the niffy side.'

He turned to me again: 'No offence taken, I assure you,' he said and looked back out of the windscreen again.

About halfway home, we turned a corner to see that a car had run off the road a little way ahead and crumpled a wing against a power pole. I pulled up and went over to see if any medical help was needed.

The only person in the car was Connie, who I had seen several times in the surgery. She was distressed but uninjured. It seemed that a tyre had blown and she'd lost control on the bend. She had already called for a tow truck and was just waiting for it to arrive. In fact, it appeared only a few minutes after I did and her severely wounded vehicle was carted away.

Connie didn't live far out of my way, so I offered to run her home and she accepted gratefully.

She opened the door and said: 'Good God! What on earth is that?'

'Oh, that's my new dog. I've just picked him up,' I replied.

'Really? Well I hope you didn't pay anything for him,' Connie said as she hopped in the back.

'He's a bit on the nose,' she said after a few minutes.

'Sshh!' I replied. 'He's a bit sensitive about that.'

'No I'm not,' the dog said as he looked at me.

'Well, sorry,' said Connie, 'but would you mind if I opened the back windows?'

'Not in the slightest,' said the dog, turning round to look at her.

'So what's his name?' Connie asked through the handkerchief she held over her nose.

'I don't think he has one,' I replied.

'Well, what are you going to call him then?' she persisted.

'I haven't really thought about it.'

'Pick a name that makes him sound like he's your mate,' she said.

'OK,' I said, 'I might just do that,' and I dropped her off at her front gate.

'I bet you never get the smell out of the upholstery,' she called out cheerily as she turned down her driveway.

It was only when I got back to the farm that I realised what extremely poor condition the dog was in. I gave him a small amount of water and a chopped-up sausage left over from my meal the night before and called the vet. Fortunately, Simon was able to fit me in later that same afternoon and I took the dog round to his surgery at the appointed time.

I hadn't thought about how the situation might look to others until I was already sitting down in the waiting room, but that twenty-minute wait for Simon was one of the more uncomfortable of my life. The dog and I were certainly the centre of attention. Everyone in the waiting room spent the entire time staring first at the dog and then at me and then back at the dog again.

'My God, look how the new doctor looks after his dog,' someone whispered on the left.

'Should be reported to the RSPCA,' said their next-door neighbour.

'I must tell the CWA ladies about this,' came a barely audible addition from the right.

And so it went on. I felt like standing up and explaining but in the end I didn't. When it came to my time with Simon, however, I was quick to explain how I had come by the dog so that at least one person didn't think I was completely uncaring and horrible.

Simon checked the dog over carefully and then stood back and scratched his chin. 'His growth is stunted,' he said. 'He has rickets and cataracts in both eyes. He has a dozen septic sores on his body and he is running a temperature. At best I give him a fifty per cent chance of survival. You may have got him for free but it is going to cost you a fortune to get him right.'

'Great,' I said.

I went home loaded with medicines and a large vet's bill and felt a dozen pairs of eyes boring into my back as I left the surgery.

At home I gave the dog some medicine and a bath and made myself a cup of tea. Then I sat down and opened the envelope. To my surprise, he was a pure-bred dog. A Large Munsterlander, no less, a breed I confess I had never heard of before.

'Well, your ancestors might have come from Munster,' I said, 'but you certainly don't look very large to me.'

I looked down at him. 'Why would anyone do something like this?' I wondered. 'And especially if they paid good money for you.'

Later that evening I was sitting by the fire and thinking of dog names. I had gone through the name of every dog I could remember; I had even looked in the back of the dictionary at children's names, but nothing seemed to fit.

I had turned on the CD player for company while I was getting something to eat and was playing some Mozart. I wasn't really listening to the music and was busying myself in the kitchen. I became aware of something against my leg and looked down at the dog, who had pressed himself tight up against me. I reached down to pat him at exactly the same time as he stood up. The result was that I got a very wet kiss across the mouth.

'Yuck,' I said as I wiped my lips. 'I now know exactly how that admiral felt in his dying moments.'

Then suddenly I had an idea. 'I'm not going to change my name to Nelson,' I said to the dog, 'but you can sure be Hardy,' and he beat the floor with his tail in agreement.

From the very beginning of my dog search I had been very clear that I was looking for a farm dog.

'One that works for a living. One that sleeps in a kennel. One that respects the house as the sole domain of humans,' I had said.

'Be soft with them and you will ruin them,' I had added to anyone who wanted to listen. 'Treat them like children and you take away their dog-hood.'

So that night Hardy slept on the end of my bed and enjoyed every minute of it.

Over the weeks and months that followed his arrival at Woongarra, Hardy not only recovered from his rickets and his cataracts but, despite his appalling start, he grew and he grew and he grew. He grew from being a really puny Munsterlander to being a really large one. He grew until he was a fine, strong animal with a lustrous coat and perhaps the best tail ever known to his breed.

He also proved to be a quick learner. Despite my breaking every working-dog rule in the book, he did whatever I wanted him to do round the farm and only ever needed showing once. He was willing, loyal and affectionate, and he got on surprisingly well with the grey cat. They never fought or squabbled, but seemed to have a quiet respect for one another. It was as if they somehow knew they were both graduates from the school of hard knocks.

Apart from fighting with the sawmill dogs, Hardy's favourite things in the whole world were running and swimming, both of which he did extremely well.

As there had been no dog on the property for some time, the foxes had become rather cheeky and had even got into the habit of taking chooks from the yard in broad daylight, before I started locking them up. Hardy changed all that. He caught a fox sneaking around the yard one day. Foxes might be quick but Hardy was quicker and he ran the fox down and killed it, only spoiling an otherwise perfect performance by rubbing himself all over it, causing his exclusion from the bedroom for a couple of nights and the need for repeated swims across the lake.

Over the week or so that followed the fox affair it unfortunately became apparent that, in addition to coating himself with an appalling smell, Hardy had also managed to catch mange from his adversary.

Within a fortnight he looked awful. Half his fur fell out again and he got ghastly looking scabs everywhere. It seemed such a shame seeing how nice his coat had become.

I tried some lotion from the produce store but it didn't do any good, so back we went to Simon. When I entered the waiting room, I swear it was filled with exactly the same people who had been there on my previous visit. To a man and a woman they pulled their animals tight against their legs and stared at us.

'Some people just shouldn't be allowed to look after animals,' someone whispered to their neighbour.

'That poor dog's no better than the last time they came in,' the neighbour replied.

'That tow truck driver was right,' said someone else under their breath. 'He might be OK with humans but he just has no idea at all with animals.'

Fortunately Simon's medication worked and in almost no time at all Hardy was looking his handsome self again.

With Hardy back in full action and with his fox-catching prowess proven, I decided to let the chooks go free range during the day again. 'It'll be healthier for them,' I argued.

'And the eggs will taste better,' my mother agreed.

For a couple of weeks the experiment was a great success. Then one day one of the chooks wasn't there at lock-up. I was very annoyed, to say the least, but didn't take much notice until a week later when the same thing happened. To minimise casualties, I decided to change the plan and only let the chooks out when I was actually there. The following Saturday I was off duty, so I gave the chooks free run of the yard whilst I busied myself with the endless chores which accompany the privilege of living on a farm.

I hadn't seen Hardy for a while but I didn't read anything into that. He had probably found himself a place to lie in the sun, I thought.

I was in the yard fixing one of the water lines when suddenly Hardy, who obviously didn't realise I was there, sauntered round the end of the long shed with one of the chooks in his mouth. As he rounded the corner he looked up, saw me and stopped dead in his tracks.

'Oh, bugger!' he said and gently put the chook down and stroked her with his paw.

Hardy looked at me and smiled ingratiatingly. The chook, who had been silent up to this moment, sensed a window of opportunity and made off as fast as her legs would carry her, swearing loudly all the while.

'Would you believe that she was lost and I was bringing her back?' he asked hopefully.

'No, I bloody well wouldn't,' I replied crossly.

'I didn't think so,' he said as he sunk to the ground.

I grabbed a bit of the black poly-pipe I was working on and whacked him twice, hard, on the haunches. It was the first of only two times I ever hit him.

There were three things about the punishment which really impressed me. The first was that Hardy neither whimpered nor flinched. The second was that he was my friend again thirty seconds later, and the third was that I never lost another chook.

He did catch the occasional wild duck on the lake, however, but I didn't mind that so much as I didn't have to pay for their feed and they didn't lay eggs for me. He would ease himself in the water very quietly and then carefully come up behind them, crocodile style, with just the tip of his nose poking out of the water. I didn't like finding these occasional offerings on the back doormat, but I guess you can't ever expect to completely take the bird out of the bird-dog.

Whilst I regarded Hardy as wonderful in almost every way, even I will admit that he had one serious defect. He was an inveterate thief. Food could simply not be left around when he was in the vicinity, and he was tall enough to lay his head sideways on any table and sweep huge areas clean with his tongue in the blink of an eye. But his speciality was as a sandwich thief. It seemed as if he could pick up the scent of a sandwich from a hundred metres away and, like a shark at a kill, was unstoppable within about three metres.

I warned everyone who worked on the farm, when they first started, about Hardy's little weakness, but then left them to their own defences. It was a regular occurrence for the peace of lunchtime to be shattered by some shearer or contractor shouting: 'That bastard animal!' and waving his fists at a fast disappearing dog with a packet of sandwiches in his mouth.

Hardy loved the farm. He loved every nook and cranny of it. He loved farm work so much that he would jump into the back of the ute whenever I started it up, just to be sure not to miss whatever fun was about to happen.

Once, when my mother's car had gone in for a service, the garage phoned her to say they had found a problem and wished to keep it for a day or so. On that very same day she had been keen to come up and attend a meeting of the local CWA.

I suggested that she catch a train and she could borrow the farm ute for the day while I was at the surgery.

'I've never driven a ute,' she said. 'Is it automatic?'

'No, Mother, it is not automatic.'

'Does it have electric seats and windows?'

'No, Mother, it does not have electric seats or windows.'

'And how will I climb into it in a skirt?' she asked.

'Firstly you hitch it up and secondly I will put a hay bale out for you to use as a step,' I replied.

'You just get worse and worse,' she said, but she accepted the offer.

On the morning of the meeting, my mother successfully climbed the hay bale into the cab, adjusted her seat manually, got the vehicle into gear and went off to her meeting. When she arrived, the association secretary apparently looked at her in a puzzled manner and asked: 'It's lovely to see you, Rose, but why the dog?'

'What dog?' replied my mother.

'The one that just jumped out of the back of your ute and is standing next to you,' came the reply.

I am not sure to this day whether Hardy thought my mother was going off to do a bit of fencing or stock work, or whether he was simply a bit bored at home and fancied meeting the CWA ladies.

As far as I know, it was the first CWA meeting that Hardy ever attended but I understand he behaved perfectly and even, on occasion, contributed to the conversation.

Rodney's back went on him from time to time and occasionally it left him twisted in a painful spasm, unable to move. A short time after Hardy's attendance at the CWA Rodney had a really bad attack.

'Could you please come to the house and see him after the surgery?' his wife had asked. 'This one's a real doozy. I think he might even need an injection.'

Marianne had never abused the system or asked for unnecessary house calls. Therefore, when she said 'doozy', it was safe bet that a 'doozy' is exactly what it was, so I arranged to go round that day.

It was early evening when the afternoon surgery came to an end, and in the fading light I headed round to see Rodney. I attended to him, gave him some anti-doozy medication and took my leave, promising to call back the following day to see how things were going.

I had closed the front door behind me and was halfway across the verandah when the family dog attacked me. He was an ugly-looking brute with mean eyes and a chewed ear. I might not be exactly clear what a 'lurcher' is, but this dog certainly fitted my image of what one would look like.

He timed his run to perfection and I was totally off my guard when he launched himself at me. At the very last moment I saw him coming and held my bag up to deflect him. As he sailed through the air, cheated of my throat as his primary target, he tried to grab the hand holding the bag as a minor prize. Fortunately he failed in even this secondary mission, but his teeth caught the skin and left some painful red stripes across the back of my hand.

The lurcher landed in front of me and immediately turned to attack again. As he sprang, in a desperate bid to save myself, I swung a foot at him. By the chance of a thousand to one against, I connected with him perfectly under the jaw. His forward momentum and the upward movement of my foot created a moment of balletic beauty. The dog did a complete backward somersault high over the verandah railings and landed heavily on the lawn. He got up with a loud yelp and beat a rapid retreat into the gloom, leaving me to complete my departure without further molestation.

As I got in my car, I happened to glance up. The whole family, who had clearly seen the entire episode, were staring at me from the front room window.

The following afternoon I visited Rodney once more. I looked round carefully as I got out of the car, but there was no dog to be seen. I kept a keen vigilance whilst waiting at the front door, but the coast remained clear.

After a few moments, Marianne answered the door and must have seen me looking around. 'Don't worry,' she said. 'I've locked him in the garage. I'm not having you being cruel to him like you were yesterday.'

'But, but . . .' I spluttered.

'I didn't believe it when I was told how cruel you are to your own dog,' she added as she stood aside to let me in, 'but I do now.'

'But, but . . .' I spluttered again.

For weeks afterwards I protested my innocence and outraged sense of injustice to anyone and everyone, but the only response I ever got was: 'I hear you kicked Rodney and Marianne's dog. Pretty upset about it, they are.'

'I remember you kicking my dog years ago,' my mother chipped in when I tried to recruit her sympathy.

'What!' I spluttered at this untruthful indignity, but no one was listening.

Despite public perception, Hardy continued to live a privileged and pampered life at the hands of his besotted owner. He paid for his keep by helping out around the farm and was never backward in getting himself involved in anything that was going, but his real specialty was working sheep.

Whatever the weather, he came out with me to feed them, move them, bring them in and put them out. Best of all he liked running from flank to flank and keeping the mob bunched together.

For a few years I tried my hand at breeding lambs. In late autumn, Hardy would come with me to check on the mothers and their babies. Two years after he arrived there was a particularly wet and cold winter. Merino ewes are very ordinary mothers at the best of times but especially so in poor conditions. If the going gets tough they just up sticks and walk away, leaving defenceless lambs behind them.

There were many abandoned lambs that season. Every day, Hardy and I would check the flock, gathering whatever lambs had been abandoned and taking them up to the house in the back of the Flying Banana. There we would warm them up by the fire in the kitchen and then put them in an old woodshed at the back of the house for bottle rearing. The bottle rearing was far from a hundred per cent successful, but it was a whole lot better than leaving day-old lambs to fend for themselves in the cold and the wet.

One evening I was rather late leaving the surgery and decided it was too dark to check the flock. I would have to get up early and check them the following morning before work. When eventually I got home I found that I had accidentally left the back door open all day. I was about to get cross with myself but found that the kitchen wasn't too cold as, luckily, the fire was still burning.

I closed the door, turned on the light and stood still in amazement. There in front of the dying embers was a row of half-a-dozen wet, cold lambs with Hardy licking them dry.

He turned to me with that funny smile of his and said: 'You were a bit late back so I hope you don't mind but I checked the flock on my own. And lucky I did. This one's a bit weak,' he indicated one of his charges, 'but I think the others should be OK.'

Apart from the time when he stank of fox for a few days and the occasion when he had had fun rolling in a dead kangaroo down by the creek, Hardy slept on the end of my bed every night he was with me. I know it's supposed to be the wrong thing to do, but it never seemed to affect either his willingness or cooperation.

Anyway, he liked it and I liked it too.

7 Phill

THE LEARNING CURVE OF those first years of country practice was steep indeed. There was so much that was new and so much to remember: patients, staff, where everything lived, how to get help and, in particular, how to operate the X-ray machine. I am good at it these days, and even have a certificate to prove it, but it was very new to me back then and every time I used it I found another way of stuffing it up.

It wasn't just the X-rays, though. I struggled with much else besides. The practice was much busier than I had imagined and there was much stitching and plastering and attending accidents, and many a broken night's sleep. I would often reach the end of the week quite exhausted.

And then there were weekends. We didn't hand over to a locum agency. There was no locum agency to hand over to. We did weekends ourselves and they were often busiest of all.

When Felix and Delphine were away, by a process of elimination, Saturday and Sunday belonged to me. In those days there was no administration staff at all rostered on at weekends. For twenty years or so Felix had managed perfectly satisfactorily on his own and I was expected to do exactly the same. I didn't have a Delphine to help me, so, before I found Heather, my parents often came up for the weekend with my mother taking calls for me.

On a Friday evening, as we all headed off to our respective abodes, whoever's turn it was to be on call would be handed the maps of the area, the keys to the surgery, a torch to find the way and a book in which to write the names of patients seen.

'Bell, book and candle' we called it.

Whoever was on call would also be reassured by everyone else that the weekend was going to be a quiet one. It is indeed true that Saturday morning would often pass peacefully enough and the patients would all be very polite and appreciative of not having had to take time off work.

When it was my turn, after finishing Saturday morning surgery I would tidy up my paperwork, touch base with my mother and then go round the corner to a nice little restaurant set up in someone's sitting room. There I would dally over some pleasant homemade food and hope that things stayed quiet.

'I'm famished,' I said to the last patient one Saturday when we had finished the consultation, 'and I'm going out right now for a bite to eat,' I added as I put my coat on.

'Well don't go too far, will you,' she said.

'What do you mean?'

'Well, I presume you know that today is the day of *the* football game.'

'And which football game is that?' I asked a little suspiciously.

'The Demons and the Rednecks.' Then, to make it a bit clearer when I wasn't catching on, she added: 'Dixon's Bridge and Rushby.'

'And?' I queried.

'Local derby,' she said. 'Turns nasty every year.'

'Oh,' I said with a sinking heart.

I did go round the corner for a bite to eat but I had barely touched my focaccia when the owner of the sitting room tapped me on the shoulder and told me my mother had phoned to say I was needed back at the surgery.

I hastily swallowed a couple of scalding mouthfuls and then returned to the practice to find two very muddy players sitting in the waiting room; widely spreading bits of playing field from their boots, holding towels to their heads and glowering at each other. One was dressed in blue whilst the other was dressed in red.

The clash of heads had left them both with sizeable head wounds and an ill-disguised mutual enmity. I cleaned them both up as best as I could and repaired their wounds.

They couldn't let one another alone the whole time and sparred across me as I worked.

'You were ugly enough before, but God, look at you now,' said blue to red.

'Don't bother with any local for him, doc. Where there's no sense there's no feeling,' answered red.

'I'm surprised your eyebrow split seeing how soft your head is,' said blue again.

'Doc, when you've finished stitching up his head, could you do the mouth as well?' red replied.

Heads repaired, I sent them both back to the front lines to rejoin the fray and had just finished cleaning up the treatment room when an ambulance backed up to the surgery door. The doors opened and out came another player whose left forearm did not look at all as nature had intended. He was grey and sweating and obviously in a great deal of pain. The arm was damaged beyond my healing skills so I gave him a shot of painkiller, checked that the arm was safe for the journey, adjusted the splint and dispatched him off to Melbourne.

After the ambulance left I hoped that would be it and I made myself a cup of tea. I was just starting to relax when there was a screech of tyres in the car park. A moment later a very tall man with a blue demon on his chest came into the waiting room cradling his arm.

'Hi, doc,' he called through to me, 'can you have a gander at my shoulder? I took a mark and got smacked.'

It didn't take long to check him out and it wasn't a difficult diagnosis.

'I think it is dislocated,' I said knowledgeably.

'I *know* it's bloody dislocated,' he replied, 'I've done it before. What I'm here for is for you to put it back in again.'

'We'd better just take an X-ray first,' I said, 'to make sure there's nothing broken,' but really wanting to delay things a bit whilst I revised how to reduce a shoulder.

'Be buggered with a picture, doc. Dr Turnbull doesn't fart around like that. Just stick it back in for me, there's a good lad. It's smarting a bit.'

OK,' I replied, 'not a problem. Now would you like something for the pain?'

'Nah, be buggered,' he said, 'just get on with it.'

So I pretended I needed something from the consulting room, then closed the door, opened my orthopaedics book at the right chapter and quickly reminded myself how to reduce a shoulder. Then, full of new confidence, I simply sauntered back and put it in as if it was the sort of thing I did every day.

He was really muscle-bound and there was certainly a lot of huffing and puffing on my part before anything happened. Then, suddenly, just like it said in the book, there was a most satisfying clunk and the shoulder popped back in.

'That's grouse, doc. Thanks a lot,' he said with a shake of the head.

'But now I'd like to take that picture just to make sure that there really are no breaks,' I insisted.

I popped the arm in a sling and sat him down by the X-ray room. I had just turned the machine on to warm it up when I heard the waiting room door open again.

'Do you mind waiting a little? I just want to see who's come in,' I said and left him to it.

The new arrival was a slightly built man in his early fifties. He was wearing neither red nor blue. I beckoned him to come into the surgery and he carefully tiptoed across the waiting room, studiously avoiding the worst of the dirt on the carpet.

'I see we've had some muddied fools in, have we?' he asked rhetorically.

He shook my right hand with his left and sat down.

'Phill White,' he introduced himself. 'Phill with two "Ls", the second one is silent. White, as in pure.'

He looked at me with a great big smile. 'Oohh! Aren't you gorgeous,' he said. 'I heard you were good-looking but not this good-looking.'

'And I love bald,' he added as he screwed up his nose.

'Exactly how can I help you, Mr White?' I said, feeling my space had been invaded a little.

'Please, please, please, please!' he protested.

'Please what?'

'Please call me Phill. "Mr White" makes me sound so old. Makes me sound like my father.'

'OK, Phil.'

'Phill,' he corrected.

'Sorry, Phill. Exactly how can I help you?'

'Well, you see, I have injured my bod. I have done myself a mischief and I hope that you have the skills to return me to my former glory. I am a waiter and I have to work tonight.'

'And what is the injury?' I asked. 'What is the mischief?'

'Roland, my better half, is a wonderful man in many ways but he is not domesticated. Don't get me wrong, I am not saying he is lazy. He is always happy to walk the whippets, but you know what men are. There are just some things about which he digs his little heels in and won't budge.'

'So who do you think has to carry all, and I do mean all, of the firewood in? *Moi*. Well, the last load of wood wasn't split very well and I said to the fellow: "This wood's not split very well." And do you know what he said? He said: "I agree. It's not very well split, is it." Well! But he didn't do anything about it.

'So today I lifted a piece which was far too heavy for me, I knew it at the time and I said to myself: "This is far too heavy for you, Phill." But I was stubborn and I did not listen to myself, and I have gone and hurt my wrist. I heard a crack and now it has gone all limp,' and he held out his right arm perfectly horizontally with the wrist bent down and the fingers dangling.

Then he jiggled the hand and made it wobble. 'See.'

I concentrated on being as serious as possible. I examined the wrist carefully, but I couldn't find a lot wrong with it.

'I can't find a lot wrong with it,' I said, 'but perhaps we'd better do an X-ray just to be on the safe side.'

We walked down to the corridor and I sat Phill next to the man with the devil on his chest.

I was about to start taking pictures when the ambulance arrived yet again with another casualty.

I took a deep breath and apologised to both men about the further delay. I promised I would return as soon as possible and went to check the most recent arrival.

The most recent arrival's right ankle was a horrible mess. It clearly needed specialist care so I gave him something to soothe the journey, commiserated with the driver about a second trip to Melbourne and sped them on their way.

When I returned, Phill was sitting on his own.

'Where did the big fellow go?' I asked him.

'I have no idea,' he replied. 'I was just being my usual friendly self and showing him my wrist when he suddenly remembered something he had to do and left at the speed of a thousand gazelle.'

I did not see the big boy again that day, or indeed for some while, but I have seen him since and am delighted to report that his arm seems to work just fine, despite not having been X-rayed.

'Who on earth was that fellow who came and sat next to me that day?' he asked. 'And what the hell are whip pits?'

Eventually that Saturday afternoon surgery came to an end. Somewhere over in the park a whistle blew to indicate the end of hostilities and the flow of casualties dried up. I did the best I could with the carpet in the waiting room and then tottered off home to see my parents and start preparing the meal I had planned for them.

'Thank God that's over,' I said to my mother, 'at least for this year.'

I spiked the sausages, peeled the potatoes and was checking that I had enough beans when the phone rang.

''Ave you got a bag needle?' a voice asked down the line.

I had absolutely no idea what a bag needle was and I said so.

'Jack's come out of the pub after the game,' the voice continued, 'and was on his way home when the bloody pavement rose up, right in front of his eyes, and smacked him square in the face. Made a bit of a mess. You better come round with a bag needle.'

The voice was very slurred and it was only with great difficulty that I managed to write down an address that made sense. I arrived back in Dixon's Bridge fifteen minutes later, where the address turned out to be one of the old Victorian weatherboard houses down by the bowling club. It was in a very poor state indeed.

A verandah, which ran the full width of the house, was filled from floor to roof with empty beer bottles which completely blocked out the windows but had been formed into a surprisingly intricate archway around the front door. It may well have been those bottles that were keeping the place up, I thought as I approached. I rang the bell and, after a short wait, was admitted into the third messiest and dirtiest home I had ever visited.

The occupants comprised three old soldiers, all ex-comrades in arms, and a fox terrier called Digger. The old soldiers were all holding beer bottles.

Jack, who had made contact with the rising pavement, was easy to identify and I set about stitching him up.

'So what's the celebration?' I asked as I worked away, trying to make myself heard over the men's singing.

'We won,' they all cheered, 'just for once we beat those bloody Rednecks.'

'I can see that it's all very exciting, but could you please keep still, Jack, at least until I've finished?' I pleaded repeatedly.

Despite working on a constantly moving target, I eventually got the job done. I stood up and looked around. The four-legged member of the household seemed to be in good shape but the other three looked awful. They were grubby and dishevelled and their clothes were in rags. They were also on the nose. The years of dedicated effort they had put into smoking, drinking, and personal neglect had certainly borne fruit.

On the way out of the house I suddenly remembered something that had puzzled me. 'By the way,' I asked, 'what *is* a bag needle?'

'It's a needle you use to sew bags up with, of course.'

How silly of me, I thought, why hadn't I thought of that?

To my surprise, when I inspected Jack's head a week or so later, the wound had healed very well. To my further surprise, all three of the diggers were still going strong some years later.

'Why are you so surprised?' Felix replied to my frequent expressions of astonishment. 'They've all been well smoked and then pickled in alcohol.'

The only one who didn't make the grade was the dog who was bitten by a copperhead under the house the following Christmas.

'Sorry to have been so long,' I said that night when I finally got back home, and started to put the food on.

'Let's not be bothered cooking now,' my mother replied. 'Is there anywhere we can go out to eat?'

I popped the sausages back in the fridge, put the beans in the pantry and confirmed that, luckily, there was a table available at Kaminsky's.

Kaminsky's, just down the road from the surgery, was not much to look at from the outside. It wasn't much to look at from the inside either, really, but it had a good atmosphere and country-sized meals.

We were met at the door by the manager who showed us to our seats. The waiter who attended us shortly after was wearing an extraordinary jacket and seemed to have a bowl of fruit on his head. His wrist was heavily bandaged.

'Hello Phill,' I said.

He pretended to have only just recognised me, gave my father an extravagant 'Hello' and fussed over my mother the whole evening.

Somewhere between the entree and the main course Phill leaned over my mother's shoulder and said: 'You have a lovely boy, Mrs Carter.'

'Yes, I know,' she replied, looking a little taken aback.

'And it's wonderful to see a boy enjoying his mother's company,' Phill added.

'Well, we've always got on really well,' my mother replied. 'It's just such a pity that he lives here now and we have to go back to Melbourne.'

'Just like my legs,' said Phill with a sigh.

'What on earth do you mean?' asked my mother.

'Well, you and he,' he said in clarification. 'You're just like my legs.'

'I'm sorry, I still don't understand,' she replied.

'My legs are the very best of friends, Mrs Carter,' he explained, 'but we all know that there are times when even the best of friends must part.'

I laughed out loud, then caught sight of my mother's startled expression and tried to wipe the smile from my face.

'Is there something you need to tell us, son?' asked my father.

'No, there isn't,' I said emphatically.

'Because, if there is,' he continued, 'it wouldn't be a problem for us.'

'Don't be bloody daft,' I replied.

When we got home we had a cup of tea before going to bed.

'What was that bizarre outfit that waiter was wearing tonight?' my mother asked.

'I have absolutely no idea,' I said, and went off to bed.

Over the years, I have become firm friends with both Phill and Roland and have even become chummy with all the whippets. Roland is a lovely, talented man who completely renovated all my curtains. It was a big job, and apart from falling off his ladder on one occasion, the job went off without a hitch. I was surprised that he fell off the ladder, actually, for he had recently spent quite some time practising balancing on the top of one.

Phill had gone for an audition with the local amateur thespians for a part in an upcoming production of *Noises Off*.

When I saw Phill in the surgery shortly afterwards I asked him how it had all gone.

'Wonderfully,' he replied. 'And not only did I get a part,' he smiled, 'but Roland has been cast as the burglar, too.'

It had been very foggy on the night of the auditions and since Phill apparently hated driving when it was like that, Roland had been roped in as chauffeur. Roland had been quietly reading the paper waiting for Phill to finish when the director realised they were a male role short, and the rest of it can be imagined.

I took my mother to the play and what particularly caught my eye was how good Roland was with his ladder work.

'And that's not all,' Phill would often say of Roland. 'He also cuts a fine swathe.' And for all I know he is right.

Whenever there is a dinner party or get-together at the farm I always ring Phill to see if he is able to help. I love it when he can, for he is funny and entertaining and really good at what he does. He makes parties far more memorable than I ever could.

And when I call to check his availability he only ever imposes one condition, which I am always happy to accommodate: that he be allowed to wear his Carmen Miranda outfit.

8 Clayton

THE FINAL RESTING PLACE for Clayton, or at least his outer covering, is the middle of the sitting room floor. He looks handsome there and attracts many favourable comments from visitors. On cold winter mornings I am always careful to walk on him, rather than on the surrounding slate which seems to suck the very life out of you through the soles of your feet. The rest of Clayton, of course, finished up in the freezer and became the excuse for many noisy and alcoholic dinner parties. Occasionally I would excite the more squeamish guests by putting his ear tag next to their plate.

Towards the end of a dinner party I would tap a glass and propose a toast. Phill would solemnly charge everyone's glasses and all would rise and join me in: 'Clayton!'

Clayton came into my life courtesy of Fred who, against very considerable odds, made it to his ninetieth birthday. And not only made it, but surprisingly made it with both his feet still attached to the rest of him. In honour of my contribution to helping Fred achieve this significant milestone, complete with feet, Ida invited me to his birthday party.

Fred and Ida lived in quite a beautiful place on the top of the range, which Fred inherited from his father. It is a long way out of Rushby but the views alone are worth the drive, albeit a bumpy one. The road that winds its way up Mt Miranda and across the pass is still not sealed and is often in poor condition.

Ida and Fred had been married for only ten years or so. Fred's first wife had died of cancer and Fred had spent many years on his own. There had come a time when Fred had needed some operation or other and, because his diabetes flared up after the surgery, he wasn't well enough to go home afterwards. Ida was the matron of the institute where Fred was sent to recover.

Fred liked Ida from the start, but I have often wondered whether it was love at first sight for Ida. She was very much the old-school style of hospital matron and didn't seem at all the type to go wobbly at the knees or experience fireworks going off. Nevertheless, Ida was obviously very fond of Fred and she certainly looked after him with kindness, albeit with a rigid attention to detail that drove Fred barmy. In all the times I went there, I never visited the house once without being shown a detailed chart of Fred's bodily functions.

The first time I met Fred I actually did think that his feet would have to come off. Luckily, in the end, he only lost a couple of toes. He hobbled into the surgery one morning and showed me a matching pair of bright red, swollen feet possessing toes which ranged from dusky red to jet black.

A stint in the Lockridge hospital on intravenous antibiotics, and some fire and brimstone lectures from me about the potentially disastrous approach he was taking to the management of his diabetes, improved things dramatically. Only the black bits fell off and the rest came back to life again.

Ida took it upon herself from that time on to be the guardian of Fred's toes and sugar levels. Even then it wasn't all smooth sailing and from time to time Fred's feet got out of hand again, as it were. Inevitably, the resulting infection would destabilise his diabetes and inevitably he would become confused.

I well remember the occasion when he insisted on wearing a cushion on his head, thinking it was the nicest hat he had ever seen, and also when he pulled the cuckoo clock off the wall in the kitchen and put it in a bucket of water to douse the evil spirit inside. On reflection, he might have been right about that clock—the way it sounded the hour was tiresome in the extreme.

Apart from his medical condition, Ida and Fred shared two other things in common: the literalness of their religious views and their joy in sharing their home with other creatures. A magpie with an extraordinarily large vocabulary lived in the sunroom; a large cage of canaries graced the centre of the kitchen table, and cats slept on every chair. In addition, the back door opened straight into the chook run; there were always hand-reared calves in the garden, and it was impossible to get out of your car without being mobbed by a pack of assorted dogs.

As Fred became more frail, and because of the complicated nature of his problems, I often went to visit him rather than have him visit me. He didn't really fit into the normal visiting round, because of his remoteness, so I usually made a special expedition. Ida would often have lunch ready for me on my arrival and I never left without a carton of eggs and an armful of homemade preserves and butter.

Not once did I ever hear Fred grumble about his medical condition. The only comment he ever made was: 'I was born in this bed, and I wish to die in it.' And eventually his wish was granted.

The Saturday of his birthday party was perfect. It was one of those really hot days where even the blue of the sky seems to have been bleached away by the sunlight. The house was packed and every room had been filled with tables and chairs. There were friends and relatives and well-wishers as far as the eye could see. I waved to many familiar faces and was ushered to my seat at the end of the table between Father Frank and a life-sized, blue-cloaked plaster Virgin Mary. She had stood in the corner of the dining room for at least as long as I had been visiting, and she smiled sweetly at us all while we ate. Across the table were Sisters Margaret and Bernadette from the primary school.

I knew them well. Our paths often crossed for all sorts of reasons and, although my Sunday attendance card was unfailingly blank, I got along famously with all of them. I can't remember much about the conversation except that we seemed to spend most of the time laughing.

'I have no idea why I was put on this table,' I said during a lull in the merriment. 'I don't believe a single word any of you lot say.'

'Perhaps that is precisely the reason why,' replied Frank with mock solemnity and that wonderful twinkle in his eye.

'Are you trying to frighten me?' I asked, and we all laughed again.

'It's lovely that you could be here, Paul' said Ida, leaning over my shoulder.

'Yep,' I replied, 'and unlike Sister Margaret and Sister Bernadette here, I'm off duty for the rest of the weekend.'

'Not on call at all?' queried Sister Bernadette.

'Nope,' I replied emphatically. 'It's Felix's turn. And the best part is,' I continued, 'that nobody, barring present company, even knows that I am here.'

As I finished speaking, the phone rang and Hettie, a friend of Ida's, tapped me on the shoulder and said into my ear: 'Heather's on the phone. Can she speak to you urgently, please?'

'But I'm not on duty,' I protested as I got out of my seat. 'And how did she know I was here?'

Hettie shrugged her shoulders, 'I've no idea, but she did say "urgently".'

There was no point in arguing with the messenger so I rather reluctantly went to the phone.

'Yes, Heather?' I asked a little petulantly.

'The surgery, now! Please!' she said. 'Felix needs you. Straight away.'

I left immediately.

I have done the journey from Fred's to the surgery on many occasions and often kept note of the time I took. That Saturday I cut the previous record by a very long way.

I arrived to find Felix on the floor of the waiting room, performing resuscitation on a small child who had been brought in by neighbours. Apparently he had been staying with them whilst his parents were out shopping. He had fallen off the verandah at the back of their house whilst trying to walk along the hand rail and had suffered severe head injuries when he landed in the rockery.

Felix looked up and nodded me a quick 'thank you' as I came in. He looked exhausted so I took over the CPR while he had a break and got a line up.

As I was doing the pushes I suddenly recognised the child.

'This is Nicholas, isn't it?' I asked.

Felix nodded.

Nicholas had spent a day at the farm only the week before. He had come up with his mum who was delivering gravel. She had gone back to get another load and he had stayed on to play with Hardy. He had had a great time throwing sticks into the lake and cheering Hardy when he got them. It had been very useful for me too for Hardy had smelled a whole lot better afterwards.

Sadly, despite all our efforts and the arrival of the paediatric team by helicopter, we weren't able to save him. Nicholas put up a terrific fight for around an hour and a half, but just five minutes before his parents arrived, the battle was lost.

Nicholas's parents were ripped apart by their grief. I would like to say that we comforted them but we were all so overwhelmed with our own emotions that I wasn't totally sure who was supporting whom. The waiting room looked like a war zone. There was equipment scattered everywhere and there was Nicholas lying peacefully in the middle. Felix looked utterly drained, as did the paediatric team, whilst Heather and Lesley, the clinic nurse, who had arrived just a few minutes after me, were weeping openly. It was a long time before anybody left and even later before we had finished tidying up.

Much later, back at Felix's house, Delphine poured us a Scotch each.

'I think I'm getting too old for this,' Felix said.

'How can anyone make any meaning out of this,' I asked, 'when the one who's celebrating a birthday is ninety and the one who won't have any more is eight?'

'Over the years,' Felix replied, 'I have found it best just not to think about it all,' and he drained the last of his whisky and poured himself a second one.

After I left Felix's, I went round to Heather's place for a meal.

'You'll probably not feel like cooking for yourself tonight, pet,' she said, 'so I thought I would invite you round. And besides, Robbie's getting too fat and it would be good for him to divide the meal into three rather than just two.'

I murmured my thanks and got stuck into the pie. I was just finishing my meal when a thought occurred to me.

'Heather?' I asked. 'How on earth did you know where to find me?'

'Och, that was easy. Eve happened to see you driving up the Mt Miranda road and phoned to tell me. I knew it was Fred's party today because we all prayed for him at mass last week, so it wasn't hard to put two and two together.'

'But why on earth would Eve have phoned you?' I asked in surprise.

'It happens all the time. Didn't you know? People assume that I want to know where you are all the time, so they phone in and tell me.'

'My sainted aunt!' I exclaimed. 'I had better never be where I'm not supposed to be, had I?'

'Definitely not, doctor,' said Rob with a big grin.

When I got home that night I patted Hardy on the head and told him that he had lost a mate that day.

'Oh! Who was that?' he asked.

'Nicholas.'

'Oh, how sad,' he said, then after a short pause he added, 'he was a really good stick thrower.'

I made a fire, poured myself a drink, put *Rigoletto* on the CD player, selected the quartet and turned the volume up as loud as it would go.

It was a week or two later that I next visited Fred. He was obviously buoyed up by the party. He was clinically very stable and I made no changes to his medication. I was about to leave when Fred said: 'Ida has something to say.'

'Sorry you had to leave the other day. I heard what happened,' said Ida. 'Poor little lad.'

'Now, you've been so good to Fred,' she continued, 'that we would like to give you a present, something really special, as a thank you.'

I felt a bit embarrassed and indicated that this was quite unnecessary and that they had already given me lots of things. I also added that I looked after Fred because I saw it as a privilege to do so.

When I had finished there was a pause and then Fred said: 'Nevertheless we have decided that we would like to give you a calf to grow up for your freezer.'

'It is already organised,' said Ida before I could demur, 'and we would like you to pick it up next Saturday.'

'Well thank you and how wonderful,' I said, feeling a little overwhelmed. 'Next Saturday will be fine.'

I borrowed a float from Meaghan, who is into horses, and appeared early next Saturday at Ida and Fred's.

'Oh, no. Sorry, I didn't explain. No, the beast isn't here,' explained Ida. 'It's at my cousin's place,' and she gave me directions for a farm around a hundred kilometres away.

I was a little surprised, but happily set off and eventually found the place. The cousin lived on a dairy farm and a nice-looking little Friesian-cross steer, calling loudly to his mum, was penned up by the driveway, all ready for me. With the help of the cousin, it took just a few moments to load the steer onto the float and then I headed off home again.

'Ida and Fred,' I said when I phoned them that evening. 'Many, many thanks. He's a lovely present and I really appreciate what you've done.'

The calf settled in well. I liked having him around and I especially liked chucking a biscuit of lucerne into the back of the Flying Banana and taking it out to him.

For a week or so he remained nameless. I just couldn't think of anything that seemed to suit him. Then a couple of weeks later, after getting home from work, I was idly going through the mail whilst thinking whether to have beans on toast or Chicken Tonight. I came across a letter in a hand I did not recognise, so I opened it and found a fairly sizeable bill from someone whose name I didn't at first recognise. Initially I thought it was a mistake, but suddenly I realised that it was a bill for the calf from Ida's cousin.

'The cheeky bugger,' I said. 'I'll lay odds that Ida and Fred know nothing about this,' and got out the cheque book.

Later that evening, when I had finished my beans and was clearing away, it suddenly came to me. In a split second I knew exactly what the calf's name should be.

Some years before, some bright spark had had the idea of launching non-alcoholic whisky and marketed it as the drink you're having when you're not having a drink. It always seemed to me a contradiction in terms, since the whole point of whisky, as I understand it, is that it *is* alcoholic. I have no idea whether the drink took the world by storm or not, but the name has passed into the Australian lexicon for everyday use.

So Clayton he became: the present you're having when you're not having a present.

He was a great success and he was ever the gentleman. He never dug holes and he never pushed through fences. He ate whatever I gave him and he grew and he grew until he was huge. He lived with me for almost two years and became so tame that I would move him from paddock to paddock leading him by nothing other than an ear.

When his time was up, he went the perfect way. He had absolutely no idea what was coming. It was simply blue sky and knee-high grasses one moment and nothing the next. Depending, of course, on what you believe.

He tasted good too.

I had never got a hide tanned before and didn't realise how long the process would take. I delivered the hide to the tannery and then, over the following weeks, forgot all about it.

'Your rug is ready,' Madge said to me one day at the surgery.

'What rug?' I asked. 'Ah!' I added on enlightenment. 'That rug. I'll pop over on the weekend and pick it up.'

So late on a summery Saturday morning, after a round trip to the tannery, I arrived home with my prize and laid it on the floor. It still had a bit of the tannery smell, so I opened all the French doors, made some tea and went out into the garden.

I was sitting by the lake, enjoying the sunshine, when Hardy dropped a stick at my feet. I threw it in for him and watched him swim out and retrieve it. I threw it a couple more times but then got bored and wouldn't throw it any more.

'You're not as good as Nicholas,' Hardy said.

'Thanks, Hardy,' I replied. 'Funnily enough I was just thinking about him. I think about him often,' I continued, 'but mostly when we're by the lake.'

'Not a bad place for memories to finish up,' Hardy added thoughtfully.

'Not a bad place at all,' I agreed, and we turned back towards the house.

When I came in to admire the latest addition to the furnishings there was a grey cat without a tail lying on his back on the rug.

'Oh hello,' I said, 'so you've finally decided to come indoors, have you?'

The cat rolled onto his side and looked at me. 'Yes, I have,' he said after a long pause. 'But I want it clearly understood that it is on three conditions.'

'And what might those be?' I asked a little snootily.

'Firstly, you recognise my right to sit nearest the fire in winter,' he said. 'Secondly, you always put my food where that dog can't reach it and, thirdly, you never ask anything of me but cupboard love.'

'Hang on a minute,' I said, 'until now you've stayed out in the sheds without even so much as a hello.' I glanced at Hardy, who was standing beside me taking all this in. I put a hand on his head. 'This is our house, you know.'

'Not anymore,' the cat said authoritatively.

When it comes to it I can brawl like a street fighter but, like Trevor's dogs before me, I can also recognise unwinnable battles. I was about to tiptoe out and leave him sprawled on the rug but instead I turned and said: 'By the way, I didn't catch your name.'

He looked up and yawned. 'Livingstone,' he said.

'Well, hello then, Livingstone,' I replied.

9 Edwin

TEDDY FELL THROUGH HIS glass-topped coffee table around two in the morning and he and I met at the surgery half an hour later. Teddy, being a really big chap, not only completely demolished the table but made quite a mess of himself as well. A large gash was visible through his open pyjama jacket and the top of his dressing gown was soaked in blood. Despite Teddy's impressive appearance, exactly what had happened to him was surprisingly difficult to elucidate, for his speech was slurred and he was having difficulty standing up. With the ease of much practice, I manoeuvred him onto an examination couch in the treatment room and started to get my gear ready. Michael, who had brought him in, sat fuming in the corner.

'So how did it happen?' I asked as I started to pick pieces of glass out of the wound.

'I tripped over the cat,' said Teddy in a thick voice.

'You don't have a cat,' interjected Michael.

'All right, all right,' said Teddy, 'I was going for the paper.'

'At two o'clock in the morning?' said Michael. 'I don't think so.'

'I was—'

'Teddy,' said Michael sternly, 'you fell into the coffee table for one reason and for one reason only, which you know full well.'

'Yes, I tripped over your slippers,' retorted Teddy.

'What a disgusting idea, I have never worn slippers in my life,' came the reply.

As I cleaned and stitched, the bickering went on.

Teddy had only moved into the area a short while before and, apart from a prescription or two for sleeping tablets, I had hardly seen the man. I knew of both Teddy and Michael by reputation, of course, as they and their city restaurant had featured in just about every epicurean magazine and good food guide over the last few years. And what had made them an especially winning combination, according to the write-ups, was their teamwork. Michael had looked after the kitchen and Teddy the cellar.

I had, on one occasion, even dined at Capers with friends. It had been a memorable evening with great ambience, good company, and food and drink to die for. We had all declared that Capers was well worthy of whatever hats, stars or Amex awards had been showered upon it over the years.

'So, how's the restaurant?' I asked brightly, partly to stop the quarrelling but mainly to show off what little society knowledge I possessed.

For a few seconds complete silence fell across the room and I looked up from my work.

'Disaster,' said Teddy, tossing his head.

'Absolute disaster,' said Michael quietly.

'Absolute *fucking* disaster,' added Teddy, as if the matter hadn't been quite clarified.

Then the flood gates opened. Whilst I knuckled down to the job in hand, I was given the goods, the whole goods and nothing but the goods. Fifteen minutes later I had a tray full of glass shards and enough background information for a complete new TV series by Gordon Ramsay.

Apparently the building in which the restaurant was located had changed hands and the new owners had decided not to renew the lease. Another site, not nearly as nice, had been hurriedly found, but then the landlords doubled the agreed rent, the chef left to open up his own place, staff cheated on them, customers deserted and Michael and Teddy finished up losing everything. The upshot was that Capers closed and the boys parted company. Michael stayed in town but Teddy decided to leave Toorak and lick his wounds in the country for a while. It seemed that Teddy had managed to salvage just enough money for a deposit on the pretty little weatherboard cottage that sat on the rise above Three Chain Creek. Michael occasionally came up from town to visit, but never stayed for long. Teddy had initially coped with the Capers collapse and the transition to the country had gone reasonably well, but on the evening in question, in response to yet another demand from some solicitor or other for unpaid fees, Teddy had taken to the cellar again.

'Glad I asked then,' I said with a wry smile as I finished off my needlework. I dressed the wound, cleared away all the debris, organised for Teddy to come back the following day, turned out all the lights and then locked the surgery behind me.

By the following week, the wound had healed well and the stitches were ready to be removed. When the last one had been taken out and a clean dressing applied, I decided it was time for the big health lecture. I was about to launch into my usual spiel when Teddy held up his hand.

'I know, I know, I know,' he said.

'What do you know?' I asked.

Teddy sighed and rolled his eyes. 'Stop smoking, stop drinking, lose weight, all pleasure is forbidden,' he said in a tired voice. 'It's all you medicos can ever think to say.'

'Yes,' I agreed, 'and what is more, we are paid to say it. Teddy, you're a medical volcano waiting to blow, and when you do finally explode, your surviving loved ones will probably get some smart lawyer to sue me for not having pointed out this screamingly obvious probability clearly enough to you. Teddy, you are the medical equivalent of the Hindenburg about to land in New Jersey. At the very least, I ask you to bear in mind that unless you change direction, then you're going to end up exactly where you're going.'

'Wow,' he said, nodding his head as he gazed at the floor. 'Some speech! The bit about going was sensational.'

'Unfortunately that bit isn't mine,' I admitted. 'I read it on a church noticeboard.'

There was silence for a few moments, and then he looked up at me.

'OK, OK, OK,' he said, 'from this moment on I swear that nothing shall pass my lips but bread and water.' And then he added: 'And just to please you, I'll cut out the bread.'

'Good,' I said brightly.

'Now on to more important things,' he continued as if he had not heard a word I had said. 'Would you like to come to dinner one evening?'

'Does the sun set in the west?' I asked, and we fixed a date there and then.

On the evening of the dinner I spent quite some time pondering what to take as a house present. Not wine, I decided, for Teddy was an expert and I didn't want to make an idiot of myself. Then I thought: 'If you live on a farm then you can't go wrong sticking to home-grown produce.' So that's what I did.

I had known the cottage previously but hadn't seen it since Teddy had moved in. As I got out of the car, I was impressed with the changes he had effected in such a short time. The path leading to the front door had gone from dull and dusty to an enchanting little walk through lavender bushes, and the front of the house had been transformed from a drab facade to a riot of colours and hanging baskets.

But the real magic was inside—magic because it was the exact opposite to my house. The furniture was just so; the decorations all seemed to have a purpose; the kitchen pulsated with vivid yellow, while the dining room was a hot stippled pink. It all looked so elegant and comfortable. And everything matched.

'Bon giorno,' he smiled at me in greeting.

'Hi,' I said and handed him some eggs in an old ice-cream container and a frozen haunch of venison. It crossed my mind, as I looked around, that the eggs might have looked better on a bed of straw in a wicker basket and that the venison could have been wrapped in hand-dyed calico, but the presents were accepted with much enthusiasm nevertheless.

'I have just the recipe for this,' said Teddy, weighing the haunch in his hand.

I had spent the previous few years in a country community where conversation, inevitably, was largely dominated by the raw necessities of life. Where silence was widely equated with strength. I had wondered as I set out that evening whether I might be out of practice with small talk, but I needn't have worried. From the moment we met there was not so much as a moment's break in the conversation. I don't think that either of us drew breath until well after midnight.

This was no gradually getting to know one another, but an instant blossoming of friendship—as if the friendship had been quietly sitting around for ages just waiting for this evening to happen. Teddy was amusing and well read and thoughtful. I felt as if I had known him all my life.

I didn't get home until very late but, even so, I didn't go straight to bed. I looked round at all the bricks and beams and animal skins and chunky mismatched furniture that was my home and it all suddenly looked so dull. There was no flair to it at all. Everything shouted 'Cro-Magnon!' This had never been an issue before, of course, but I couldn't get it out of my head how nice Teddy's place had looked.

I did try a few touchy-feely changes over the weeks that followed, but I just don't have what it takes. Teddy had hung a silk scarf on a wall hook and it looked sensational. I did the same thing and it looked as if someone had accidentally left an old rag hanging on a nail. Teddy had placed his furniture at exciting angles to one another and made magical transformations. I did the same thing and then banged into it repeatedly until I moved it back again. The only thing I ever did that really worked, and gained universal praise, was moving the garden furniture back out into the garden and buying some proper indoor stuff. So that, despite all my efforts, the house, beautiful though it was on the outside, remained a monument to unbridled nineteen-eighties masculinity on the inside. And it stayed that way until much later when Helen took it under her wing and transformed it with her genius for beauty and elegance.

There followed, over the succeeding months, a series of marvellous evenings at Teddy's house. The two of us would eat and drink and laugh and then sit in front of the fire and talk of people and books and music and opera. We also talked about ourselves.

I learned, to my surprise, that Teddy had spent many years in the army, had risen to the rank of full colonel and had even been decorated in Vietnam. It had only been at the end of his military career that he had met Michael and opened Capers.

I came to know Teddy as an intelligent, creative, principled and amusing man who hated humbug and mediocrity. He said he had enjoyed his rich life of overseas postings but was now glad to be in retirement. His sole regret was that he had been forced by army regulations into a complicit secrecy about his sexuality during the whole of his military career. He also said he had come to see losing Capers as simply an opportunity to move on and do different things in life, and that the years of living with Michael had simultaneously driven him mad and kept him sane.

Through Teddy being so open, it felt right to talk about myself. In his company, I felt as if a neglected part of me was being raised up, the part that had sunk like an old treasure galleon to the floor of the ocean. As we sat in the dark sipping Tokay by the fire, I gradually learned to tell stories about myself, of my undergraduate days in London, of my hospital years, of meeting Linda, of the baby, of the move to Australia and of the parting.

Maybe it was the alcohol or maybe it was the warmth of the fire, or maybe it was the sense of total relaxation that I felt in Teddy's company, but as we sat there in the dark sipping liqueur, I suddenly started telling him a story.

'Linda caught my eye right from the start. She was small, she was pretty, she was intelligent and she was bursting with energy. There was an immediate attraction between us and we started seeing one another as often as our medical rosters allowed. The relationship blossomed and we got married a year and a half later. It was a big social do. The ceremony was in the small Norman church across the village green from where my parents-in-law lived, and a nearby medieval coaching house was hired for the reception. There was a huge roll-up from both families and the event was widely reported in the papers—largely because of the prominence of my father-in-law.

'When Amy was born, about two years later, it seemed as if we had a marriage made in heaven. Things simply couldn't have been more perfect— Amy was just like her mum. She was petite and pretty and joyful and affectionate. She was healthy and strong. She was so full of life that her death was beyond being unexpected, it was completely unbelievable.

'Exactly ten months after her birth, on a Sunday morning, we found her dead in her cot. She had been quiet for once when we had woken and Linda and I had taken the opportunity of that rare peace to make love. It had been lovely and unrushed and we lay in one another's arms for a while. Then Linda went through to get Amy for her feed.

'I think what I mostly remember is the noise, for even now I can hear Linda's screams. She just went on and on and on without stopping. I jumped out of bed and raced through to the nursery. Linda was sitting cross-legged in the middle of the floor clutching Amy to her. Linda hadn't wanted to let go of her at first but I begged and she let me take her. I looked down at our daughter as I felt for her heartbeat. She was such a pretty baby, but she was cold and blue and her arms were stiff.'

When I finished, Teddy and I stared silently into the embers for a while and Teddy gave me time to dry my face. He was a man who had seen and heard it all before but whose heart had not been hardened by the experience.

Teddy said softly: 'Have you told that story before?'

'Not like that,' I said simply. 'I think about it often, of course, for there isn't the slightest detail that has been lost from my memory. It's more that I just don't talk about it.'

'I feel very privileged you chose to share it with me this evening, then,' he said.

During our friendship, I continued to see Teddy professionally, of course, but I'm not sure that I ever achieved much. He never stopped smoking, he never reduced his alcohol intake and he certainly never lost any weight. But despite all of that, it still took him almost eighteen months to have the heart attack I had promised him.

He spent a week or so in one of the cardiac units in Melbourne and when he came home I was determined to be much stricter with him. This time he did stop smoking, some of the time; he did cut down a little on his drinking, and he did actually lose a kilogram or two.

'Get some more exercise,' I bullied.

'Ever since the army I have always hated exercise,' he replied.

'Exercise or die,' I said fiercely.

There had never been any question of Teddy jogging or cycling, swimming or doing circuits. The big challenge was to find something that he was prepared to do. Then, just when I was running out of suggestions, he found it for himself in the form of his garden.

Teddy redesigned his entire garden, breathing new life into every corner of it. A delightful archway of golden roses sprang up to grace the front path; new flowerbeds appeared everywhere, and there was a new-found vitality in the vegetable garden behind the kitchen.

'This is wonderful,' I said as we wandered round the garden one balmy evening, glass of local white in hand. 'How did you know how to do all this?'

'I borrowed Michael,' Teddy said, so the next time Michael was visiting for a few days I tackled him on his gardening skills.

'Well, my dear,' Michael said, 'perhaps you didn't know, but before the food game I was into interior design. Oh, yes! Graduated from Sydney Uni. They tried to make me do architecture at first, but it didn't work. There was this part of the course where you had to build a wall. Can you imagine it? Me? Putting bricks together? Anyway, my wall fell over, so I was shifted to interior design, which is what I had asked for in the first place.'

'What's all that to do with gardening?' I asked.

'Absolutely everything,' he said somewhat enigmatically, and that was that.

Once Teddy got the exercise bit between his teeth, there was no stopping him and the vegetable patch was further transformed with unending activity. Under Teddy's industry it became a square of complex and verdant beauty. I once stayed at an old priory in the south-west of England that had the most stunning walled vegetable garden I have ever seen. Teddy's veggie patch wasn't quite as good as that, but it certainly gave it a bit of a nudge. Teddy had plans to go commercial, producing spices and herbs for all his old mates in the restaurant business.

With Teddy back on deck again, our dinners resumed. At the end of one evening Teddy turned to me and quietly said: 'So what happened then?'

'How do you mean?' I asked.

'Well, I never got to hear the end of the story. I mean, what happened after Amy died?'

'Ah,' I said, taking a breath. 'Looking back I suspect we were both on autopilot. We did all the right things, of course—attended all the right groups and had all the right counselling—but something inside each of us died that Sunday morning. And it was as though neither of us was able to make it better for the other.

'We stayed on in London for a couple of years but knew that we were simply going through the motions. So we looked around for a sea change, something so different that we could make another start. At about that time Linda had a resident's job at one of those dismal Victorian workhouse-style hospitals in Northern London. My job was fairly easy at that time, so I used to go up and join her at the hospital for what masqueraded as dinner.

'The hospital was poorly equipped and in an unfashionable part of town. For some time, therefore, it had had a lot of difficulty recruiting local medical staff, so they had decided to advertise overseas. Apparently that had been a successful strategy in the various antipodean journals, for the place was full of Aussies and Kiwis. They were terrific. They were loud and they were lively. They worked hard and they played hard and they were in charge of the mess bar. I had never drunk Foster's before, but I sure learned fast since Foster's was the only beer on offer.

'Those raucous residents were just what Linda and I needed. In fact, I think that run-down leftover from the Victorian era was the best mess I have ever been a part of, and somewhere between enjoying the Aussies' company and listening to stories of Down Under, we decided it might be good to move across the world and reinvent ourselves in Gondwanaland. Then, out of the blue, an exchange opportunity arose and I grabbed it with both hands.

'Perhaps moving to Australia was running away from ourselves and we should have recognised that you can't do that. That wherever you go you always take yourself with you. And maybe that is why our relationship didn't work in the end.

'We were happy enough here of course, who wouldn't be? But whatever died that Sunday morning in London never came to life again, especially for Linda. She gradually withdrew from the relationship, though I never noticed her slipping away, and then she finally decided to go her own separate way. Perhaps I withdrew too.

'And perhaps it would have been best if we had stayed put and fought whatever demons we had to fight on home soil. But it's all water under the bridge now.'

I hadn't talked about Amy and Linda for a very long time. In a small country community I had never even thought of sharing my story with people who were patients as well as friends. Somehow Teddy was different. I knew that he could be trusted implicitly.

Then suddenly one morning, Michael, up for a few days on one of his visits, woke to find that Teddy had died in his sleep. I went to the house in response to Michael's urgent call. He was waiting for me in the garden.

'I am so sorry,' I said as I gave him a hug.

'Thanks from both of us,' he replied.

I went into the house and completed the clinical formalities. It felt very strange, as it always did, performing that final examination on someone I knew well. But I've never had the feeling so strongly as on that occasion.

Despite everything, I was profoundly shocked by Teddy's death. Although he had constantly flaunted medical advice, he had at the same time been so full of life and so positive about the future. Sometimes with big men you imagine they are indestructible. Sometimes you imagine they'll be around forever.

There was a huge turnout at the chapel for the cremation service a few days later and many eulogies were read by friends, loved ones and former colleagues from the services. Teddy was clearly highly regarded and loved by a wide circle of people indeed.

I stood during the period of silence and reflected on the generosity he had shown to me. The space he had created for me to visit my story again.

I also remembered all the sessions when he tried so hard to teach me about food and wine. Some of it went in but I was never a star pupil and I have never managed to successfully recreate that wonderful pink thing he used to do with white peaches and champagne.

Teddy was in my life for a brief three years but I still think of him often and miss him greatly. I especially miss his wisdom, his hospitality and his generous gift of listening that gave me the space to reopen chapters that should never have been closed.

10 Show Girls

IN A SMALL COUNTRY town, everyone becomes involved in local activities sooner or later. Even in the relatively short time since I had made the move from Melbourne, I had spoken to the Rotary Club about mental health and to a packed Lions meeting about sexually transmitted diseases. In addition, I had attended emergency practice sessions with the local fire brigade and had presented prizes at the local daffodil show. I had even hosted treasure hunts and painting afternoons at Woongarra for local schoolchildren.

It didn't come as a great surprise to me, therefore, to receive a letter from the organising committee of the local show. With hindsight it might have been better if I had not opened the letter at all and simply dropped it in the bin. But hindsight can, of course, only be gained with hindsight, so rather than drop the letter in the bin, I opened it and read it.

It was an invitation to act as one of three local notaries to judge the Miss Show Girl competition at the Rushby show scheduled for about six weeks hence. The letter informed me that the other judges, who had already agreed to participate, were to be Barry and Gayle, the local shire president and his wife. Since their youngest son was often not well, I had met them both on a number of occasions and liked them a lot. Yes, I thought, I could happily spend a day in their company.

The letter went on to inform me that the local show was part of a national competition to select a young woman to act as an Australian ambassador abroad. The winner would be chosen for her community commitment, presentability and personality. It all sounded very worthy. Lunch and wine were included and the kick-off was at nine-thirty.

'Sounds like fun,' I said to Madge, who was the receptionist on duty that morning. 'Could you please phone back and accept on my behalf?'

Madge looked at me in what I thought at the time was a rather odd way. She said nothing but simply took the letter from me in a somewhat exaggerated fashion, lifted an eyebrow, and then went quietly about her business.

Yes, it will be fun, I thought, as I went through to my room to start the day's work, and I was already looking forward to it. I had been to shows before a few times and had really enjoyed myself. The judging wouldn't take long, I imagined, and then I'd be free to wander around and have a look at all the other events. I had half-planned on going to the show anyway and this was a nice excuse to do just that.

I didn't give the matter much further thought apart from simply turning up on the appointed day some six weeks or so later. I arrived quite early, keen to get a good park but also keen not to be late. I showed Ken at the front gate my judge's pass.

'Yes, I heard you was doin' it. Well, best of British,' he said a little enigmatically as he waved me in.

It was a beautiful day. There was hardly a breath of wind and it felt good being there watching the show getting itself ready. There was a lot of activity with everyone putting the final touches to ensuring a successful day, and by nine o'clock there was already a steady stream of cars coming in through the gate.

At a quarter past nine, with a nice hot coffee in my hand, I went over to the tent which had *Show Girl—Proudly Sponsored by The Country Times* written in large green letters on the roof.

To my surprise the tent was already full of frenetic activity. The woman who had written me the invitation caught sight of me through the crowd and waved. She had to fight her way across the tent and was a little breathless by the time she reached me.

'Thanks so much for helping, Paul, and thanks so much for being early,' she smiled. 'The other judges haven't arrived as yet and we must get started or we're going to run behind. You don't mind starting on your own, do you?'

Without drawing breath or giving me the chance to even comment, she continued: 'Good. That's settled that then. Now you probably already know that the day begins with Miss Tiny Tots. They're all getting ready as we speak.'

A very uncomfortable feeling went down the back of my neck and I said: 'What do you mean "the day begins" and who exactly are the Miss Tiny Tots?'

'Oh, we have a very full day's work ahead of us,' she said as she handed me a programme. 'As you can see,' she pointed to the top of it, 'we start with the littlies and then gradually work our way up through the age groups.'

'I thought I was here to help judge the Miss Show Girl competition,' I said, trying to keep the panic out of my voice.

'Oh you are, you are. Don't worry about that. That's the highlight of the whole day. And unless we run late, we should get to it shortly after lunch. But this morning it's all the younger grades.'

I couldn't move, I could hardly breathe, and I began to perspire as the full implications of the day ahead gradually dawned upon me. In every class, I suddenly realised, there will be one winner and lots and lots of losers.

'Are the mothers of Tiny Tots good losers?' I muttered to myself under my breath.

'Like hell they are,' I replied.

'Will I make friends here today or will I make enemies?'

I thought darkly, and the answer came back very loud and very clear: 'Just a few of the former and lots and lots of the latter.'

'By the way,' I asked my hostess a little pointedly, 'where exactly are Barry and Gayle?'

'I'm afraid I don't know. I tried to contact them a little while ago, but without success. Their phone's been engaged since first thing.'

'Funny that,' I said with a rather tight smile.

'Don't worry,' she continued. 'You'll be fine on your own. It really only takes one judge anyway.'

'Would Barry and Gayle have known that?' I asked.

'Yes,' she nodded brightly, 'they may well have done.'

Looking a little stunned I was led to a trestle which stood in front of the small makeshift stage. It was covered in a white cloth and looked an awful lot like a sacrificial altar. At one end was a pile of sashes and a row of small awards mounted on polished wooden bases. I sat in the middle of the three seats provided and looked through the programme that had been thoughtfully left there for me. By the time I was even halfway through, I knew for sure I was in big trouble indeed.

As soon as I put the programme down and looked up, a dozen or so four-year-olds were led onto the stage by their mothers. They had all been dressed for the occasion in period costume and they all wore bonnets. Even through my panic I could see that they did all look rather cute. A surprisingly large crowd of grandparents and other assorted admirers pressed in behind me. Many of them nodded or waved me recognition and there were quite a few calls of 'Hi, doc'.

To the constant flashing of cameras, the Tiny Tots were led, one by one, to the front of the stage where they were given the choice of singing, dancing or reciting a poem. Despite much encouragement from both onstage and offstage, not every tot proved equal to the task, but most of them made a surprisingly good fist of it.

I remember one little maid singing a song called 'How does a little froggy go?' She got as far as the end of the first line, which was the same as the title of the song, and then abruptly stopped.

She turned to her mother and said, 'Mummy, how *does* a little froggy go?'

To which, in a loud stage whisper, her mother replied, 'On a lily pad, all day long, darling.'

'Oh yes,' said the maid. 'That's right,' and sang, On a lily pad, all day long, darling.'

The completion of each offering was greeted by enthusiastic applause and yet more camera work from the audience, which had built up to such a size that it overflowed the tent. It was obviously widely regarded as a lovely occasion and I was probably the only one present who wasn't enjoying it. I wasn't even in the moment. I was somewhere else entirely, preoccupied with the decision it would be my lot to announce to the assembled throng in the increasingly imminent future.

And suddenly there it was, the performances were completed, the competitors were lined up, and everyone was looking at me. A sort of silence had fallen across the tent, when suddenly I had a flash of inspiration.

'The standard was so high and so consistent,' I said as I stood up, 'that I would like to make all these beautiful young ladies equal first.'

I smiled at the crowd through my brilliance, but it was not to be.

'You can't do that,' said my hostess. 'There's a trophy.'

'Well,' I said as I gripped the back of the chair tightly, 'out of all these equal firsts there is perhaps one especially shining star,' and I named the froggy song girl.

There was a lot of clapping, the trophy was handed over and the child's mother and all four grandparents shook me by the hand.

For just a few seconds I started to relax until I realised that I was being tapped on the shoulder. I turned round to face a young woman with a face like thunder.

'I cannot believe,' she said with her face close to mine, 'that you have just picked someone who couldn't even remember her words, when my Erin stayed up for the last three nights making sure that she knew hers perfectly.'

Then from behind her someone added, 'And didn't you notice the dress? That was the same one her sister used last year. I make Tayla's costume new for every show. Have you any idea how long that takes me?'

As my life has unfolded, there have been a few rough patches along the way, but I have never, so overwhelmingly, felt the wish to run and just keep running as I did at that precise moment. Or maybe just sink into the ground until I vanished from sight.

Instead, however, I smiled bravely at the disappointed members of the assembly and then found my way back to my seat to compose myself for the next event. I was pouring myself a glass of water with a somewhat shaky hand when I became aware that a woman clutching the hand of yet another unsuccessful Tot was standing in front of me.

'We'll be changing to another doctor, won't we, Chantelle?' she said simply as she lifted her nose and swept off into the crowd.

Eventually, however, my tormentors left me alone and the area round the stage cleared once more. My hostess came over and said: 'Well done, well done. You did really well. I thought you handled that really well, but we must press on. Tempus fugit and all that. Well now, it's time for Master Tiny Tots.'

There may have been longer mornings since the world was created, but if so then I had not been asked to live through them. It was unrelentingly ghastly, right up to Miss Country Teen, the last event before lunch. I am sure that most Country Teens are perfectly nice girls who grow up to look after their parents and help the elderly across roads. This does not necessarily apply, however, to the ones who enter themselves into country shows. The advantage they had for me over the Tiny Tots in not having their mothers on stage with them was completely offset by the fact that all but one of them felt completely comfortable about being directly abusive to me after the awards were announced.

'What did you see in that slag?' they said, pointing at the winner. 'Sleep with her mother, do you? Or maybe with her,' they added.

'Is that what you have to do round here to get noticed: sleep with a dirty old man like you? You should be reported to the authorities, you should. You should be struck off.'

By the time the last of the morning's trophies had been handed out and the tent had finally emptied, I felt like something that had been dragged off the floor of the Colosseum.

I staggered off to the refreshment tent, keeping to the shadows wherever possible to avoid fresh encounters with any wandering Country Teens, and fortunately arrived unscathed. To my delight, the refreshment tent was exactly what it purported to be. It was light and it was cool and bit by bit my spirits revived. A glass of chardonnay and a local string quartet very creditably playing Schumann and Brahms, were unction to my wounds.

I was well into my second glass of wine when, to my great surprise, my co-judges casually sauntered into the tent, waved hello to everyone, organised themselves some food and drink and came and sat down next to me.

Before I could say 'And where the hell were you two?' Barry smiled at me and said: 'How's it going? Still in one piece? Still able to hold your head up in society? Still got a practice?' and then they both laughed until they had to dry their eyes.

When they had finally settled down, I took my chance: 'And where the hell were you two? I'd like you to know that I am now the most unpopular person within a fifty-kilometre radius, I have post-traumatic stress disorder and a whole new insight into what the poor buggers went through at the Roman games. Have you the slightest idea what it was like in there?'

'Well actually we do,' said Gayle as she speared a prawn and started to laugh again. 'Some years ago we did what you did. We accepted the invitation to judge and then actually turned up. It was ghastly. Barry was coming up for re-election with the shire at the time and nearly didn't make it as a result.'

'We wouldn't dream of making that silly mistake again,' chuckled Barry. 'There were even fellow councillors who didn't talk to us for ages. So these days we do it differently. We accept the invitation and then simply turn up for the lunch, giving, of course, profuse apologies to the organisers for running late. Been doing it for years. Works really well. Very nice lunch this year, by the way,' he added.

'The main trick,' whispered Gayle, leaning forward in a conspiratorial manner, 'is to remember to take the phone off the hook when you go to bed the night before.'

'But, but . . .' I spluttered.

'Sorry not to have warned you, old boy,' said Barry as he lifted his glass, 'but someone had to do it. Someone has to actually sit in there.'

'Oh, and by the way,' Gayle continued. 'I assume you'll be OK on your own this afternoon for the Show Girl? Barry and I have a prior engagement,' and they both started laughing again.

'How d'ye go?' asked Heather and Rob when I dropped in on them on my way home.

'Ghastly,' I replied. 'It was completely horrible from start to finish. I have been publicly insulted, humiliated, sworn at and threatened. I will certainly never make that mistake again.' I took a large restorative sip from the glass that had been poured for me.

'D'you know,' Rob said to Heather, 'I think that's word for word what Barry and Gayle said when they dropped in on their way home from the show some three or four years ago.'

Then they leaned their heads on one another's shoulders and laughed until they sobbed.

11 Peter

TWO DAYS A WEEK it fell to me to drive up and do the surgery in Rushby, a small township which picturesquely nestles in the foothills of the Great Divide.

During the gold rush, the road to the Lockridge diggings went through the town and then zigzagged up over the ranges before turning northwest towards the goldfields. In that rugged terrain, however, bushrangers proved impossible to control and a new road was eventually built to the west, bypassing the ranges altogether.

With the opening of the new road, Rushby was simply no longer required and slipped gently into the quiet retirement it has enjoyed for the hundred and more years since. In the blink of an eye, Rushby went from a bustling town with a population of thousands, thirteen pubs and four barber-surgeons, to the sleepy backwater it is today.

Like the town itself, many of the inhabitants seem out of step with modernity. It is as if the tidal surge of humanity that washed up to the hills with the gold rush left behind it a wonderfully rich tradition of individuality which has been passed on down, generation by generation, to the present day.

And in this unique setting, where the plains and hills shake hands, different ways of looking at the world have not only been tolerated but actively nurtured. This liberal attitude has been preserved, at least in part, by the relative isolation of the area. Only a few years ago it was common to find local folk who had never travelled more than a few kilometres from Rushby, and it was rare to find anyone who had been on an aeroplane.

Early in the piece I had attended Frank who lived on his sheep farm in the foothills of the Divide and who had a rather unpleasant eye problem. I wanted him to see a specialist and organised things accordingly.

'Is this in Melbourne?' Frank asked as he squinted suspiciously out of his good eye at my referral.

'It certainly is,' I replied brightly.

'Well then, you might as well know that I shan't be going,' he stated adamantly. 'I went there once in 1956. Didn't like it. Never been back.'

And that was that.

When I first started visiting Rushby I felt a little as though I was in the Wild West for, in those early days, I attended many gun-related incidents and wounds. One such incident involved Nigel and James who were living out a peaceful retirement from the postal service in one of the side streets behind the primary school. They spent their days keeping the house tidy, maintaining a sensational vegetable garden and doting on Versace, a small white fluffy thing that they took turns to walk early every morning. One day, late in December, it happened to be Nigel's turn. Apparently, everything went like clockwork until the pair reached the halfway point.

It just so happened that three likely lads, who had been out all night after foxes, were, at that very time, returning home. They had grabbed some coffees from the milk bar to wake themselves up and were returning to their car when Nigel and Versace strolled by.

I am not sure if it was due to tiredness or trying to balance guns and polystyrene coffee cups, but as he crossed the nature strip one of the lads tripped over the kerb and fell. When he hit the ground two things became immediately obvious. The first was that the gun he was carrying was loaded, and the second was that the jar of hitting the ground was sufficient to activate the trigger.

If it hadn't been for Versace I hate to think of what would have become of Nigel's legs. They were a big enough mess as it was, but Nigel was largely saved by his small companion, who took the full force of the shot in the midriff. It is my understanding that dogs are greatly upset by loud noises and I am comforted at least to think that Versace may have been spared such distress by the relative speeds of lead and sound.

I have since been told by passers-by that the dog just seemed to disappear, but I know for myself that was not true. When I attended Nigel a short while later to organise drips and helicopters, Versace was very obviously still present, only in a different configuration. I looked across the nature strip and I looked up at the trees. There were white bits everywhere.

Then there was the occasion on which Syd presented himself to the Rushby Bush Nursing Hospital late one Saturday night. I had been watching *Predator* on TV and was a bit grumpy about being called out just at the bit where the thing takes its helmet off and shows all its dreadlocks. I immediately felt at home, however, as Syd's face, which was a mass of cuts and glass, didn't look much better. Unlike the predator, however, he smelt heavily of the sort of liquid I would rather have been at home supping.

Syd's story was that he had been on his way home from the pub in his ute when he had suddenly realised he was being stalked by a panther.

In response to my raised eyebrows he grabbed my collar, pulled my ear down to his lips and confided in me that at the end of the war, when it was time for the Americans to go home, they had released their regimental mascot into the Mullaways.

'Wouldn't it be a bit long in the tooth by now?' I asked.

'It had babies,' he replied, tapping his nose.

'Oh, I see,' I said, intending to be funny. 'You mean there were two regimental mascots?'

'And probably many more,' he replied darkly.

'So how did you know you were being stalked?' I asked as I set to work cleaning up his face.

'The eyes,' Syd replied. 'As I was driving along Milroy's Track I suddenly saw these eyes looking at me from over the bonnet and however much I turned on the gas I just couldn't shake that panther off. Even when I swerved. So I pulled the shotty from behind the seat and gave it both barrels. Dan happened along at that very moment, saw the mess the panther had caused and drove me over to see you.'

It took me well over an hour to finish my work. I sadly realised that the tussle in the South American jungle would be well over by now and that Arnie would have had to cope without me this time.

I tidied up, feeling that there was something about the story I hadn't quite grasped. I walked outside with Syd and found Dan waiting for him.

'So what actually happened?' I asked Dan.

'I'm not absolutely sure,' he said. 'We left the pub together and I followed Syd up the track. He had given me a hard time about the Devils recent form so I decided to raz him up by sitting on his tail. Next thing I know he accelerates, but he doesn't get away from me. Then he's all over the place and I hear the gun go off.'

'Right,' I said.

Milroy's Track wasn't far out of my way home so I did a little detour to see if I could see where Syd's car had finished up. I couldn't find it at first but then there was a shift in the clouds and suddenly I saw it. It was down a small slope near a hedge and it was in a terrible mess. The rear-vision mirror, the windscreen and a surprising amount of the front part of the roof had simply been blown away.

'Well, well, well,' I chuckled and then wended my weary way home.

On my days in Rushby the waiting room was always pretty full by the time I arrived. One morning there were a few of my old regulars to whom I would normally have waved a friendly hello, but on this occasion I hardly even glanced at them. Sitting right amongst them was Vermeer. I love portraiture and I am especially fond of Vermeer's work, so it was an especial and completely unexpected pleasure to find him in my waiting room. It wasn't really him of course, but the floppy tasselled velvet cap, the beard, the ruff, the baggy slashed sleeves and the pantaloons were all perfect. I guess what gave it away, however, was the footwear. As far as I know, Vermeer never wore red and yellow runners.

It transpired that the brush-man himself was first cab off the rank that morning and two seconds later we were in the surgery introducing ourselves.

'I don't think we've met,' a smiling Vermeer said as we shook hands. 'But we have now,' he added in his thick Gloucestershire accent. 'Name's Peter.'

'Nice to meet you, Peter.' I replied. 'How can I help?'

'Full medical,' he replied. 'Without that finger thing,' he added after a moment's pause.

'Not a problem,' I said. 'Any special reason?'

'I am going on a journey,' Peter replied, 'and I want to make sure I'm fully fit.'

'Great,' I nodded as I took his blood pressure. 'Where are you off to?'

'To find myself.'

'Wow,' I said.

'I'm going to find myself, cleanse my system and give up tobacco, choof and alcohol. I intend to walk for forty days and forty nights.'

'I think you'll find that's been done,' I joked.

'Yes,' he said seriously, 'but not for a very long time.'

Peter informed me that he was going to tuck eight dollars into his sock for emergencies, draw a straight line on a map and cross Victoria with as little deviation from this route as possible.

'Wow,' I said again.

Fortunately, it turned out that Peter was completely fit, so I reassured him that, from my point of view, there were no impediments to him striding out across the state. In fact the only unusual finding of any note in the entire examination was the ironing board tattooed on his right arm.

The rest of that morning surgery never quite lived up to the promise with which it had started and I spent a fair bit of it daydreaming over not only Peter's project but also the previous time I had seen him. Peter had been right in that he had not met me, but I had definitely come across him.

Late one afternoon some weeks before, Bill had phoned the surgery and requested a home visit for his wife. Consequently, when I finished the day, I drove the two minutes round to see her. Bill and Violet are a delightful couple who spend their latter years behind a large and immaculately kept rose garden across the road from the mechanics hall.

I dallied for a cup of tea after Violet and I had completed our medical matters and it was dark when I left. I was surprised to find the street full of cars and annoyed to discover that I had been boxed in. I crossed the road to the hall, with the intention of finding someone to 'unbox' me, and found it full of people expectantly waiting for something to begin. What I had intended to do was locate the culprit, get them to move their car, go home, feed Hardy and watch something crappy on the TV. What I did was sit down with the others and wait.

I have embraced serendipity many times, often with only modest rewards, but on this occasion I struck gold.

Within a few minutes of my sitting down, the lights were muted, the chatter died away and a man of about my own age, brightly dressed as Harlequin, strode to the lectern. He put on his glasses and shuffled the papers in front of him. When he looked up at the audience the bells on his hat tinkled and caught the stage lights.

'There is no such thing as a village idiot in Rushby,' he started by saying. 'For every bugger has had a go at it.'

And then, for the next forty minutes or so I listened to an emotionally charged exposé of local gossip and disappointed ambitions. I found out later that, when Peter and Joyce moved to Rushby some years before, Peter had fallen in love with the place and then decided to express this love by forming himself into a one man militia against local humbug and insincerity. In fact, so moved was he by his concerns that he wrote down his thoughts as a series of short stories which he then became keen to share with the public at large. On the night in question, Peter had hired the mechanics hall and given the first public reading of his 'Ugly Stories'. I had never heard of the stories before that evening but have read them in their entirety since. It is true that they have many strengths, and show much insight, however I think it unlikely they will ever be regarded as pillars of literature. But the big turnout that night had nothing whatever to do with literary merit. That night the hall was packed simply because everyone wanted to find out whether they had been mentioned or not.

The reading was a sensation and made all the more lively by the fact that the audience clearly thought it best to give Peter feedback as he progressed. I am afraid to say that poor Hardy dined late that night.

There were a number of other readings over subsequent months and, although I didn't attend, I understand that every time the hall was more and more packed. As can be imagined, much local discussion was generated by the stories. Many different points of view were aired, but the final consensus was that the indignity of being referred to in a scurrilous manner paled into insignificance against the indignity of not being mentioned at all.

I saw Peter several times more in the weeks leading up to his walk. Once he was Dylan and once a surprisingly passable Pagliacci. I loved all the outfits but I think Vermeer remains my favourite. It suits him down to the ground.

With each visit Peter would politely invite me to dinner and I would just as politely turn it down. There came a time, however, when my repeated refusal started to sound a bit like rudeness, so I eventually accepted and a date was duly set for a Saturday after he returned from his walk. Peter told me he was having a few of his mates over and that the dress code was 'favourite frock'.

On the evening of the dinner I was ready in plenty of time for once, so I stopped off at the Dixon's Bridge drive-through where I picked up a bottle of wine and some wolf whistles.

Peter lives a fair way up into the Divide. It is a beautiful drive out to his place along a curving, rising road with views on either side. Although not far from Rushby as the crow flies, the area is surprisingly isolated and the land has been tightly held for generations by a handful of families who are all sprung from the same stock. Just a few years ago the local primary school, which at the time was looking after the academic future of thirty-two young souls, boasted the distinction that every child shared the same surname.

I hadn't visited Peter's place before but it was not hard to know when I had reached my destination. Not only was the letterbox a large pointy pair of stainless-steel breasts, but the front lawn was covered in sculptures, dominated by the central piece depicting, in surprising detail, a couple making love.

I sat in the car for a while and drank it all in, thinking how useful that centrepiece could have been to Steve and Erica.

Steve and Erica were a lovely couple in their mid-thirties, both of whom worked for an electricity supply company and were clearly very much in love. They had come to see me some years before Peter's dinner party with the problem that, although they had been married for ten years, there was still only the two of them. They both came from staunch Catholic families and their respective parents were starting to put pressure on them.

I organised tests for each of them and then set a time to discuss the results. It so happened that all the results came back completely normal so I decided to give them both a physical. When it was Erica's turn, I immediately realised that in one way at least she was more like an old-fashioned bride-to-be than a woman who has been married for ten years.

'How often do you have sex?' I asked them.

'Every night,' they replied.

'Really?' I asked doubtfully.

'Yes,' they nodded in agreement. 'Every single night we sleep together.'

'Aahh,' I said after a fairly long pause. 'I tell you what. I'm going to draw you a diagram.'

So I did. I am good at drawing and when I had finished the drawing showed exactly what I wanted it to. They both leaned forward and silently looked at my artwork for a long time. Then they both looked up at me and Erica said: 'You're pulling our legs, aren't you?'

There are some things you can joke about and some things you can't. I assured Erica that the current discussion fell into the latter category. However, despite being given the diagram for future reference, they went off looking very unconvinced indeed.

For all the world, they reminded me of a young lad who, on the occasion of the arrival of his sister, had asked his dad how babies were made.

'And what did you say?' I asked the dad when he told me.

'Well,' he said, 'I decided to tell him the truth so I told him *exactly* how babies were made.'

'And?'

'He said he thought it sounded really gross and didn't imagine he would ever be trying it.'

I still see Steve and Erica from time to time. They are both forty-odd now, still very much in love, and there are still just the two of them. These days, however, as I understand it, their having no children is no longer an issue with either family due to the frenetic activities of their younger siblings.

I came out of my reverie and drove up the gravel driveway to where Peter's house came into view from behind a rise. It could probably be best described as 'interesting' for, under the jumble of roof pitches, it was not quite clear where the house started and it was equally uncertain where it ended. When Joyce and Peter had parted company, sadly not long after coming to Rushby, Peter had found that he had just enough money left to buy a bare block of land, so that was exactly what he did. Realising that this did not satisfy all his needs, he then tackled the task of putting a roof over his head by visiting the local tip. Bit by bit, over several years, he recycled society's cast-offs and built a house with them. And, as he went, he improvised. The windows were panels of beer bottles set horizontally in mortar; the coffee table was an old millstone; the loo was a small garden shed at the end of the kitchen, and the landing was connected to the bedrooms by a trapeze.

Despite the eclectic nature of the supply system, the construction of the house went surprisingly well, apart from a mouse plague which had slowed things down for a while due to chewed pipes and cables and eaten insulation. Just a short way up the road from Peter's place some old hay bales had been removed from a farm shed to make way for the new season's harvest and a billion mice had trudged down the hill to find a new home.

Peter threw himself into mouse war with the same enthusiasm he brought to everything else and, mainly through the use of sprung steel and anticoagulants, eventually dispatched every *Mus musculus* within a kilometre radius to the big cheese in the sky. I understand that the only downside of the campaign was that the construction site finished up about a foot deep in small furry bodies.

Probably, I would have simply got rid of them, but Peter, firmly following the philosophy of waste not want not, took a very different tack.

He transformed the vanquished hordes from liabilities to assets. He cast them as the main players in a series of small dioramas exemplifying various forms of suicide and other forms of violent death and then sold them off at local art galleries.

I crunched to a halt next to a large unfinished concrete ammonite, parked next to what I took to be the side of the house and got out. Peter, in a full-length gown of peacock blue, appeared from nowhere, bid me welcome, admired the floral number Susie had lent me, and took me inside where I realised that I was far from the first to arrive. I don't know what it is about blokes and frocks but they are not a good combination. Later, watching the DVD Peter made of the evening, confirmed my worst fears that I was no exception. Hairy chests and plunging necklines just do not go.

Nevertheless the evening was a great success. The company and food were excellent and I sat next to a very pleasant retired banker in a cream gown with whom I danced later in the evening.

'How did the walk go?' I asked Peter above the background din.

'Complete, fucking shambles,' he replied.

'What sort of a shambles was it?' I asked, pretending not to have heard.

'Complete and also fucking,' he confirmed.

'What went wrong?'

'Oh nothing went wrong,' he said. 'It's just that I had really wanted to find myself, cleanse my system and give up tobacco, choof and alcohol.'

'Yes?'

'Well, I still haven't got the faintest idea who I am, I am far from clean and I haven't given up anything.'

I was sorry to hear this. The jury might still be out on alcohol and marijuana, but everyone wants to find themselves and everyone, apart from the people who own the companies, knows that tobacco kills.

Not that cigarettes were always on the outer. When I was at medical school every patient had an ashtray on their bedside table and the morning ward-round coffee break invariably involved everyone from the professor to the student nurses lighting up.

Things have certainly moved on since then, but just occasionally one chances upon someone who remains intransigent.

Fairly recently I saw a lady who wanted to have a grumble about a GP in a town on the other side of the Divide.

'And what exactly is the problem?' I asked, not knowing what was coming next but feeling strongly that I didn't want to get involved.

'Well,' she said, 'I didn't mind that he had a full ashtray on his desk and I didn't really mind that he had a cigarette in his mouth when he examined me. What I objected to was that as he bent over to listen to my chest he accidentally burned a hole in my new head scarf. Do you think I should ask for a replacement?'

My discussion with Peter continued and we were joined by several other guests. Peter repeated to the enlarged caucus that he wanted to find himself, and over the next hour or so, assisted by a continual stream of alcohol, was given quite a number of anatomical suggestions as to where he might start his search.

It was a great evening and I didn't leave until long after the bewitching hour. I'm ashamed to say that I was loose as a goose and didn't stop laughing all the way home. The only fly in the ointment was getting out of Susie's number. She and I are very different shapes and, despite having left the zip undone, it cut me cruelly under the arms.

I woke the next morning with the usual regrets, had a couple of Panadol and sat on the patio with a cup of tea. Peter's quest had got me thinking about the journey of self-discovery on which we are all embarked.

'And where do you reckon we should be looking to find ourselves?' I asked Hardy as I rubbed his head.

'I don't think it's like that at all,' he replied.

'Oh?' I said, looking down at him. 'I am all ears.'

'Very funny,' he said, flicking his. 'The answer is not out there,' he continued, looking from me to the hills and back again. 'So looking out there will only ever prove to be a futile quest for the holy bone. Inside. That's the place to look. Being at peace with who you find there, that's the only way to lasting happiness.'

I stared at him, open-mouthed in amazement.

'And for some reason,' he said, 'we dogs get all that and you humans don't.' And he rolled over so that his black bits glistened in the sun.

12 Domestic

SOME SUNDAY SURGERIES ARE a breeze and some just seem to go on forever. This one was a shocker. I had worked flat out from the moment I walked in and the entire morning had seemed like a re-enactment of Custer's Last Stand. The more patients I saw, the more they kept coming. There were even a few patients left in the waiting room at two o'clock in the afternoon when the police phoned.

'Call for you,' Meaghan said chirpily.

I had already fielded an uncountable number of calls that morning, so I suggested she deal with this one herself.

'I don't think so,' she said. 'It's the police,' and put the call through.

I apologised to June, who was lying on the couch, and put a blanket over her.

'I'm afraid I've got to take this call,' I said.

'What, another one?' she replied, slightly exasperated at the continual interruptions.

'G'day, doc,' said Sergeant Hogan. 'There's been a domestic in Kimpton Street. We would greatly appreciate it if you could attend as soon as possible.'

'It's not who I think it is, is it?' I asked with a grimace.

'I'm afraid it is, doc.'

'Oh, Lord. Are you sure you need me there? Do I really have to go?'

'Well, we'd appreciate it very much. There are already two officers at the house, so you will be in no danger,' he added reassuringly.

'What do you mean: "danger"?' I asked with alarm.

'Ah, didn't I tell you?' he continued. 'There's been another stabbing.'

There really wasn't an answer to that. Over the years I have been given many different reasons justifying requests for house calls and over the years I have come up with many plausible excuses for not doing them. I do know when I have met my match, however, and a request to attend 'another' stabbing is game, set and match.

I apologised to June, grabbed the emergency bags, asked Meaghan to reschedule everyone who was left and headed out of the clinic.

'Best of luck,' she said with a cheeky smile from behind those huge glasses of hers. 'I'll hold the fort until you get back.'

Kimpton Street was not far from the surgery and it didn't take me long to get there. I didn't need directions as it had only been a couple of months since my last visit. On that occasion there had also been a stabbing. I had arrived late one evening to find the place looking as if it had been hit by a whirlwind. The big window next to the front door was completely shattered, and a rubbish bin and its contents were scattered across the sitting room floor in a sea of broken glass. Brook, sporting a black eye, showed me through to the bedroom where Jack was lying down.

Jack appeared very much the worse for wear. There were a couple of empty flagons on the bedside table and the whole place reeked of alcohol. What immediately caught my eye, however, was the impressive and gaping wound in Jack's upper left arm which was still bleeding freely.

I checked the wound and found that fortunately it was not as bad as it looked. I stopped the bleeding without too much trouble and then sewed it up without the need for anaesthetic. When I finished, Jack and I went through to the kitchen and sat and drank the coffee that Brook had made for us.

I asked them what had happened. Like all really good stories it had the essence of simplicity. Brook had waited for Jack to go to sleep, then taken the bread knife from the wooden block in the kitchen, walked through to the bedroom and stabbed him in the arm.

Nothing to it, really. I am sure there are lots of people who feel like doing that sort of thing to their loved ones all the time. The only difference in Kimpton Street was that Brook and Jack converted dark thoughts into dark deeds.

Not that they were bad people at all. In fact, I found them extremely likeable and had quite a soft spot for the both of them. It's just that neither of them had the faintest idea how to run a relationship in a way that didn't involve chaos and violence. I guess that was all they had ever had the opportunity of learning.

'By the way,' I asked, 'where are the boys?'

'They've gone off with my mum,' Brook replied.

'Good,' I nodded. There was clearly a piece of the jigsaw puzzle missing, so I looked at Brook and asked her the obvious question: 'So why did you stab him?'

'Because he beat me,' she said.

'I did not beat her,' Jack said to me. Then he saw the look of disbelief on my face and continued: 'Well, yes, OK, I did beat her, but only because she'd started drinking again.'

'But I was only drinking to calm my nerves,' she said.

'If your nerves were so calm, how come you were screaming at the top of your voice?'

'I was screaming because you threw the dustbin through the window.'

'But I only threw the dustbin through the window because you locked me out.'

'And I only locked you out because you killed Rupert.'

'That,' said Jack emphatically, 'was an accident. You know it was. You know that I only sat on him accidentally when your mother pushed me.'

'But she only pushed you when she saw my black eye!'

'And I only tripped because of the all the mess you leave lying around all the time.'

'But you didn't have to pick him up and throw him at my mum, saying: "Take your dog back, bitch."'

'And just remind me why your mum was here in the first place?'

'To take the boys away.'

'Yeah, to take the boys away, because you were drinking again.'

'But I only drink because you beat me.'

'And I only beat you because you drink.'

My head was spinning by now so I left them to it. I think they had forgotten I was even there. Circles were the only direction they knew to go in. I felt so sad for them.

As I turned into Kimpton Street that Sunday afternoon my destination would have been immediately obvious, even if I hadn't already known it. There were two police cars parked at the front of the house and a dark column of smoke drifting up from the backyard.

I pulled up in the driveway next to Jack's Falcon 500.

'Goodness,' I said, noticing that all the tyres were flat.

As I reached the front door, a young policeman in his shirtsleeves emerged from the house.

'Glad you're here,' he said. 'We're all in the kitchen.'

'Aren't you a bit cold?' I asked as we went in.

'Yeah, bloody freezing,' he replied.

I entered the house a little apprehensively in view of my last visit, but I needn't have worried. Everything was peaceful and calm. There was no chaos, no mayhem and no blood.

Jack was leaning back in the chair in the corner, dressed in a singlet and jeans and looking a little shabby. He hadn't shaved for a while and his hair, which was normally pulled back in a ponytail, straggled greasily over his shoulders.

'Hi, Jack,' I waved and when he smiled back I realised he hadn't as yet had time to put his plate in. He silently pointed to a bandage round his right upper arm.

Near him, sitting at the kitchen table, was a policewoman; she was stroking a fluffy ginger kitten on her lap. She looked up at me and waved a friendly hello.

Brook, wearing a policemen's jacket, was perched on a stool at the breakfast bar. She put down the large screwdriver she had been playing with and smiled at me from under her shock of impossibly red hair.

'Hi, doc,' she said breezily. 'Would you like a cuppa tea?'

'Well, yes, thanks, if everyone else is having one.'

Brook slid down off the stool to make the tea and, as she did so, I realised that the jacket, which she had obviously borrowed from the constable, composed her entire wardrobe. I also realised that she was covered in dozens of small bruises.

I stared at her in surprise for a second then looked away, a little embarrassed. I sat down, composed myself and then asked if anyone could tell me what had happened.

Everyone spoke at once and it was a little hard to follow, but I gathered that the previous evening Brook had asked Jack to take her to a party at her cousin's. Jack had been working at the upholstery factory all week and had said that he was too tired to go. The upshot was that Brook went to the party on her own and Jack stayed at home watching the footy. During the course of the game he finished off the slab he had brought home with him and then went off to bed without waiting up for Brook.

The following morning, Jack apparently woke to find that he was alone in bed. He heard Brook singing in the shower and decided to make her a cup of tea. When he opened the shower door to give her a good-morning kiss and tell her he'd put a cup of tea by the handbasin, he noticed, much to his surprise, that Brook was covered from head to toe in dozens of lovebites.

Now Jack knew, as we all would, that you do not get covered in lovebites just from going to a party at your cousin's place. To Jack's great credit, however, he kept his temper. He neither shouted nor screamed. He neither ranted nor raved. He did not even let on that he had recognised the little bruises for what they were. He simply gave Brook a peck on the cheek, calmly closed the shower door and then, methodically, went through the entire house, visiting every cupboard and drawer. He collected up every single stitch of Brook's clothing and footwear, piled it all up in the middle of the back lawn, poured petrol over it all and chucked on a match.

When Brook eventually emerged from her shower and found that every article of clothing she owned in the entire world was on fire in the middle of the back lawn, she, like her husband, acted decisively.

Dressed only in the suit she was born in, she went to the workshop at the back of the garage, found the largest screwdriver possible, walked round to the front garden and stabbed to death every one of the tyres on the Falcon.

Garry and Amanda live two doors down from Brook and Jack. Garry used to be a photocopier service man, but since he had retired a couple of years or so previously he had contented himself with transforming his house and garden into the neatest in the district. He was giving the grass round a bed of succulents on the front lawn a final clip when Brook's attire and actions caught his eye.

Like Jack and Brook before him, Garry didn't cause the slightest trouble. He just quietly turned off his mower, went indoors, called the police and told them that there had been a stabbing.

'Bloody typical,' said Brook, screwing up her face. 'Garry has been dying to get even with me ever since that fuss about finding his cat dead in our garden. When he saw me, he must have thought that all his Christmases had come at once.'

'By the way, where are the boys?' I asked.

'Oh, they stayed overnight at a friend's.'

'Good.'

I sipped my tea and wondered what I was doing there since I was not much chop at putting out fires or fixing tyres. I was just about to voice my concerns when the policewoman said to Brook: 'So what did you finally decide you wanted for him?'

'Ten dollars,' said Brook.

'OK, I'll take him, but I haven't got any money on me. Could you lend me a tenner, David?' the policewoman asked her colleague.

Money changed hands and Brook tucked the notes under a pepper grinder on the kitchen bench.

There was a knock on the door and Cheryl, a friend of Brook's, arrived with some clothes in a bag. The females all disappeared into the bedroom, presumably to watch Brook getting dressed, and Jack cleared away the tea things and loaded the dishwasher. The women reappeared, with Brook now clad in a fluffy pink jumper and flared skirt, and Jack said: 'You look nice in that, Brook.'

'Thanks, Jack. Yeah, thanks, Cheryl. And thanks for the lend of your coat, too,' she said to the young officer as she handed it back to him.

'Not a problem,' he replied cheerfully. 'Glad to be of service.'

'Blimey,' I thought, any more of this and we'll all be slipping in it.

'By the way, Brook, have you got a cardboard box?' said the policewoman.

'I think there's one in the garage,' said Jack and went to get it.

He reappeared a few minutes later and was handing it over when Brook suddenly leaned forward, grabbed the box and repeatedly stabbed it with the screwdriver. When she had finished, she stood there for a while, screwdriver raised, looking at us all and breathing hard.

There was a moment's intense silence and then Brook said: 'Fucking air-holes,' and we all laughed.

A few minutes later the house was almost deserted. The police had both disappeared, taking the kitten with them, and Cheryl had departed with the promise of bringing Brook some more undies the following day.

I was the last to leave and halfway down the path a thought occurred to me and I turned back to ask Jack a question. He and Brook were standing on the front verandah with their arms around one another, the picture of domestic bliss.

'What about the bandage?' I asked, tapping my arm.

'Oh, that,' he said, looking down at it. 'I got a new tattoo a couple of days ago and it's a bit sore. But thanks for asking.'

I was just getting into my car when Brook shouted: 'Thanks for everything, doc, you were terrific. I don't know what Jack and I would do without you. Don't you worry about us, we'll be fine. I needed some new clothes anyway.'

Over the years there had been many occasions when I had put in a back-breaking effort which has gone completely unnoticed or unrecognised. Accordingly, on an occasion when I received praise and flattery for having done absolutely nothing at all, I felt no qualms whatsoever about accepting it graciously. I did a little bow, said that it had been my pleasure, and drove away.

Back at the surgery Meaghan asked how it had gone.

'Apparently I was terrific,' I said, 'Apparently they don't know what they would have done without me.'

'Fancy a cup of tea then?' Meaghan asked.

'Yes, thanks,' I replied. 'But you're up against a bit of competition.'

'And why's that?' she asked.

'Well my last one,' I replied, 'was served by a naked woman.'

There was a moment's silence. 'So what Medicare number do I put down for that?'

'Very funny, Meaghan,' I said.

Things settled down for Brook and Jack for a while after that. Largely because, despite the scene of domestic bliss on the verandah, they parted company a short while later. Jack stayed in Kimpton Street and Brook went to Melbourne with the children.

Apart from very occasional contact with Jack for blood pressure pills and bumping into Brook one night on Southbank, I eventually lost contact with both of them. I didn't know how they were going for a long time, apart, that is, from reading about them in the papers.

Then, one Thursday afternoon, some three years or so after being served tea by Brook in the raw, she and Jack came back into my life once more.

I had been feeling quite smug that particular afternoon. Just for a change, I had actually been running on time and had not had to apologise to a single person all day for keeping them waiting. I had even managed a couple of fit-ins. It didn't happen often, but it was happening today.

'I'm going to get off on time today,' I said to myself. 'And just for once, I shall even be on time for dinner with my mother.'

I finished a consultation and walked my patient back to reception. I bid her goodbye and looked up to call in the next patient. To my surprise I saw that the waiting room was full of policemen, and before I knew it they were all in my consulting room.

'What on earth is going on?' I asked in alarm as I heard one of the comedians in the waiting room yelling out: 'They've got you this time, doc.'

'We'd like your help,' Sergeant Hogan began.

'Help with what? Help with inquiries? Help with an investigation?' I gibbered, for in all truth my conscience was far from clear.

Some months before, I had had the privilege of helping Dana's dad through his last illness. Given the circumstances, his last few months were made as comfortable as possible and the whole family had been very grateful. Dana left a message at the surgery for me that she had put a couple of pot plants in the back of my ute as a thankyou, and when I got home that night I planted them. I am not a great gardener so I simply put them on either side of the patio at the back of the house and promptly forgot all about them. They grew into large healthy bushes, though they looked like dull plants to me. Certainly there was lots of greenery, but there were no flowers to speak of.

At about the same time, a patient had died in what I thought were rather odd circumstances. I caused quite a stir by refusing to sign the death certificate and the matter was duly referred to the coroner. He, in turn, passed it on to the homicide squad. They wanted a statement from me so I organised for them to come up to the farm.

The day before their visit, an old friend of mine dropped in on his way back to Melbourne and I invited him to stay for dinner. We poured ourselves a stiff Scotch and stood by the French windows, admiring what we could see of the view through the rain.

'Fabulous place you've got here, Paul, absolutely fabulous,' Christian purred, then suddenly went stiff and leaned forward. 'What in God's name have you got there?' he said, pointing at Dana's bushes.

'I've no idea of the botanical name, if that's what you mean,' I smiled at him. 'But they were a 'thank you' from a patient.'

Christian dashed through the rain, pulled off the end of a sprig and dashed back again.

'You idiot,' he said, showing me the leaves in his palm. 'Here's some advice from a close friend: get rid of both of those little babies as soon as possible.'

'Yes, right, I will,' I replied, a little shaken. 'I had no idea. I'll dig them up as soon as the rain stops.'

'Good,' said Christian and we went through for dinner.

The next morning three members of the homicide squad arrived at the appointed hour. I ushered them into the living room and they organised their laptops. They wanted to know what had made me suspicious in the first place, what I knew about the family and a host of other things. We had been going over the case for twenty minutes or so when I suddenly had an unpleasant prickling feeling down the back of my neck, my heart started pounding and I broke out into a sweat.

I realised two things. The first was that I had forgotten to remove the bushes from the patio when the rain had finally stopped. The second was that, the way we were all sitting, a glance past my right shoulder by any of the three young policemen would have afforded them an uninterrupted view of what I now knew to be two of the tallest, healthiest marijuana plants in the district.

Casually and slowly, still answering every question in as calm a voice as possible, I got up as though needing a stretch. I then slowly crossed to the other side of the room, taking three pairs of eyes with me, and sat down again, hoping to look as if I did that sort of thing all the time.

We talked for a little while longer and then there came a time when all the questions had been answered. They stood up, packed away their computers and told me I had been very helpful.

They were about to get into their car when one of them turned to me and said as he looked around: 'Bit of a gardener, are you?'

I simply smiled and mumbled an agreement. To this day I have no idea whether he was giving me a nudge-nudge, wink-wink about Dana's gift or whether he simply liked the garden. Either way, the bushes were out of the ground and hidden in the shed within fifteen minutes of the police car disappearing down the driveway.

'Gawd, you must have a guilty conscience, doc,' said the sergeant, bringing me back to the present. 'We're not here for you,' he added with a smile. 'No. What we've come for is your help. Yes, we'd like your help with a domestic.'

'A domestic?' I asked, more than a little relieved.

'Yes,' he repeated. 'There's been a local domestic and it's turned a bit nasty. In fact, the tactical response squad has been deployed and they are now officially calling it a "situation".'

'A "situation"?' I asked, startled. 'And how on earth can I be of help?'

'Because,' came the calm reply, 'the bloke holding the gun to the lady's head has made it quite clear that he will only speak to you.'

There was a pause for a while and then I looked at him and said: 'Please tell me it's not Jack and Brook.'

Every policeman in the room looked at his boots and smiled. Sergeant Hogan glanced down and then back at me. 'I knew you was our man, doc. You got it in one.'

'Oh God!' I said as a million bonus points for being on time for my mother for once just flew out of the window.

I picked up the phone and asked Meaghan to cancel the rest of my afternoon.

'Are you OK?' she asked in a whisper. 'You're not in trouble, are you?'

'Don't be ridiculous,' I replied. 'Pure as the driven snow, I am. Whatever made you say a thing like that?'

'Well, your room's full of policemen for a start,' she answered in a conspiratorial voice. 'And then there were those plants from Dana,' she added in a whisper.

I was about to ask how on earth she knew about them when I was whisked away.

'Let's go,' said the sergeant, and I trooped out through the waiting room surrounded by policemen. There was complete silence from the assembled patients at first, but as we headed out to the car park I heard someone say: 'I suppose they had to catch up with him eventually,' and the entire waiting room burst into laughter.

'Lord knows what rumours will fly round for this one,' I muttered darkly to my companions as we got into the police car.

Whilst driving the few minutes to Kimpton Street I thought about Jack and Brook as the scenery flew by and the siren blasted my ears.

Two years before, after a sensational production of *La Traviata*, I had bumped into Brook on Southbank on a beautiful, gentle Melbourne evening. I was having a late coffee with friends in one of the restaurants that open directly onto the esplanade when I saw Brook walking along the riverbank, hand in hand with a huge Pacific islander.

She saw me at about the same time I saw her and we gave one another the big 'Hello!'

In answer to my questions, she told me that she was doing fine and that the boys were well. 'Growing up fast,' she said. 'You wouldn't recognise them.' Then suddenly she added: 'Oh, I don't believe you've met my cousin.'

I said I didn't believe that I had either, and my hand was shaken by a large dusky paw.

'Well, nice catching up with you, doc,' she said after we had exchanged pleasantries for a few minutes.

Brook turned and waved to my friends, and then, like Desdemona and Othello, she and her cousin, hand in hand, continued their stroll along the esplanade.

'Cousins?' said my friends with knowing grins.

'That's what she said,' I nodded. 'And be careful what you say about him,' I added, 'because I happen to know that he bites.'

I hadn't seen Brook since that night, but I had certainly been kept abreast of events by the papers.

Apparently, not long after I bumped into Brook, Jack found out where she and her cousin were living and decided to give them a bit of a shake-up. He borrowed an arsenal of weapons from various friends and acquaintances, loaded them into the boot of his car and headed off to Melbourne with darkness in his soul.

Whether or not you see this as an acceptable way of venting displeasure depends very much upon your point of view. What is certain, however, is that the plan went pear-shaped when, being so pre-occupied with the task at hand, Jack accidentally ran a red light and hit a petrol tanker, which exploded on impact.

The upshot of all this was that instead of teaching Brook and her cousin a lesson or two, Jack lost his right eye, several of his fingers, suffered extensive burns and did irreparable damage to the Falcon. He also caused a traffic jam which took hours to clear, made the headlines in every newspaper and even featured on the evening news.

Jack was airlifted to the burns unit and remained there for some months as the recipient of repeated plastic surgery.

I hadn't realised he was back in circulation until I was called out at the end of an evening surgery to the Swinging Arms to attend to a bloke who had collapsed near the pool table.

When I arrived, there was a bit of a crowd standing round a fellow on the floor. One of them was Jack.

'Hi, Jack,' I smiled. 'Good to see you back.'

Fortunately, the fellow who had collapsed had already regained consciousness. I checked him over just the same, but there didn't seem very much wrong.

'I think you're OK,' I said reassuringly. 'Just a faint. What happened?'

'It was the most horrible thing I've ever seen,' he replied.

'What was?' I asked.

'Well, I was playing pool with that fellow over there,' he said, pointing at Jack, 'he was about to take a shot when a mate of his comes in, shouts, "Hi, matey" and gives him a great slap on the back.'

'So?' I said.

'His eye fell out onto the pool table and when it had finished rolling he potted it into the top pocket.'

Jack looked a bit sheepish. 'Actually I must come and see you about that, doc,' he said. 'The eye they've given me is a bit small and falls out as easy as wink.'

I was brought back to the present as the police car screeched to a halt in Farm Avenue, just round the corner from Kimpton Street. I got out and looked around as I was fitted with a big heavy jacket. There were police everywhere. They were crouched behind walls, they were crouched behind vehicles and they were all looking at me.

A senior officer came over and shook my hand. 'Thanks for coming, doctor. We really appreciate your help.' Then he lifted his loud speaker. 'Dr Carter is here,' he boomed at the house.

'Send him in,' came the faint reply.

'Off you go, then,' said the officer.

'What do you mean: "Off you go then"?' I asked in alarm. 'I thought I was here to speak to him. I imagined it was going to be through a loudspeaker, round a corner.'

'No, no. He wants to speak to you face to face,' the officer replied. 'Off you go, up to the house.'

I peeped round the corner and then withdrew.

'But he's got a gun,' I protested.

'Don't you worry,' said the officer.

'But it's a fair way in the open,' I protested.

'Don't you worry,' said the officer again. 'We'll be behind you all the way.'

'That's exactly my point,' I replied a little sarcastically. 'I'd feel a hell of a lot better if you were all in front of me.'

I peeped round the corner again. 'Jack!' I called.

'Yes!'

'Are you planning on shooting me?' I asked.

'What on earth would I want do that for? Don't be stupid!'

'Is that a no?'

'Yes!'

'Oh, well, that's all right then,' I said sarcastically. I turned the corner and walked across to the house.

I am delighted to say that Jack kept his promise and I reached the front door in one piece. The door was open so I walked inside.

'We're in here,' called Jack from the front bedroom.

It took my eyes a few seconds to adjust to the darkness of the house and then I saw them. Jack had a shotgun and Brook had another shiner.

'Fancy meeting you two again,' I said brightly. And then, after a small pause, I continued: 'Jack, if that thing's loaded, then please empty it. Loaded guns make me very nervous.'

To my surprise there was no argument of any kind. Jack simply broke the gun and ejected the cartridges. I sat down on a bedroom chair with a big sigh of relief.

'Can I ask a few questions?' I enquired.

'You always do,' Jack said in a vague attempt at humour.

'Firstly, where are the boys?'

'With my mum,' answered Brook.

'Well, thank the Lord again for that,' I sighed. 'But tell me, how in hell did you two get together again after the petrol tanker business?'

'It was my doing, I suppose,' said Brook. 'I felt sorry for Jack stuck in that hospital, missing his fingers and his eye and all, so I started to visit him. One thing led to another and, well, before you know it, here we are again.'

'Aren't we just,' I said as I shook my head.

'And the cousin?' I enquired, just in case he was also in the house.

'Who?' Brook looked puzzled for a moment and then her brow cleared. 'Oh, him. I got rid of him a long time back.'

'But why all this, for God's sake?' I asked, and Brook just pointed at Jack.

'When I got out of hospital,' Jack said, 'I found she had sold what was left of the Falcon for scrap and blown the dough at the casino.'

'I could see that would be annoying,' I said, 'but I'll ask again—why all this?'

'Brook just didn't see that she'd done anything wrong,' said Jack. 'I didn't do anything at the time, but today she joked about me not having a car so I roughed her up a bit. She started packing her things. I realised that I couldn't have her leave again so I decided to keep her here with me.'

'Cheryl happened to come over to see how we were getting on,' Brook continued, 'saw the gun and called the cops.'

There was a long pause.

'Jack,' I finally said. 'You've always trusted me, so here's what I want you to do. I want you to throw the gun into the front garden, then I want you to let Brook leave and then I want you to walk out with me and give yourself up.'

And he did. Just like that. The whole thing was over in little more than a minute. After all the build-up, the ending was, fortunately, a complete fizzer. Jack was very cooperative with the police and within moments was being driven away in the company of three beefy officers. Within a quarter of an hour, just about everyone had left and the street had gone back to sleep again. Deserted, that is, apart from Garry who was mowing round his succulents.

I was dropped back at the surgery by the police late in the afternoon. The waiting room still had plenty of people in it, and every eye was fixed on me.

This time I got in before any of the comedians: 'Released early for good behaviour,' I called out, and shot into my room.

On the way out that evening, I asked Meaghan how she knew about Dana's present.

'But everyone did,' she said with a surprised look on her face.

I was about to go into this further with her, but then decided to leave the lid on Pandora's box. I simply shook my head and picked up the phone to let my mother know that I was running hopelessly late again.

To my surprise, Jack was bailed out after the shotgun episode and, to my even greater surprise, he and Brook moved back in together yet again. It would be fair to say, however, that the first flush of excitement had left their relationship and, not knowing how to fill the void, they sought my advice on how to recapture the magic.

Now, I am no relationship counsellor, but since I knew them both very well, I gave them a few general sessions on developing listening and communication skills. The sessions went surprisingly well and both of them frequently contributed to the conversation in very positive ways. Over the weeks that followed they even learned not to quarrel in front of me or interrupt one another continuously.

I felt very pleased with the success of the meetings and also a little smug that I had helped reduce the sum of human suffering, albeit in such a small way. After the sessions finished I didn't see either of them for a couple of months and then one day Brook came to the surgery for an appointment.

'How can I help?' I asked.

Brook sat smiling at me.

'I bet you can't tell what I'm here for,' she grinned.

'Well, when a girl says that and looks like the Cheshire cat,' I replied, 'it usually means she would like me to do a pregnancy test.'

'Bulls-eye, doc,' she said and handed me a specimen.

The test was positive and I said: 'This is wonderful, definitely cause for you and Jack to celebrate.'

The smile disappeared from her face. 'What do you mean?'

'Well isn't it usual for the happy couple to celebrate together on occasions such as this?' I asked, a little puzzled.

'Oh, I see,' she said, her smile returning, 'you obviously haven't caught up with the latest. Jack and I parted company on the night of our last counselling session with you. When we got home, Jack said he was sick of all this shit, smacked me about a bit and left. That's the last I've seen of him. No, this baby is nothing to do with Jack. This,' she said, patting her tummy, 'belongs to Brent.'

'And who is Brent?' I asked.

'A fellow I met down the pub the night Jack left.'

'Well, there you go,' I said.

I have never seen either of them since that day. I have no idea what happened to Jack, but I do know that Brook sold all of Jack's metal-working tools, went back to Melbourne on the proceeds and had another boy.

Susie has taken excellent care of the more domestic aspects of my life for quite a few years now, since shortly after I moved to the farm. She is lovely. She is also reliable, hardworking and trustworthy. I have come to like her very much indeed and do not know how I would manage without her.

I am usually at work when she comes to the house so our paths don't often cross. Shortly after the debacle in Kimpton St, however, it just so happened that I had come home early from the surgery and she was still there.

'Oh, by the way,' Susie said as she turned off the vacuum. 'I hope you don't mind but I took some of your oregano home the other day.'

'Fine,' I replied. 'You know you can always take anything you want from the garden.'

'Well, thank you. It was for the CWA Italian lunch,' she explained. 'I made lasagna.'

'And how did it turn out?'

'Extremely well. In fact it was probably the best lunch we've ever had. For some reason everyone was in a really good mood, even old Mrs Morwood, and that's saying something.'

'Good,' I nodded, and we went about our respective businesses.

An hour or so later, we sat down for a cup of tea together in the kitchen.

'Where did you find the oregano by the way?' I asked, impressed by the mysteries of my own garden. 'I didn't realise I had any.'

'Of course you do,' she replied with a smile. 'In the shed. You know, those shrubs you've been drying out for the last few months.'

13 Good Choice

AT THE END OF my living room is a large open fireplace with a wonderful rough-hewn mantle. Hardy and I, and occasionally Livingstone, have sat and toasted ourselves in front of it on many an evening.

On the wall above the mantle, Prince Rupert of Hentzau, monarch of the glen, gazes unblinkingly down upon the room. Well, at least the front part of him does. But even from the head and shoulders it is easy to see that he was a giant of a beast and his antlers reach up almost to the clerestory windows. Underneath him there is a small polished wooden plaque which I made myself. On the plaque a large cartridge is mounted above a small brass plate inscribed with the words: *Good choice.*

Prince Rupert is so impressive that he draws almost universal acclaim, apart from Heather, who thinks he is 'fewsty'.

Before the front part of Prince Rupert finished on the living room wall, there was a time when I got to know a chap called Russell. He wasn't at all well and he visited the surgery frequently.

'How are things?' he asked on one of his visits.

'I'm fine,' I replied. 'But it looks like you've bled into this knee again,' I said as I prodded it very gently.

Russell completely ignored my concern.

'A little birdie whispered in my ear that you have some deer on your place, these days,' he said.

And it was true.

Although it was hard work, initially the farm did well with the clip from the flock I bought with the property. Then, suddenly, someone removed the floor price. It had to happen, of course, but overnight everyone in the entire industry went from a comfortable profit to a very uncomfortable loss.

People urged caution when I originally did my sums on what a clip was worth, but I didn't understand why anyone could be worried. It all seemed ridiculously easy: so many sheep to the hectare, so much fleece per sheep, so many dollars per kilogram and Bob's your woolly uncle.

It was clearly child's play. All one had to do was have a few sheep, sit on the back patio reading the paper and just a few months later someone would deposit a good-sized cheque into your bank account.

'Look at the margin,' I said excitedly to my accountant.

'I don't know anything about sheep,' he said with a shake of his head. 'But I do know one thing.'

'What's that?'

'It's a brave man who goes into business with God as his partner.'

So I paid him a goodly sum of money for this advice and then completely ignored it.

The first snag I hit was finding that, unlike my predictions, merinos aren't optimistic. Not in the slightest. When a merino comes up against adversity, it does not burrow deep into its personal reserves, bring out a will to live, maintain a stiff upper lip, or dig its little heels in and bravely fight on. No, when a merino comes up against adversity its first reaction is to instantly hand in its dinner pail.

There is an old saying that the only thing a merino does well is die. This is not quite true and I would like to create a new old saying: the only thing that a merino does well is die, after first costing you a great deal of money and causing you endless anguish, drama and rides in the Flying Banana in disgusting weather.

In summer it is all pinkeye, worms, scabby mouth, lice and fly-strike. In winter they simply rot. Their feet rot, their fleeces rot and, believe it or not, even their pizzles rot.

The whole year becomes an expensive and time-consuming continuum of husbandry. When you are not stamping out fires you are building firebreaks. If you are not vaccinating and drenching, then you are jetting and dipping; and if you are not crutching and wigging, then you are delousing.

Then, when you have completed the animal husbandry, you start pouring money down their throats because the autumn rains are late.

Over the years after the floor price disappeared I gradually became heartily tired of working hard for the privilege of operating at a loss. When the opportunity presented itself of sending the entire flock on a one-way cruise to the Middle East, I grabbed it with both hands.

Then, after a while of doing nothing, I acquired some young stags and decided to try my hand at growing deer velvet.

'There are a lot of little birdies round this district,' I replied.

'Yes,' Russell responded, 'there sure are.'

Then he looked down at his knee. 'Must have happened when I was clearing rocks yesterday.'

'What!' I exploded. 'You know you're not supposed to be doing things like that.'

'Yeah, yeah, yeah,' Russell replied.

Lesley put a pressure bandage on the knee and I said: 'There, that should be fine until you do something stupid again.'

'So any time you need some help with the deer,' he said, changing the subject, 'just give us a yell.'

'Working with wild animals would almost certainly come under my definition of you doing something stupid,' I laughed.

'Yes, but remember that I have the advantage of being very experienced. After all,' Russell said as he got off the couch, 'I used to be married to one once.'

Russell and I had clicked from the time we first met. Perhaps it was that we were both on our own, or had similar interests, or maybe we just had the same silly sense of humour.

Russell had retired early from the banking business because of his health and now spent his days on his farm to the west of Rushby. Despite my reservations, we got into the habit of doing farm jobs together on those occasions when two blokes are better than one. So we would sometimes spend a day over at his place and then another one back at mine. I enjoyed working with him and he obviously felt the same about me. We always knew exactly what the other was trying to do, when to push, when to pull, when to talk and when to shut up. In all the times we were together, I don't think we ever had a cross word.

Russell never seemed to mind that I always got the better end of the bargain in terms of jobs done, and he even occasionally helped by picking up my post from Ros on the way through.

'Don't worry, we're not keeping score,' he would smile. 'You're chained to a stethoscope while I'm as free as a bird.'

I came to like Russell a lot. He was intelligent and funny and good company of an evening.

Of course Russell did help with the deer; I don't think I could have stopped him, and he proved to be a natural at it. In the shed he knew exactly when to force them and exactly when not to, when to close the crush and when to leave it open. Over the three velvet seasons we worked together we put many hundreds of animals through the shed without so much as a single injury either to them or to ourselves and it simply would not have been possible without Russell.

My dear old dad was helpful around the place in many other ways, but there were some things he did not do and deer, he said, were definitely on that list. After the sheep went, and before the deer arrived, I considered having cattle on the farm and my father came with me early one morning to have a look at some young bulls. It was bitingly cold and the wind cut like a knife. Neither of us knew the first thing about cattle buying but my father, in an attempt to appear knowledgeable, bent down and peered at the nearest animal's undercarriage.

'He hasn't got very big balls,' he observed to the stock agent.

'I don't suppose yours look too flash this morning either,' came the instant reply.

With Russell and myself on the job, the deer flowed through the shed as smoothly as if they had been oiled. Almost all the time that is, for in every mob of animals there is always one bugger that's not interested in flowing, however much oil you put on him.

Prince Rupert was our bugger. He might have had royal Hungarian blood flowing through his veins, but he wasn't a prince. He was mean and he was ugly and he was big. He was hard to get into the shed and even harder to get out of it. And, as the seasons rolled by, he got bigger and stronger and ever more difficult to handle. Although we got to know him well, he also got to know us. He would stand there, all two hundred and eighty kilograms of him, looking at us sideways, poking out his tongue and clicking his teeth.

'This is not looking good,' I would say to myself as he crashed into my shield and sent me flying against the wall for the umpteenth time. 'Russell,' I called out as I picked myself up and dusted myself off. 'I've done all the hard ones. There's just one easy one left for you.'

'Ah,' said Russell as he peeped round the door. 'I think I recognise him. Sod off, Paul.'

Prince Rupert was the only stag we ever gave up on. He was just too obstinate and dangerous, so we turned him back out into the paddock and decided to work out what to do with him later. We didn't, of course, and in a few weeks his velvet changed to hard antler and he started bullying the rest of the herd.

'We'll just have to move the Prince into a paddock on his own,' I said.

'You mean *you'll* have to move him,' replied Russell.

'I'm not doing it on my own,' I protested. 'If I'm going to die, I'd prefer to do it in company.'

Russell put up a few more feeble objections but I overruled him and, shortly after, we entered the paddock in the Flying Banana. For a while all went well as we quietly made our way through the herd towards the delinquent. When he first got wind of our intentions he didn't seem to mind too much, but as we got closer he poked out his tongue again and clicked at us.

'I don't like the look of this,' said Russell a little nervously.

'You're a worrier,' I said in my best calming, air-hostess manner. 'Just tighten your seat belt and make sure that your tray is in the upright position.'

Russell was in the middle of reminding me that we didn't have any bloody seat belts when Prince Rupert charged.

In the excitement I missed a gear and by the time I had the vehicle spun round and underway he was almost upon us. I'm not sure what the top speed of the Flying Banana is on soft ground, but I do know that it is exactly one kilometre per hour slower than Prince Rupert. Moment by moment, he gained on us.

Russell, I thought, summed the situation up particularly well. 'Oh, shit! Oh, shit! Oh shit! Oh, shit!' he shouted as a large and angry beast with two sets of daggers on its head came to within a few centimetres of his backside.

Then, fortunately, we demonstrated why the industrial revolution was such a success: machines don't tire whilst animals do. Slowly at first, but then with increasing speed, we gradually pulled away from him.

'I will never forgive you, you bastard,' Russell said to me back at the house.

'Garbage,' I replied. 'You loved every minute of it.'

'People have nightmares about being chased by killer animals,' he replied.

'Well, think of the positives,' I said. 'You no longer need to have nightmares about it. You've got memories.'

In the end we did get Prince Rupert away from the herd and we did it without anyone getting killed or even scared half to death. On the second attempt we tried cunning rather than full-frontal attack and we used the oldest trick in the book: sex. We borrowed half-a-dozen young hinds from Tony who had a deer farm nearby, put them in the next paddock, left the gate open and Prince Rupert walked quietly through all on his own.

Just a few days later Russell had been over at my place to put out some feed when he phoned me at the surgery.

'The Prince has gone!' he said.

'What do you mean?' I asked. 'He can't have gone.'

'Well he has. You had better come and see for yourself.'

Fortunately I was nearly finished for the day and managed to delegate what I had left to Felix. I drove home in a bit of a hurry, threw on some farm clothes and went down with Russell to inspect the damage.

The fences were all intact and the females were still quietly grazing under the trees, but of Prince Rupert there was neither hide nor hair.

'What do you reckon made him do that?' I asked. 'Weren't those hinds attractive enough?'

'Perhaps he's gay,' laughed Russell.

Russell and I spent a frantic afternoon checking both of the creeks and as much of the forest as we could reach by vehicle, but there was not so much as a hoof-print or even a scrap of fur on a tree stump. He had vanished without trace.

I badly wanted him back. Not only had I never lost an animal before, but I was worried about him roaming around the district. Besides, I'd paid good money for him.

Every spare moment after work and on the following weekend I searched the whole district, but never so much as caught a glimpse of him.

The first sighting came after two months. Some friends with a farm higher up in the ranges phoned and told me that they had seen him grazing amongst their cattle, but by the time I got there, of course, he was long gone. After that there were any number of reports: a repair crew working on an electricity line up in the forest reported he had now grown into full antler; a motorist on the main road to Lockridge apparently missed him by a whisker late one night, and a woman phoned the surgery to report a sighting in Ellerstone.

'Are you the doctor with the escaped stag?' she said in an irate voice.

'Yes, I am. Have you caught him?' I asked hopefully.

'No, I haven't caught him, but I'm looking at him out of my kitchen window right now. He is in my vegetable patch eating my lettuces. Could you please come over and get him right now?'

If only it was as easy as that. 'I'll see what I can do,' I said, and did nothing.

I was enjoying a rare lie-in the following Saturday when the phone interrupted my dreams.

'Did you ever catch that stag of yours?' asked Tony.

'No, I never did.'

'I didn't think so, because he's at my place. He has jumped the fence into my farm . . .'

'Yes, he can do that,' I muttered.

' . . . chucked my stag over a fence and taken over the herd.'

'Well that rogers Russell's theory,' I said.

'What?' said Tony, but I told him not to worry.

I arrived at Tony's half an hour later to find him very agitated indeed.

'That bloody stag of yours,' he said. 'Come with me and I'll show you what he's done.'

We drove onto his farm and down to an area that looked like a battleground.

'God, this looks like a battleground,' I said, perhaps unnecessarily.

'That's because it is one,' said Tony. 'This,' he continued as he gestured towards the wreckage, 'is where your boy trashed my fellow and then chucked him out. My bloke must weigh over two hundred kilos and your boy lifted him up with his antlers as easy as anything and threw him over what was left of the fence, fortunately into another paddock. I wouldn't have believed it except I saw it with my own eyes.'

'Much damage to your fellow?' I asked, wincing at the possible answer.

'Not to him. No, luckily just a few cuts and bruises. But when I came to his rescue that bloody stag of yours attacked my vehicle and made a right mess of it.'

'Don't worry, Tony. I'll get that fixed for you,' I replied a little unconvincingly. 'But where is he?' I continued, looking around.

We drove further down the lane and rounded a corner. Suddenly, there he was. He looked magnificent. He had grown much bigger in the forest and he was carrying a full head of spectacular antler.

'You'll have to drop him,' said Tony.

'What?' I replied in surprise.

'You'll have to put him down,' repeated Tony.

'But . . .' I tried

'Let me see,' Tony said. 'He's a fence jumper, he's huge, he's in full antler, he's so aggressive that you can't get within a hundred metres of him, he's trashed my fences, he's damaged my stag, he's pushed the passenger door in on my ute, he would be impossible to get back to your place and he would escape again even if you somehow managed to.'

'Now that you put it that way . . .'

'Paul, he's a lawsuit waiting to happen. Sooner or later he's going to kill someone. Need I go on?'

'No, no,' I replied. 'I'll arrange something straight away.'

That evening I made a few phone calls and early the next morning the shooting party assembled at Tony's. It comprised Tony, myself, Bob and Bob.

Living in the city certainly has many advantages, but living in the country has some of its own. Quite apart from the open spaces and the fresh air, it is also easy to put together a shooting party. With only a couple of calls I located and enlisted Bob, a professional hunter, and his son Bob, also a professional hunter.

Bob opened the boot of his car, revealing an armoury the SAS would have been proud of.

'I'm presuming you want a trophy?' he asked.

'Of course,' I replied, thinking of it for the first time. 'I might as well have something to show for all this trouble.'

'Then go for a heart shot, son,' said Bob.

'OK, Dad,' said Bob, and pulled a very impressive piece of equipment indeed out of the boot.

'Bob's a good shot,' Bob said proudly. 'That bugger will never know what hit him.'

And he didn't. One shot, one echo, one stag on the ground.

Bob opened the chamber on his firearm and ejected the cartridge. He caught it in midair and handed it to me. 'Stick this in your pocket, doc, as a souvenir.'

We all walked over to where Prince Rupert lay and stood looking at him. He was a big boy indeed.

The two Bobs set to work immediately. In just a few minutes, or so it seemed, the insides were down the creek for the foxes, the body was in the back of Bob's ute, and the head and antlers were lashed to the grill behind the cab on my vehicle.

'Bob'll take the body to the butcher, won't you, son?' said Bob.

'Not a problem, Dad,' Bob replied.

'So,' Bob continued, 'if you bring the head round to my place, we'll get it ready for the taxidermist.'

As soon as I arrived at Bob's place on the back road to Jackson's Crossing, he got to work with skill, speed and a variety of tools I didn't even know existed. His wife invited me in for a cup of tea while Bob went about his business and we drank our tea under the watchful gaze of whole herds of motionless animals. There wasn't a square metre of wall in the entire house that did not have an animal poking out of it. The passage to the loo was a walkway between noses, and from either side of the fireplace two huge water buffalo stared unflinchingly at one another.

'See that one?' Raylene said pointing to a deer by the front door. 'I got that.'

The sight of one of the local medics driving through town with a deer's head tied to the back of his cab had not gone unnoticed and I had been at Bob's for less than half an hour when the first arrival showed up.

'Hear you got a deer, doc,' he said.

I nodded whilst the new arrival looked over the head. 'What a beauty,' he muttered.

In a trickle came the others, until by the end there must have been twenty or more. When Bob finished his work, the outer part of Prince Rupert was smothered in salt and put away for safekeeping. Someone lit the brazier and we all stood round it in a circle telling hunting stories. I had never actually been hunting, so I simply stood and listened.

There were stories of pigs and goats and buffalo and ducks and kangaroos, but most of all deer. Deer, it seems, are the bee's knees when it comes to this business and there was general admiration for Prince Rupert and the size of his antlers. The record book came out and we found that he was the fifty-fifth largest set of antlers ever recorded. I felt a warm glow of proprietorship.

Suddenly someone on the other side of the circle said: 'So what did you fetch him down with, doc?'

It was at that precise moment I realised I had somehow omitted to mention that he had not been shot by me. I am a poor liar at the best of times and was about to come clean about the whole affair when my fingers felt something metallic in my pocket.

Without so much as a word, I pulled out the cartridge case and threw it to the inquirer. I wouldn't have had the faintest idea what sort of cartridge it was, but he held it up knowingly, squinted at it, showed it to his neighbour and then threw it back to me.

'Good choice,' he said and a circle of heads nodded in agreement.

A few months later I got a call from Heather during a weekend on call.

'I've had a very peculiar call,' she said, 'which I don't fully understand, from a man who wants to know what expression you would like on your head.'

I had no idea what she was talking about at first, then suddenly the penny dropped. 'Well that depends on what's available,' I replied.

'He said,' Heather continued, rather primly, 'that "Monarch of the Glen" is his speciality.'

'Well, in that case, could you please let him know that "Monarch of the Glen" it is,' I said brightly.

Some while after, Russell was in the surgery again. I told him I was taking a short break and I asked if he would mind giving me a hand with some drenching the Sunday I got back.

'Of course,' he said. 'Love to.'

I had organised to visit some friends in Gippsland who had taken on the job of being lighthouse keepers. It was a wonderful and relaxing break. I bushwalked and read and wrote and painted. I sat with my friends as we gazed at the sun setting over the ocean and sorted out the world's problems over a bottle or two of red.

I came back with my batteries fully charged. Sunday morning dawned clear and mild, a perfect day for handling deer. I brought the animals we needed up to the shed, got the drench ready and waited for Russell. When he didn't arrive, I drew up the tally book, re-greased the hydraulic crush, cleaned up the shed, made a cup of tea and waited for him again.

I gave him a call but his phone rang out.

Drenching deer is not really a one-man job but the animals were in the shed and it seemed too good an opportunity to miss. By the time I'd finished the last one, I was exhausted. I tried Russell's number again when I got back to the house but without luck.

Back in the surgery the next day I was busy, busy, busy catching up with all the regulars who had been hanging out for my return. At lunchtime, after I had battled with the inevitable mountain of accumulated paperwork, I suddenly realised that Russell had been booked in to see me that morning but had missed his appointment.

I phoned through to the desk. 'Could you please let Russell know he missed his appointment this morning and ask him to make another time.'

'I'll just pop in,' Meaghan replied, and a few seconds later she and Madge were sitting by my desk.

'You don't know, do you?' Meaghan asked.

'Know what?' I asked in reply.

'He died,' Madge said in a whisper.

'What!' I felt as if I had been struck in the face.

'Well, the day after you went on holiday he had another bleed. A bad one. Into his tummy. He was rushed to the hospital, but they couldn't stop the bleeding and he died two days later.'

'What!' I exclaimed again.

'You weren't told because no one wanted to spoil your holiday,' Meaghan said quietly. 'The funeral was last Thursday.'

I thought of nothing else all day and at home that night I gave Russell a toast: 'You bastard, how dare you die on me. Especially when I loved you.'

In fact, I gave Russell a lot of toasts as the evening wore on. I had known that he was gravely ill, of course. I had known that he walked on thin ice every day. But he was always so full of life. How dare he do that. How dare he go, without even a chance of saying goodbye.

Two weeks later there was a message on my answering machine from Bob telling me that the head was ready and that Angelo, the taxidermist, would deliver it the following Saturday. I had been waiting months for this to happen but I felt too flat to get excited.

Right on time the following weekend, Angelo pulled up in front of the house.

'Can you help me get your one out?' he asked. 'It's near the bottom of the pile,' he added as he threw off a large tarpaulin revealing a mountain of animal heads of all shapes and sizes.

Prince Rupert was located and carefully disentangled from the antler puzzle. He was then carried into the house and hung on the nail I had knocked into the brickwork in honour of his impending arrival.

We stood back to admire him.

'He looks magnificent,' I said.

'He certainly does,' Angelo agreed, 'and it is always nice to see my work going to places where the artistry is appreciated.'

'Monarch of the Glen,' I said in awe.

'Monarch of the Glen,' Angelo nodded.

There was a pause and I thought he was about to leave when he said those words that send shivers down any doctor's spine. 'You're a medical man, aren't you?' he asked.

'Yes I am,' I replied cautiously.

'Well, I would like to seek your opinion on a matter of some delicacy.'

'Yeees,' I said even more cautiously.

'Down in Melbourne a short while ago, a pedestrian was knocked down by a tram which ran over his leg and chopped it off. The hospital was going to throw it away but the man sought legal advice and apparently the leg still belongs to him. He has asked if I would be prepared to stuff it and mount it on a wooden shield for him. Apparently the hospital has frozen the leg pending my reply. I understand that the leg is very hairy and that is putting me off a bit, but are there ethical considerations here? What do you think I should do?'

'Well it all depends,' I responded.

'On what?' asked Angelo.

I dug deep into the experience of a medical practitioner with many years tucked under his belt: 'Well, it all depends on how much the chap is offering you,' I replied.

Without Russell, I was lonely and sad for many months. I missed his wit and laughter. I missed his company and his enthusiasm for being alive.

I also missed our evening chats when we would talk about anything and everything. But that's not true, not everything. For in all the times we talked, not once did either of us ever refer to the past. Perhaps in time we could have done, but it wasn't to be. I would have liked to have heard his story and I wish now that I had told him about Amy.

'I miss him,' I said to Hardy as we sat by the fire.

He looked into the flames and didn't say anything for quite a while.

'I know,' he replied eventually. 'I know you're feeling sad right now, but having had him in your life, having had him as your friend, was a really good choice.'

There was a long pause.

'You really have a knack with words,' I said and he thumped the side of the chair with his tail in agreement.

14 Heather

I DON'T KNOW HOW many duty weekends I have done over the years but it must be hundreds. Although they were often tiring and emotionally draining, and although they always seemed to come around surprisingly frequently, they were largely bearable because of Heather. If still short of pleasurable then she at least made them do-able. I may not have looked forward with happy anticipation to yet another weekend of hard work and interrupted sleep but, with Heather looking after me, neither did I look forward to it with dread.

I had no Delphine at home to field calls, and mobile phones didn't work reliably round the hills in those early days. The staff at the local bush nursing hospital did their best, and my mother was a brick, often coming up to help out. Nevertheless, things were still a bit of a headache until I 'found' Heather. Once she was onboard, everything became a breeze. She was always so beautifully organised with paperwork and messages, and she kept me under control as well. I would phone in at regular intervals from wherever I was to see what was happening and what calls she had taken. And if I forgot to let her know where I was it didn't matter, for she always miraculously seemed to know how to get hold of me anyway.

'Don't you ever think of putting a toe out of line, mister,' she would say, 'because I will know about it even before it has happened.'

'Anyone would be crazy to even think of putting one atom of a toe out of line whilst living in this goldfish bowl,' I replied.

'Yes, well, plenty do,' she said in her schoolmarm way. 'So you just mind yourself,' she added, 'or I'll be onto you, doctor.'

And I did mind myself. In fact it never even crossed my mind to do anything else, but I did rather enjoy having a de facto baby sister who bossed me about and checked that I stayed on the straight and narrow.

I had met Heather that very first day when Felix asked me to do a home visit. She was pretty blue in those days and spent her housebound life attached to the end of a plastic line. We got on well from the first. Despite how ill she was, she was always cheeky and witty. She always sparkled. In her beautiful Lowland brogue, she only ever made the best out of anything. She was, even then, extremely positive. In all the time I have known her I have never once heard her grumble about anything.

Because she was so unwell, I started visiting her on a regular basis and, over the years, we gradually came to know one another well. I happened to visit her one Saturday I was on call. Whilst I was at her house I phoned the hospital to get my messages and work out where my next house calls were. Unfortunately one of them involved me travelling all the way back out to Murrum Vale whence I had just come. I expressed some frustration, knowing full well it was no one's fault. Just the result of poor communications.

I shared my frustrations with Heather, who said: 'Why don't you switch the phone from the hospital to me. I may be dying but I can still answer the phone. Call me when you're finished out at Murrum Vale and I'll let you know what else has come in.'

So we did and it was a great success, and for the rest of the weekend I didn't have to backtrack once. And the weekend reins were handed to Heather forthwith.

On the Saturday nights I was on duty, I would often go over and have dinner with Heather and Rob and their two extremely badly behaved fur-children. Wire-haired Foxies they were, who jumped everywhere. Actually, that's not quite true: they were forbidden to jump on the table while we were actually eating, but they certainly jumped everywhere else.

Unlike the dogs, I was very well behaved. I never said a word about all their shenanigans, but if I so much as raised an eyebrow when they walked across the back of the settee or stood on top of the television, Heather would scoop them both up and say: 'Oh, so the clever-dick doctor doesn't approve. Well, come to Mummy, my poor little babies, and don't be frightened of the nasty man because I love you even if he doesn't.'

Then she would cover them in kisses and put them out into the garden where they would immediately bite something to pieces or dig yet another hole.

'She kisses those dogs more than she kisses you, Rob,' I said one evening.

'Och aye, it's been like that for years, doctor,' he would say with a smile. 'I used to think she was growing a moustache, you know, a side effect of one of her pills, but then I realised it was just dog hair round her mouth. Care for another wee dram?' he added as he ducked a cushion thrown at his head.

The fur-children jumped all over Hardy too when he came. Hardy often did the rounds with me at the weekend. He thoroughly enjoyed doing house calls and the house calls seemed to thoroughly like him too, so he was quite often with me when I went to Heather and Rob's for dinner. He didn't like it one bit.

Heather didn't mind being stuck at home answering the phone for me at weekends. As she always said: she was stuck at home anyway. In fact she loved it, for it helped to fill in the time whilst waiting for her new lungs to arrive. She had a frustratingly long wait for those lungs and was therefore my weekend organiser for quite a few years. And being the smartie she was, she got really good at the job and in no time at all was even triaging calls. She loved the work, loved the sense of community, loved being useful and loved bossing me about.

'After all,' she would lilt through her blue lips, 'what on earth other job could I do?'

From the very first time I met her she was already on the active transplant list and we all knew that the weekend arrangement would have to be abandoned if she got the call to arms. She did get the call eventually, but it was not for a long time and there were quite a few false starts along the way.

I went round one Monday to do a routine house call, only to find Heather very flat indeed. Apparently over the weekend she had been phoned and told that a donor had become available. She and Rob had thrown some things in a bag and shot down to Melbourne quick smart. Heather had got as far as being wheeled into theatre before the whole thing was called off. The new lungs were apparently too big to fit into her chest. I understood later, speaking on the phone to the specialist, that the donor had been a bikey in his twenties. I never saw the bikey, of course, and he might not have been a particularly big bloke, but Heather is tiny and I was surprised that the issue of size hadn't surfaced before things went as far as they did.

Heather had never had children. Her lung problem having first presented when she was a teenager, she had been strongly advised against motherhood and had acted accordingly.

'Not to worry, you've got Rob and me and the dogs,' I would say, only to start her throwing cushions again.

'Have you ever been married?' Rob asked when the excitement died down.

'Well, as a matter of fact, I have,' I replied.

'Do you still keep in touch with her, doctor?'

'Not really,' I said. 'Perhaps I should, but I don't.'

Twice more Heather was called down to Melbourne on a wild-goose chase. The first time the organ had come from interstate. Unfortunately there had been delays along the way and by the time it reached Melbourne it had gone past its use-by date.

The second time the organ came from interstate again. On this occasion, keen not to repeat the previous problem, the ambulance making the pick-up from the airport tried to get to the hospital in record time. On the exit road from the freeway, the driver misread a curve, clipped the central safety zone and flipped the ambulance onto its side. Sadly, not only was this organ lost too but also the life of one of the officers travelling with it.

A few evenings of commiserations with Rob and Heather were required, along with a few hugs and more than a few drams of Scotch.

In all the time that I have known her, I have often tried to get Heather to call me by my first name, but I have never been successful.

'"Doctor" sounds so formal,' I said once.

'And what's wrong with that?' she asked primly.

'Well nothing, I guess, apart from the fact that, unbeknownst to you, I've completed all the necessary paperwork and have now officially adopted you as my baby sister,' I replied.

'Oh get away with you, you silly man,' she laughed.

Nevertheless, she decided that she couldn't come at 'Paul'. It was just too informal for her. For a while she experimented with 'chucky', but I wasn't too keen on that so in the end we just went back to where we started.

Heather and Rob migrated just a year or two before Linda and myself. Like us, there had been an element of running away and like us they had fallen in love with Australia. Rob had been a little reluctant at the start, apparently, and would have been happy to stay in Scotland. He had acquired a couple of international rugby caps along the way and was a bit of a hero in his home town. In the corridor by the loo at the back of their house is a photograph of Rob, with long hair tied back with a headband, and much less waistline than now, doing a drop kick for Scotland at Murrayfield. I didn't recognise him at first, for these days his hairstyle is very similar to my own. In the end Rob's love for Heather was much greater than his need for local accolades and he happily came along with her for the ride.

'What were you running away from?' I asked one evening.

'Hah,' interjected Rob, 'you've obviously not met Heather's family.'

I admitted that I hadn't had the pleasure and spent the next hour having Heather and Rob firmly filling in the gaps in my knowledge. The family were presented as ghastly. They were this, they were that and they were definitely the other. In fact, it seemed as if there was nothing derogatory that the whole bunch of them weren't. By the time Heather and Rob had finished, I could quite see why they felt it best to be on the other side of the world from them.

Some time later, when Heather eventually got her new lungs, her mother came out to help look after her when she was discharged from hospital. I was expecting to meet an absolute dragon. Rather to my surprise, however, Heather's mother turned out to be a pleasant little jenny wren of a woman who busied herself round the house all day, fluffing up Heather's pillows and being unfailingly polite to me.

'See what I mean, doctor?' Heather said when her mother had gone home.

I said I did, but really I didn't. I guess that's families for you.

Heather was fourth time lucky with her donor. She went to hospital in the late evening and this time was wheeled right into theatre without any hiccoughs. The operation took all night. Rob had initially planned to stay at the hospital but there really wasn't much point, so he came home to feed the dogs.

He gave me a call to let me know what was happening and, as I was nearby, I popped in to see him. We exchanged all the usual pleasantries and I was about to go when he asked if I would like a wee dram. I'm not sure I have ever said no to a wee dram with Rob, or indeed anyone else, so I said yes.

One dram, of course, became two which became reminiscences which became old rugby videos. We didn't get drunk but, over the course of the night, we certainly toasted the surgeon, the anaesthetist, the transplant team, the founders of the hospital and probably quite a few others as well.

In the early morning light we made ourselves coffee and then Rob headed off to the hospital whilst I headed off to work.

The operation was a great success and Heather sailed past every possible complication and reached every desired milestone well ahead of schedule. Even so, she was in the hospital for quite a while and I popped down to Melbourne a few times to see her.

'This is my doctor,' Heather would proudly tell the ward staff.

'And why is he here?' they would ask in a puzzled way.

'Because he loves me,' she would reply, holding my hand as they raised their eyebrows.

When she was well enough, and when she had stopped spending one hundred per cent of her life having blood tests or seeing specialists, Heather came home again. Her feet had hardly got in the door when she was demanding to be on weekend phone duty again.

'Heather,' I said, 'it's wonderful having you back. I've missed you badly.'

'Get away with you, you daft man,' she replied, blushing with her new pink colour. 'And can you and Rob please stop fussing round me,' she added as though she didn't love every minute of it.

Over the weeks and months after leaving the hospital, Heather's strength grew steadily day by day. Since she no longer needed to be attached to an oxygen cylinder, she eventually reached the point where she could go out. She and Rob had both been so kind to me that I invited them over to the farm for dinner. We were just sitting down at the table when Heather looked up.

'God in heaven,' she said looking down the room. 'What on earth is that awful fewsty thing above the fireplace?'

'That,' I said proudly, 'is Prince Rupert of Hentzau, Monarch of the Glen.'

'Well it just looks like an awful fewsty thing to me,' she said. 'If I lived here, that thing would be the first to go,' she added with determination.

'Well then I guess it's lucky for the Prince that you don't,' I replied.

Heather's recovery was remarkable and she continues to remain well to this day, constantly setting and then re-breaking transplant survival records. In a few short months after her operation, she went from respiratory cripple to fit and energetic woman. It was miraculous, and within a year of her operation she was chomping at the bit to rejoin the out-of-home workforce.

At about the time that Heather was ready to work again, there was a vacancy for a receptionist at the surgery. When Meaghan left to have her baby, she had been replaced with Sheila. Unfortunately, this had not been a happy appointment and Sheila had left only a few months later under somewhat of a cloud. I decided to ask Heather if she was interested in the position, figuring that whatever she did she would have to fit in better than Sheila.

'How would you like a job at the surgery?' I asked Heather the next time I saw her.

'Well what do you think, you daft pillock?' she squealed and gave me the best sisterly hug I have ever had. 'I thought you'd never ask.'

Heather's joining the staff was a great success. Not only was she fabulous at her work but she got on well with Madge and even, thank the Lord, continued to look after my weekend work as well.

All was going well until a few months later. A patient came to me and said that she wished to make a complaint about a staff member. I still felt a little raw over the events surrounding Sheila's departure, so I groaned inwardly and asked what the problem was.

'The other day, I needed to see you and couldn't get an appointment,' the woman said.

'Perhaps I didn't have one available,' I replied reasonably.

'But it has never been a problem before. The others always fit me in with you, but not this one, oh no. Mrs High and Mighty just said there was a time available next week but nothing sooner. I said I wasn't happy with that and she said that she wasn't happy with the way I constantly abused your good nature by pushing in on you and that it had to stop.'

'Which staff member are we talking about?' I asked when she had finished.

'That one,' she said, pointing at Heather. 'The one with the Italian accent.'

15 Neighbours

FRIDAY EVENING SURGERIES WERE often rather difficult. Not only did they usually drag on forever but I was always tired by that time of the week. There was one Friday I remember when I was feeling especially jaded and the surgery seemed unending. Eventually, however, I managed to empty the waiting room and was really looking forward to going home with a takeaway and having a whisky by the fire with Hardy. I was nearly at the front door when the phone rang.

'Tell them I've already left,' I whispered to Madge.

Madge grabbed me by the sleeve and held me tightly as she picked up the phone. She and I had become good friends over the years but she never missed an opportunity to reaffirm her pecking order. 'Medical Centre, Madge speaking, how can I help?'

With a completely impassive face, she 'mmmed' and 'aahhed' as she listened. Then she nodded a few times, put the phone down and let go of my arm.

'Well? Can we go to our respective homes and relax by our respective fires with glasses of whatever takes our fancy?' I asked, with what I hoped was a winning smile.

'I can,' she said, giving me a winning smile back, 'but you can't.'

'Please don't do this to me,' I groaned. 'I'm exhausted. I'm only prepared to see them if they are bleeding out of their eyes.'

'They're not bleeding out of their eyes, Paul,' she said with a straight face, 'but they are bleeding out of their stomach. Badly. There's been a stabbing. Apparently the patient is still alive but the police would very much like you there. "As soon as possible", I believe is the phrase the officer used. Here's where to go,' she added as she wrote down the address.

' I groaned to myself a few times, grabbed the emergency gear and shot up to Rushby as fast as I could. The dark countryside flew by and my thoughts went back through all the injuries and wounds I had seen since making my move.

Farm accidents were a dime a dozen and domestic ones were even cheaper, so while I saw lots of wounds of one kind or another pretty much on a daily basis, the overwhelming majority of them were accidental. Almost all were pretty straightforward, such as arms caught in wool presses or hands injured whilst slicing pumpkin and arguing with children at the same time.

A few of them were severe. Fortunately they were not common, but there had been the time when the four year old who was riding on the front of the ride-on mower had fallen underneath it, and the other time when Dennis had put his hand in a wheat auger to free a blockage without turning the motor off first. The hand did surprisingly well after it was stitched back on, actually, but it had been very difficult getting it out of the auger to send to the hospital in the first place. The four year old also did surprisingly well, needing only sixteen operations to put the pieces back together again.

Nevertheless, apart from when the boys got excited at the Arms on a Saturday night, I saw very little in the way of wounds that had been deliberately inflicted by men on other men. A man was brought into the practice one day with a butter knife poking out of his right eye, it having been put in there by a friend during a dispute about money, but that sort of event was rare in our practice.

Men inflicting wounds on women, by contrast, I sadly saw quite often. It was not unusual to have to stitch up eyebrows and cheeks late at night on a weekend and I once banned one of the shearers from ever coming back to the farm when I saw what he had done to his poor wife's face. And late one night, I was busily picking pieces of glass from the face of a lady who had had her head smashed into the Welsh dresser when her husband came looking for her.

It had always been my habit to lock the front door when I was attending a patient out of hours, simply because it felt more secure, and I had done so on this occasion. As I worked away, I could hear him rattling the door. The rattling became increasingly violent and then suddenly there was a huge crash of splintering glass.

I raced through to the waiting room to discover that, finding the door locked, the man had decided to gain access by headbutting the front window. He was very drunk indeed, there was blood streaming down his face and he was coming for me.

'Where the fuck have you got my wife?' he bellowed.

'Where I can take the glass out of her face that you put there, you arsehole,' I shouted back. I don't often swear at patients or their husbands, but I was riled up. 'And look at the mess you've made, you bullying prick,' I continued. 'Whatever else happens, you'll be paying for that in the morning.'

To my surprise he turned round, looked at the destruction and said he was sorry.

'And what's more, you moron,' I shouted angrily, 'I won't be able to go home when I have finished your wife's face, because now I'll have to look after yours as well.'

And he really did pay for all the damage and his wife did finally leave him.

I followed Madge's instructions, and when I arrived there were several police cars parked outside and the house was vividly lit up by their headlights. I parked on the nature strip and as I ran up the driveway towards the house a young constable leapt out of the darkness and put his hand on my chest.

'Jesus!' I exclaimed, jumping about a metre in the air.

'Sorry sir, but no one is allowed in. Please go home.'

I thought of my single malt Scotch waiting for me at home and was very tempted to take his advice when Sergeant Hogan spotted me and hurriedly escorted me into the house.

Eddie was lying on the floor of the sitting room, clutching some very bloody towels to his middle. Sandra was kneeling on one side, holding his hand, and Martin, their son, was sitting on his other side.

I knew them all well.

'Hello, doc,' Eddie said faintly.

'Hi, Eddie,' I replied as I spread my gear out on the floor.

Eddie was looking pale and frightened and I found that he had very little in the way of blood pressure. I gently pulled away the towels to see what was underneath and saw that he was bleeding freely from a small but deep wound in the middle of his tummy. I reapplied some fresh towels and asked Sandra to press hard.

'Can someone call the ambulance?' I asked.

'We already have,' she said. 'I understand they'll be here any minute.'

'Good,' I replied. 'But what on earth has caused that wound?' I asked as I started to put up a drip.

'A bread knife,' Sandra replied. 'A twelve-inch bread knife. The new next-door neighbour apparently got irritated about the dog barking.'

'I didn't think you had a dog,' I said as I concentrated on getting the drip working properly.

By the time the ambulance arrived a short time later there were two lines running well. Within ten or fifteen minutes Eddie was feeling a whole lot better. His pulse was less alarming, his blood pressure had become measurable and his breathing sounded less laboured. Even so, an air ambulance was organised just to be on the safe side.

I leant over Eddie and said: 'You're going to be fine, Eddie, but you'll be going to hospital so that someone can work out what the damage is inside.'

'Thanks, doc,' said Eddie with a weak smile. 'I feel a whole lot better already.'

The sergeant leaned forward and put his head very close to mine.

'This is all very well, doc,' he said, pointing to the drips, 'but do you realise that if he pulls through, this reduces the case to attempted murder?'

Eddie, Sandra, Martin, the ambos and I all said: 'What!' in loud chorus and, just for the sake of emphasis, I added, 'And for God's sake be careful of those lines.'

'Whereas, if he doesn't make it,' continued the sergeant, apparently oblivious to our consternation, 'I would be fully justified in calling in the homicide squad.'

'I guess we're going to do our best to spoil your bit of fun,' I said and adjusted the drips to make them run a little faster.

The sergeant was about to protest but was cut short by the noise of the helicopter overhead on its way to landing at the football ground. Eddie, still very much alive, was loaded onto a stretcher and whisked away by the ambulance crew for his transfer to Melbourne.

When the air ambulance eventually departed, Sandra, Martin and I went back to the house and Sandra made a cup of tea.

'What on earth happened?' I asked.

'Martin was just leaving for his night shift and Eddie and I were standing at the front gate saying goodbye to him,' Sandra said. 'Suddenly, the fellow from next door, who's only recently moved in, appeared at the gate. He was ranting and raving. "I'm sick of your effing dog barking all the time. Effing shut it up!" he screamed at us.

'Eddie tried to explain to him that it wasn't our dog, and that it belongs to the Williamsons on the other side. The man took no notice and screamed, "I don't want any more effing nonsense from you, I just want you to shut the effing dog up."

'Eddie asked him politely not to swear in front of me and he went berserk. The next thing we know, he pulled a bread knife out from under his jacket, stabbed Eddie in the stomach and ran off into the dark.'

A police constable stuck his head round the door. 'The sergeant would like you outside, doctor, if you don't mind.'

I went outside. 'Yes, sergeant?' I asked. 'How can I help?'

'We haven't apprehended the suspect yet, doc, so we're going to storm his house,' he said. 'We want you here in case there are any more dead bodies inside.'

'But . . .' I said in an astonished voice, ' . . . but we haven't had any at all so far.'

'Ah,' he said as if his plans had been thwarted, 'but we came pretty close just a few minutes ago, and I'm not taking any more chances.'

Then, in a loud voice to his officers, he shouted: 'Secure access to the house,' and an officer armed with a large sledgehammer appeared out of the night.

'Why don't we just check to see if the door is unlocked?' I asked as the officer raised his weapon. 'Maybe . . .' I continued, but it was too late.

Under the force of the blow, the front door, together with its entire frame, shot backwards into the hallway with a tremendous crash, leaving a large and slightly irregular black hole in the front of the house and a slowly dispersing cloud of dust.

'That worked well then,' I said looking at the hole, but no one was listening because there was a cry behind us and a constable ran up to say that the neighbour had been apprehended and was now in the back of the divvy van.

We all walked over to the van and, sure enough, there he was.

'That worked well then!' I said for the second time and this time people nodded their heads in agreement.

'Isn't that . . . ?' I asked, recognising the neighbour as someone I had seen on TV.

'It sure is,' replied the sergeant.

The divvy van departed a little later and within a few minutes the police had gone. All that was left to show that anything untoward had taken place was Sandra, Martin and myself standing in the front garden and a large hole in the front of the house next door.

'Mind you, I will say one thing,' I said.

'And what's that?' asked Sandra.

'The barking of that Williamson dog could really get on your nerves,' and we all laughed and went back into the house.

While Sandra was making the cup of tea we hadn't got round to having before, Martin told me that he had tried to protect his dad against the neighbour's attack and had also been wounded in the process. He showed me an ugly wound on his forearm. I asked him if he had told the police about it but he shook his head.

'Why on earth didn't you tell them?' I asked as I examined the arm.

'I guess I was so worried about Dad,' he replied.

'It's a nasty-looking wound,' I said, 'but fortunately the knife seems to have missed all the important bits.'

I popped some local in, put in a few stitches and in a few minutes the arm was back in one piece again.

I swallowed my tea, bid them all goodnight and drove home feeling mentally and physically exhausted. Despite the lateness of the hour, I lit a fire and poured myself a Scotch before chucking the takeaway in the microwave. Hardy came and pressed himself up close against me.

'Sorry I can't pour drinks or light fires,' he said.

'That's OK,' I replied, patting his head. 'You do lots of other things instead.'

There was a long pause and then I said to him: 'But there is one piece of advice that I would like to pass on to you.'

'And what's that?' he asked.

'Never, just never, bark anywhere around Eddie's new neighbour.'

I went through to the kitchen to turn off the lights, only to find that there was a message on the answer machine. It told me that Felix had a bad head cold, was not feeling at all well and could I please do the Saturday morning surgery tomorrow.

'Bugger!' I said and went off to bed.

Eddie did very well in hospital. Although the knife had penetrated a loop of bowel and nicked a small blood vessel, it had missed the aorta. The surgery was a great success and he was home just ten days later.

The incident was the talk of the town for several weeks, of course, and patients in the surgery would often say that they understood I had attended the stabbing. Their eyes would grow large when, with melodrama that improved with practice, I replied: 'The *double* stabbing, I think you mean.'

The neighbour also did well. His legal representative visited the police station within an hour of him arriving there and, unbelievably, he was released and allowed home that very same night.

I have often heard it said that the legal profession marches to a different drum beat to the rest of us. That was certainly the case this time and the matter took over a year to get to court. In all of that time the neighbour continued to live as if nothing had happened and in all of that time Sandra and Eddie lived next door in constant fear of him. He screamed abuse and threats at them over the fence on a daily basis, scattered their mail over the front garden when it was raining and lit bonfires or used his leaf blower when Sandra hung out washing and the wind was in the right quarter.

When the matter eventually came forward, the case was heard in the local county court and attracted a lot of attention from the local press. There was even more interest than there would have been otherwise as a well-known silk came up from town to handle the matter.

In his practised, eloquent way, I understand that the silk told the court how his client was a quiet, retiring man who he had been cutting a loaf to make himself a snack when a dog started barking next door, how his client had courteously asked for the dog to be kept quiet and how Eddie and Martin had viciously attacked him. The silk then told the court that his client's action was merely the sort of self-defence that any reasonable person would use in such a situation.

The locals who attended the hearing sat open mouthed at this account and then sat with even wider mouths when the court accepted this bizarre version of events and the defendant was exonerated of any wrongdoing whatsoever.

After the trial, life for Sandra and Eddie became impossible and they eventually reached the point where they were frightened even to go outside. After a year or so of increasing misery they decided they had had enough. They simply put their house on the market and moved away from the district altogether.

The Williamsons' dog, however, without the option of moving, was not so lucky. It was found dead by its owners a month or so after the completion of the court case. I understand that Simon, the local vet, thought it might have been poisoned by snail bait, but the Williamsons maintain that they always kept the dog locked in the yard and never used bait anyway.

Some time after Sandra and Eddie moved I met the new owners of the house in the surgery. They seemed very pleasant people indeed.

'My wife needs something to calm her nerves,' he said.

I said I was happy to oblige but would like to know why she needed the medication.

'Do you know the man who lives next door to us?' she asked. 'He's making our lives a misery. We've only been in the house five minutes and already our nerves are shot to pieces.'

I wrote her a script and they were about to leave the room when a sudden thought occurred to me.

'By the way,' I said, 'do you have a dog?'

'No,' they replied, looking a bit puzzled.

'Good,' I said and let them go on their way.

16 Archie

IT WAS A STINKING hot day and my car had been standing out in the sun all morning, so the drive out to Clive and Marjorie's place was really uncomfortable. The air-conditioning had sort of kicked in but hadn't, as yet, got things under anything like proper control.

'Blimey,' said Archie, mopping his brow as we rumbled along.

About a week before, Janet, from the university, had phoned.

'Would you do me a favour, Paul, please?' she said. 'A really big one?'

It turned out she had a fifth-year medical student who had planned to do his elective in Africa but now wasn't able to as his destination had erupted into civil war.

'He obviously can't do his elective there now,' Janet continued, 'and he can't just hang around, so we were wondering if you would take him on for the four weeks and show him some exciting country medicine. You said you've been toying with the idea of having students and this would be a great way to start. He's English and would be just your cup of tea.'

I had recently made a firm decision not to take on any extra commitments over the summer period. Delphine had been quite unwell for some months and needed specialist care. Felix had taken her down to Melbourne and I had been working on my own for some while.

'I want to be really strict about this,' I had said at the recent staff meeting. 'I feel that I probably need to get away for a bit of a break after Christmas,' and everyone had vigorously nodded their heads in agreement.

'Yes, of course,' I said to Janet. 'Not a problem. I'll look forward to it,' and then I promptly forgot to tell anyone else what I had agreed to.

Just two days later, when I had finished with a patient and gone through to reception to hand over some paperwork, Madge said, a little oddly I thought: 'There's someone here to see you. He says you know all about him.'

I turned around. There was a young man standing by the front door. Now Archie has apparently never been small. He has lost a lot of weight in recent times and he is still not small. But he hadn't lost the weight then. In the bright sunlight streaming through the window he looked very impressive indeed, and all the more so as he sported a long blond ponytail and his attire consisted solely of bright orange board shorts and iridescent thongs.

He smiled as he crossed the waiting room, shook my hand and said in a beautiful English public school accent, 'Thanks so much for taking me at such beastly short notice, Paul. It really is frightfully good of you. Bally civil war!'

I was completely puzzled for a moment and then enlightenment dawned. 'Ah!' I realised. 'Archie. Of course.'

'So you do know this . . . man?' Madge asked with a wrinkle in her nose as she looked him up and down.

In the end, of course, she fell in love with Archie just like the rest of us. For once we got him a little more suitably attired for our world, and despite the fact he insisted on keeping his ponytail, Archie turned out to be a wonderful addition to all our lives.

He straight away got stuck into everything. He helped out wherever possible and it was immediately obvious that he had exceptional clinical knowledge and skills. He made a big impact on both staff and patients alike and years later people still ask after him.

'He's a colo-rectal surgeon these days,' I say with pride.

Janet was right. Archie was just my cup of tea and we got on famously. Just as well, really, seeing that he lived out at the farm with me.

Putting to one side his dress sense and hairstyle, Archie was conservative in everything else. He came over as rather prim and proper, almost prudish. He was very, very English and he spoke with two more plums in his mouth than even I do.

It was the very first night at the farm that I discovered Archie's passion for cooking. Evening meals instantly hit a height not only never reached before but never even imagined.

I can turn my hand to most things and am invariably happy to have a go in just about any situation. There are three things, however, that have always eluded my grasp: golf, ironing and cooking.

Golf and ironing I simply abandoned. After endless expensive lessons in golf and endless disasters with ironing, I gave up the one and, with the money I saved, paid Susie to do the other. Cooking, however, is hard to avoid, especially if you live alone and arrive home as hungry as I do. I have tried and tried, but I have never progressed beyond bangers and mash or Chicken Tonight. Apart from baked beans on toast, of course.

My loved ones all rallied to the flag when I first started needing to cook for myself. My mother gave me a set of utensils which I still don't have the faintest idea how to use, and my friend Michelle chipped in with *A Cookbook For a Man Who Probably Only Owns One Saucepan*. As soon as I opened it, I knew this was the book for me. In bold red letters on the very first page it said: *Never use road kill as an ingredient.* I hadn't known that you shouldn't do that, but I've stuck to the advice ever since and never regretted it once.

Watching Archie cook, I felt like someone who has worked hard to score three on a computer game only to have someone else wander along and score a billion with no apparent effort. I would have to say, however, that I never let that get in the way of enjoying the fruits of his labour.

After we had eaten our fill we would go and toast the sun setting over the lake with a glass or two of red. Those balmy summer evenings, sitting by the darkening lake and watching the field bats come out to hunt in the fading light, were magical. I hadn't had close, regular company since Russell passed away and I enjoyed it enormously. I still felt rather out of practice at talking about myself, so Archie did most of the chattering and I did most of the listening.

I found out that having been at Eton, Archie had moved to Australia at the age of sixteen. Apparently his father had been transferred to the local branch of some multinational or other. Archie had transferred to Geelong Grammar and then got into medical school two years later.

There was one evening when it was pouring with rain and we stayed inside.

'Put some music on,' Archie had shouted out to me from the kitchen.

So I put on my favourite piece of music. I'm not very original I know, since it is everyone else's favourite piece as well, but I can't help that.

'Ah,' he said as the music wafted through from the sitting room. 'The old Mozart Clarinet Concerto. I love it. Used to play it a lot.'

'Get away with you,' I said.

'No, really. School orchestra, uni orchestra, doctor's orchestra. I've played it loads of times. Know it off by heart. Would play it for you now,' he added, 'except that I don't have a clarinet with me.'

'No, but I do,' I said, for a thousand years ago I had once been part of a small traditional jazz band that played at medical school hops. In all truth we had been pretty awful, but we had had a lot of fun and the liquorice stick was still in the cupboard under the CD player.

'It may not be up to your standard,' I said a little tentatively, 'but when I handed him the instrument after dinner he was delighted with it.

While Archie got the reed to his liking, I poured myself another red and settled back comfortably in the settee.

I thought he might be good but he was way better than that. His virtuosity was breathtaking and, exactly as Wolfie had intended, Archie transported me right up through the atmosphere and away to worlds beyond this one. I could hardly breathe, it was so beautiful, and I cheered and clapped when he finished.

'I know one thing for sure,' I said, putting the clarinet away afterwards. 'It's never sounded as good as that before.'

Later that evening, lying in bed and waiting for Morpheus to tap me on the shoulder, my mind went back to that evening in the waiting room with Dave. How similar he and Archie were in this one regard, yet how very different in so many others.

Archie enjoyed helping round the farm too, and during his stay we did many jobs together. We cleared fallen timber, mended fences and installed a new letterbox in honour of the new system of delivered mail which had recently replaced the rather quaint but hopelessly insecure system at the Warraweet store.

Not only did Archie do all the surgeries with me, but he came on all the house calls too, which is why we were both stifling in a suffocatingly hot car on the way to Clive and Marjorie's place.

It took us perhaps ten or fifteen minutes to reach our destination and we parked the car between the scattered remains of a dozen or so vehicles under the shade of a large candlebark. We picked our way along the winding path that leads through Clive's private scrapyard and workshop to the back door of the house.

'That workshop,' he whispered after he had glanced through the open door, 'is like one of those working museums at tourist attractions. In fact,' he continued, 'the whole place is amazing. How on earth has he been able to collect so much junk in one small place?'

'Beats me,' I replied.

'House' was rather a grand word for Clive and Marjorie's abode, for the tiny structure sat slightly off square, propped up by the rusting water tank outside the kitchen. The last vestiges of paint disappeared many moons ago; the roof had gone curly, and the unprotected window frames had fared poorly in the sun.

There was mess and weeds everywhere. Most of the fibrocement sheets had sprung their corners and there was a large hole in the back door, presumably created by the dog that poked its head out and eyed us up and down in a very suspicious manner.

Marjorie appeared at the door. 'Praise be the Lord,' she cried. 'Clive is not at all well. I have been praying for you to come and my prayers have been answered. Come on in.'

We trooped into the kitchen and I introduced Archie. The dog, very much against its inclinations, was evicted and then poked its head back in through the door and eyed us up and down again.

Apart from the kitchen table, the chaos inside the house was such that it made the garden look comparatively neat and tidy. The kitchen table, however, was an oasis of peace in the midst of bedlam. It was completely clear except for a tall wooden candlestick and a large open Bible on a lectern.

'Clive's in the bedroom,' Marjorie said. I knew where to go, having been there many times before, and led Archie through to a filthy room at the back of the house. There was rubbish piled high on either side of the bed, and the torn curtains had half-fallen down a long time before. Hanging from the ceiling, whole squadrons of model aeroplanes refought battles of long ago. A thin and wizened man lay on the bed.

'Hello, Clive,' I said cheerily as we entered the bedroom.

'Hallelujah, and praise the Lord!' replied Clive. 'Deliverance is at hand.'

Clive had had a stomach upset for a few days, apparently, associated with a lot of pain. Unfortunately, this was nothing new for Clive who had had loads of stomach operations over the years. After examining him, we gave Clive an injection for the pain and decided to wait a while to make sure that the treatment worked.

While we were waiting, Marjorie kindly made us a cup of tea and then disappeared outside for a few minutes, only to reappear with a large armful of rhubarb, which Archie accepted with great glee. Then, whilst I went back to check how things were with Clive, Archie asked Marjorie where the toilet was.

Fortunately the injections did the trick and Clive was much more comfortable, so we were able to leave shortly afterwards.

In the car on the way back, Archie was strangely quiet. I imagined he was ruminating on the huge gaps between the different worlds that people live in when he suddenly said, 'They're not on the mains sewer, you know.'

'Yes, I know that,' I replied.

There was a pause and then Archie said: 'They're not even on a septic tank.'

'Yes, Archie, I know that too.'

There was a further, longer, pause and then: 'Night-soil buckets, Paul, that's what they use.' Archie looked out of the window for a long time. Then he turned back to me and said, 'It's a really hot day.'

'Yes, Archie, I know.'

'But what you don't know,' he continued, 'is that it's been quite a while since the bucket was emptied.'

I could see that Archie had been profoundly affected by his experience, so I covered my mouth in case he saw me laughing.

'Bet that wouldn't have been allowed at Eton,' I said, and we drove back to Dixon's Bridge and got stuck into the afternoon surgery.

At the end of a rather tiring afternoon we retired to the farm only to hear the phone ringing as we walked in the door. It turned out to be a small child with a sore ear so I drove back in to see her while Archie rustled up something for dinner.

The sore ear took a fair bit longer than I expected, so Archie had everything prepared and laid out by the time I returned. After we had eaten the main course, Archie proudly served up rhubarb and ice-cream as dessert and got stuck into it with great gusto.

I sat there with my plate untouched, simply chatting away. After a moment or two he glanced up and said: 'This rhubarb we were given. It's the best I've ever tasted.'

He suddenly noticed I was not eating.

'What's the matter?' he said.

'Just not hungry,' I replied.

'Rubbish,' he said. 'When you came in you said you could eat a horse. What's the problem?'

'Well,' I said. 'The visit we did at lunchtime.'

'Yes?'

'When they do eventually get around to emptying the bucket, where do you think they put it?'

Archie stopped eating and went very quiet for a while. Then, very slowly, he lowered his spoon. He silently looked down at the rhubarb and then back up at me.

'You mean . . .'

'Yes, Archie,' I nodded. 'That's exactly what I mean.'

'Do you know,' he said. 'I think I've lost my appetite too.'

I have no idea whether rhubarb is good for chickens or not, but the next day they got an awful lot of it and none of them died.

In the second half of his stay Archie asked if his girlfriend, Liz, another medical student, could come up for the weekend and of course I said that would be fine. The next Saturday morning a tiny slip of a thing arrived and Archie showed her round the farm whilst I did the morning surgery. That evening Archie did himself proud again and we had a lovely meal that lasted late into the night.

I was waxing lyrical about Archie's virtues when Liz interrupted me: 'Is there anything at all that's not perfect about him?' she laughed.

'Well, as a matter of fact, there is.'

'And what might that be,' interjected Archie with mock severity.

'That bloody ponytail of yours. I can't stand it. It drives me mad.'

'I can see why that might be, Dr Chrome Dome,' he said. 'You're just jealous.'

'I have asked him dozens of times to get rid of the bloody thing,' I said to Liz, 'but he completely ignores me. And another thing I have just thought of,' I added. 'He's too prim and proper.'

Liz exploded in a cloud of food and laughter which took quite a while to clean up. 'Prim and proper? You have just got to be joking.' she laughed.

'Well, just let me tell you about the fourth-year social then,' she said as Archie turned bright red and tried to stop her. 'At three o'clock in the morning,' she persisted, despite his best efforts to gag her, 'Mr Prim and Proper here was dancing on the top of the karaoke machine, roaring into a microphone and wearing nothing but a bridal veil.'

Liz eventually went home and Archie's time continued to fly by. Just a few nights before the end of his stay, we were out by the lake again watching the little field bats catching their dinner, and going over everything we had seen together.

'It's been fantastic, Paul. It really has. I've learnt heaps. Apart from a delivery, I think we've covered just about everything in the book.'

On the shelf above my desk at home is a small framed photograph of a pretty little girl with dark curly hair. She looks very seriously at the viewer out of huge brown eyes on the occasion of her first communion. Her mother recently gave me the picture as a present from the family.

Occasionally I tackle the paper mountain on my desk. It's a bit like cleaning out those ancient stables for I never seem to win. I don't enjoy it a bit and happily look for any distraction, so I often glance at the photograph and remember how it all happened.

It was Archie's last day and he was being a big help, as usual, in getting through the morning's work. Despite both of our efforts, however, the waiting room remained as full as ever and we were running as late as ever.

The lady I was consulting with at the time I got the call was a very serious person whom I have never seen smile. I was obviously in trouble for having kept her waiting, and could feel her annoyance that the phone had already interrupted her consultation twice. She was reading from her list of ailments when the phone rang for the third time.

'I need you to speak to Sarah,' said Heather hurriedly.

'No, no more interruptions,' I said sternly, trying to impress my patient with my authority.

'No,' Heather insisted. 'I *need* you to speak to Sarah.'

Heather put the call through and a hysterical woman at the other end of the line screamed at me that I had better get there quick as the baby was coming.

I looked at the poor serious soul the other side of the desk and said: 'I'm sorry, but I have to leave immediately on an urgent call.'

'But I've been waiting for forty minutes.'

'I know.'

'But I only want a few scripts.'

'I really can't.'

'And an examination.'

I fled.

I ran past a waiting room full of pleading eyes which I studiously avoided. And on the way out I grabbed the emergency bag from the shelf in the corridor, the address from Heather, my car keys from Madge and Archie from the treatment room.

As we squealed our way round corners there was a tense silence inside the car but not inside my head.

'Unscheduled home deliveries! You fool! Are you crazy? There's no backup, you know. Can you even remember what to do?'

'Course I can,' another part of me said.

'But aren't you getting a bit old for emergencies like this?' the first part persisted.

'Don't be ridiculous.'

'There has to be an easier way to make a living.'

'Of course there is but, if you remember, I needed a change.'

'Well, you sure got it.'

'I sure did.'

I was thinking I must be going barmy talking to myself like this when Archie interrupted my thoughts.

'Can you remember what to do?' he asked.

'Course I can,' I replied.

'Good,' he added, 'but there have to be easier ways of making a living.'

A minute or two later we screeched to a sliding halt in front of the house. We jumped out and shot through the front door, which was held open by Robert.

'Sorry, guys, no point in calling an ambulance, she was never going to make it to the hospital,' he said as we whistled past.

The house was filled with screams and expletives. In the living room and kitchen there was a cast of thousands. Not only were the whole family present but most of the neighbours too.

The overwhelming majority of the noise was coming from Sarah, who was lying cross-wise on the bed, legs in the air, ready to give birth to her fourth. I introduced Archie to Sarah, who told me she didn't give a flying fuck who he was.

I felt like asking for hot water and newspaper but didn't know if anyone would get the joke, so I simply asked for towels and pulled on a pair of gloves.

The examination, watched with great interest by at least a dozen people, showed that Sarah was fully dilated and the head was crowning. Archie had to fight through the crowd just to get a look.

With the next few contractions I urged Sarah to push, but the baby made little, if any, progress.

The following contraction was much stronger.

'Push,' I said, but Sarah simply lay there looking a bit sweaty.

'Come on, push,' I said more loudly, but again she ignored me. Determined not to miss such a good opportunity I yelled at her, 'For God's sake woman, push!'

Sarah started to push, then screamed and stopped. She then propped herself up on an elbow, turned to me and yelled back: 'This fucking hurts, you know!'

Sarah's mum, who was standing next to me, reached over and put her hand on my arm. 'Don't take it personally, Paul, she always swears at the doctors when she's in labour.'

At that moment Sarah started her next contraction. I was wondering how to urge her to greater efforts when Rita from next door came to the rescue. She was a large woman with a sound, if rudimentary, grasp of English. She brushed Archie and myself aside and leant over Sarah until their faces were very close.

'He told you to fucking push, so fucking push, you stupid bitch,' she screamed at Sarah, 'and then we can all fuck off home!'

It may not have been quite how I would have put it, but it certainly did the trick. Sarah followed her instructions perfectly and a complete head with a good covering of thick black hair appeared a few moments later. The rest was easy, as it usually is, and with one more push, Ayesha came into the world along with a great whoosh of liquid which completely missed all the towels, hit the bedroom wall and made a slippery mess on the carpet.

Ayesha cried almost immediately and I handed her over to Sarah.

'Give us a cord clamp, please,' I said to Archie, but, after a frantic search in the emergency bag, he found that the number of cord clamps in our possession was exactly zero.

Fortunately I have seen lots of Hollywood movies so I instantly knew what to do. 'Shoelace, Archie,' I said. 'I need one of your shoelaces.'

'What's wrong with yours?' he said.

'Slip-ons,' I lied.

After a brief period of him fumbling about, the necessary item was procured and applied and the afterbirth was successfully delivered into a large mixing bowl a few minutes later.

Whilst I checked Sarah, Archie examined the new addition and pronounced Ayesha to be a perfect specimen. Having confirmed both mum and babe to be in rude health, it was time to examine the afterbirth. I turned round to find an empty bowl and a trail of blood leading across the carpet and out of the door.

Despite the large number of people who helped, it took a surprisingly long time to catch the cat. It was eventually cornered on the back verandah and the missing organ retrieved.

It was immediately obvious that the afterbirth had suffered a bit, both as a result of the cat's attention as well as the effects of the chase. It wasn't easy, therefore, to do an accurate examination, but after a bit of poking about and a fair bit of discussion, Archie and I finally decided it was probably all present and accounted for.

We congratulated one another on a job well done, washed our hands, swallowed a quick cup of tea and left.

When we got back to the surgery, the staff all wanted to know how it had gone.

'Piece of cake,' I said. 'The only really hard part,' I added, 'was getting the afterbirth off the cat.'

I glanced around the empty waiting room.

'We sent everyone home and rescheduled their appointments for later,' Meaghan said.

'What a good idea,' I said. 'Peace and solitude,' I added at the strangely empty room. 'How delightful.'

'Well,' I said loudly as I clapped Archie on the back, 'time to go and have our last lunch together.'

We were headed for the door when a voice cried out from my room: 'But before you go, doctor, I just need some scripts. And an examination.'

17 Famiglia

I HAD SEEN QUITE a lot of his family over the years but I hadn't met Mario until he nearly killed himself chopping down a tree for firewood. I'm not sure whether he got the cuts wrong, whether the wind shifted or whether it was plain bad luck. Whatever the cause, the upshot was that when the tree hit the ground it bounced back, landed on top of Mario and broke his leg.

The boys went looking for him when he didn't come in for lunch and I was called shortly after.

Mario and Constanza live on a small farm on the back road to Stoney Creek. It is a pretty part of the country with gently rolling pasture and picturesque stands of trees. The house is a weatherboard, relocated from Melbourne, and sits, rather like a castle with a moat, in the middle of a quarter of an acre of concrete.

The approach to the house is via an unsealed driveway which skirts some falling-down cattle yards on the one side and a paddock in which an assortment of animals patiently wait their turn to be eaten on the other. Beyond this, and reaching all the way to the concrete, is a large and meticulously kept vegetable garden behind which a corn plantation stretches out of sight. Every time I drive in there I smile as I think of the simplicity of their approach: meat and two veg.

When I arrived, Mario, attended by his four sons, was still trapped under the tree. Apart from his leg, which was a mess, he seemed to have got off rather lightly. One of the boys fitted forks to the tractor, gently inched off the tree limb and Mario was slid out and carried by the five of us up to the house.

As soon as I examined the leg it was obvious he needed an operation.

'Mr Gaggliano,' I said. 'You need to go to hospital.'

'Acall ame Mario,' he replied. 'Ayou ado it here,' he added nodding at the kitchen table.

'Don't be ridiculous,' I exclaimed.

'Back in Sicily . . .' he started, but I stuck to my guns, gave him a shot for his pain and organised an ambulance.

There was a bit of a wait for the ambulance and it was dark by the time it arrived. In the meantime, various members of the family had wandered in by twos and threes. The Gagglianos' kitchen is big, but by the time the ambulance crunched its way up the driveway, it was standing room only. There must have been forty or more people in there. I have no idea how they knew to come, but the bush telegraph was obviously working well.

'Agive im some coffee and sausages,' called Mario to Constanza as he was being loaded onto the stretcher.

Back in the house I was given a coffee that took the roof of my mouth off and handed a package.

'Ahere's asome sausages for ayou,' said Constanza with her wonderful toothless smile.

I said my thanks, bid my farewells and headed off into the dark. As I stepped off the verandah I felt something very squashy underneath my foot. There was a terrific scream, sixteen hot needles penetrated my ankle and I fell heavily onto the concrete. Neither of us was hurt but the cat got up before I did. He looked at me balefully, flicked his tail and stalked off under the house, making sure that I had a clear view of his daisy the whole way.

I was picked up and dusted off by twenty willing pairs of hands.

I then headed home for dinner, only to find that there was nothing in the fridge that wasn't furry.

'Looks like beans again,' I said to myself and then remembered the sausages. My spirits quite restored, I popped half-a-dozen of them under the grill, put the beans in the microwave and poured myself a glass of chardonnay.

Fifteen minutes later I was sitting in front of the Premier League with a meal on a tray. The sausages not only looked good but they smelled good too. In fact their only real drawback was that they tasted awful. They were inedible. That's not strictly true, of course, because Hardy scoffed them down very happily the next morning, but they were inedible for me. The evening wasn't a total disaster, however, since beans on toast and soccer aren't such a bad combination.

Hospital was not for Mario. He took his discharge the day after his operation and came home for the family to look after him. When he first came home he was still in a great deal of pain and his wounds needed dressing daily.

'I'll organise the district nurse to visit,' I suggested.

'Anoah way,' he replied firmly. 'No outsiders. This is a job for the family.'

'But the wounds will need cleaning daily,' I protested.

He looked at me and, in his best Marlon Brando voice, said: 'I athink of you as family.'

So that was that. Every night on my way home I did a bit of a detour so that I could call in on Mario and attend to his needs as he lay in a Jason recliner that had been specially set up in the middle of the kitchen.

That kitchen was a wonderful place. From floor to ceiling it was lined with preserves and flagons of homemade wine. It also smelled deliciously of the meats of every description that hung from hooks on the ceiling.

And every night I performed my dressings before an audience. Whenever I arrived there would only ever be the three of us, but by magic the family would arrive in twos and threes until there would be thirty or forty people, from the elderly to the very young, packed into the kitchen. In a silent semicircle, they would watch every move I made and not make a sound until the job was done.

Then suddenly everything would be laughter and chatter and I would not be able to escape without having another of those coffees or without listening to the clinical woes of at least three or four other family members. And every time I left, the cat would watch me suspiciously from the far end of the verandah.

Occasionally even Nonna attended my visits to Mario. Nonna was a diminutive figure who only ever dressed in black and wore a veil over her head. She was Constanza's mother and lived with them in a granny flat at the back of the house. She had recently turned a hundred and one and had lived in Australia since the end of the Second World War without ever learning so much as a single word of English.

Above the mantelpiece over the stove there was a wonderful photograph of Nonna and her groom scowling angrily at the photographer on their wedding day. Now it is well known that marriage is not all beer and skittles, but it is generally accepted that it is possible to take a more lighthearted view of it on the very first day. Not Nonna and her groom. Right there, on their wedding day, they were clearly preparing themselves for the hard slog ahead.

Through Constanza, I once asked Nonna what she attributed her great age to. Like mother, like daughter, she gave a broad toothless grin and said something in dialect which Constanza translated as 'guinea pigs'.

'I don't understand,' I said a little blankly and was promptly taken by a group of giggling younger family members to a shed behind the barn. There, carefully shielded from the weather, were dozens of cages, each containing a large fat guinea pig.

'Ah,' I said to them with understanding. 'She has a hobby. She keeps them as pets.'

The children squealed with laughter. 'Don't be silly,' they shouted in chorus. 'She eats them.'

And indeed she did. A quarter of a guinea pig each day. That was her elixir of youth and I am certainly in no position to refute the efficacy of her diet.

I was offered some guinea pig to try and it was certainly very tasty, but children's pets aren't really my cup of tea. Even expatriate English farmers have difficulty eating Olga da Polga.

The Gagglianos were by no means the first Italians in the district. During the war four Italian country boys who had been taken prisoner at El Alamein were billeted at Woongarra. By day they worked on the land and by night they slept in the top of a barn with the ladder taken away to prevent them from fleeing. Ridiculous really, since if they had really wanted to escape they could have done it far more easily in daylight.

I suspect that escaping would have been the last thing on their minds anyway, since they must have thought they had won the lottery. One minute they were being shot at from every direction and the next they were thousands of miles away, in a beautiful place, doing what they had in their blood all along. I believe it far more likely that the ladder was removed in an attempt to protect the local ladies.

At the end of the war, when they were all repatriated, three of them immediately migrated back to Australia and came back to the district to live. That was a long while ago, of course, but there is still one old fellow who comes up to Woongarra for an occasional shot of nostalgia.

At the end of one of my visits Mario presented me with a flagon of homemade wine. After I thanked him for the gift, I asked: 'By the way, how are you meant to cook those sausages?'

I was greeted with a blank stare. 'Ayou do anot cook those sausages, my friend,' Mario said with a puzzled look. 'Those sausages are not afor cooking. Did you try and acook athem?' he asked with a laugh.

'Athey afor hanging,' explained a smiling Constanza.

So I went home, got what was left out of the fridge and hung them up in the pantry.

I cannot remember what I ate that night but I do remember trying the wine. It looked great, it smelt great, it tasted like paint stripper.

Although I was initially a little disappointed, I decided to run a scientific experiment and am now in a position to state, with absolute certainty, that after the first three or four glasses of Mario's homebrew, the palate is in such a state of shock that it throws its arms in the air and bows down to the inevitable. I really got into that experiment that evening, and eventually tottered off to bed around midnight, leaving an empty flagon on the kitchen table and having to live on Panadol for days afterwards.

Mario's bones and wounds were a little reluctant to heal and I continued to visit the family on a regular basis for some months. I was always treated as an honoured family member and never left without being given a jar of tomato sauce, a bag of corncobs, a flagon of paint stripper and, on one occasion, a pan for cooking chestnuts by the fire.

'You alike pork and bacon?' asked Mario one day.

'I sure do,' I replied.

'Good,' he said. 'The aboys are killing Gilda on aSatday. You acan come and awatch, if ayou like, and athen atake some home with you.'

So the following Saturday at about ten o'clock I presented myself to the farm and joined the assembled throng making their way to the pigpen.

Gilda was vast. I had not seen many adult pigs up close and I was very impressed. The block and tackle was readied and the flensing knives had all been sharpened. We stood in a semicircle whilst Tony, the eldest son, went into the pen of this monster, raised a gun to her forehead and pulled the trigger.

I'm not exactly sure what I expected to see but it was something along the lines of: Gilda falls to ground, Gilda is raised on block and tackle, Gilda is prepared with flensing knives, everyone goes home some time later with piece of Gilda. All very Amish.

What actually happened was that the shot bounced off Gilda's thick skull, showering pellets in all directions and causing all and sundry to hit the deck with great speed. Gilda, incensed by this unexpected attack on her dignity, threw Tony and his gun as far as she could, scattered her pen as though it was a collection of match-sticks, and then headed for the horizon with about four generations of Gagglianos in pursuit.

Gilda did eventually meet her maker that day, but it was not until quite a bit later and not before she had knocked over an old shed, ploughed up a surprising amount of the back paddock and laid waste to around a hundred young olive trees.

The family took all this in their stride. Tony simply changed his gun for something bigger, jumped into a ute with his brothers and joined in the chase. When he was able to eventually get in a shot, the anti-tank gun he had chosen certainly did the trick and order began to prevail. Eventually the scenario began to resemble the one I had imagined in the first place.

When Gilda was hung up in the shed she measured over three metres from snout to tail. I drank some paint stripper with Mario whilst Tony and the boys prepared the carcass and, in the late afternoon, eventually found myself on the way home with a large piece of Gilda resting on the back seat.

Eventually Mario's leg started to heal and my visits became less frequent. It was at about this time that I tried the sausages again. By now they had been hanging in the pantry for a couple of months. They looked just fine, they smelt fine too but they tasted every bit as disgusting as they had before.

'How long should you hang the sausages for?' I asked innocently on my next visit.

'Ah! Along atime,' was the reply. 'Ayou ahaven't been aeating them yet, have ayou?' Mario laughed at me. 'Athey anot ready for a long atime.'

'No, of course not,' I lied.

Later that year Rosa, the youngest daughter, got married. The groom's family came from Brunswick. This was to be the Italian event of the year and, to my surprise and great delight, I was invited as a guest at the top table. It was a wonderful affair: colourful, unaffected and joyous. I loved every minute of it. I loved being seated between the groom's aunt and grandmother, neither of whom spoke a word of English, and becoming instantly fluent in sign language. I loved the flow of wine and the tables groaning with food. I loved tapping the glasses to call the bride and groom to kiss; I loved the men who wore their hats and sunglasses throughout the entire afternoon, and I loved grandparents dancing with grandchildren. But best of all I loved the constant stream of men who came up to our table, shook Mario by the hand, said, 'Eeee, Mario' in deep guttural tones and then mingled with the crowd again.

Eventually the time came for Mario and I to go our separate ways. His wounds were healed and he was able to walk without a limp.

'Mario,' I said. 'I know I have been coming here as your doctor but you have all been so kind to me, I would like to show my appreciation. I have some young stags in the back paddock and, if you would like one for the larder, I would like to give one to the family as a gift.'

He didn't understand 'stags' at first but when I repeated my offer with the word 'cervo' a big smile spread across his face. He phoned Tony on the spot and within a few minutes a posse had been organised.

In the early morning light, on the very next Sunday, half-a-dozen or so male members of the family arrived at Woongarra in an old blue F100.

Unlike dispatching Gilda, the whole exercise took no time at all. I pointed out the beast in question, Tony brought it down with a single shot, twelve eager hands loaded it into the back of the ute and they were gone, inviting me to lunch as they went.

Lunch turned out to be a big affair. As far as I could judge it was a combined celebration of Mario's return to health, the baptism of some recent addition to the family and the first communion of a nephew I had not met before.

Well into the proceedings, Mario suddenly took me to one side and said: 'I athank you for the adeer. The boys will acome over later in the week and acut some afirewood for you.' Then, with a conspiratorial whisper, he added: 'Acome awith me.'

I followed him outside and into the big shed at the back of the farmyard where all the heavy equipment was kept.

'Follow,' he said, and led me to the far corner of the shed where a stack of old hay bales was stored. Mario looked around cautiously and then released a catch hidden deep in the side of the haystack. A secret door swung open, revealing the stack to be hollow. We entered the hollow stack and Mario closed the door behind us.

'As ayou are family,' he said, 'I acan trust you,' and he proudly showed me his still. He handed me a glass of crystal-clear liquid which did something funny to my tongue and sent off a thermal explosion somewhere in my stomach.

'Athis is afor ayou,' he added, pulling a box of bottles from a pile on the floor.

'Wow, this is good stuff,' I replied. 'Thanks a lot.' Or at least that is what I would have said had I not been temporarily robbed of the power of speech. What I actually said was: 'Oohh, aagghh, eee.' But it didn't matter, for Mario had got the gist of it and helped me carry the box outside.

I drink the grappa from time to time of an evening by the fire, but only in small quantities at widely spaced intervals. It tastes wonderful but I am always worried about how many billion brain cells turn up their toes with each swallow.

Just recently I was doing something rather unusual for me. I was clearing out my pantry and in the process found the sausages hanging behind the door. They must have been there for a year or more. I had forgotten all about them. I was rather excited by my find and decided to have them for lunch.

'They've surely been hanging for long enough by now,' I thought.

I got myself all prepared and sat down with a glass of wine and the crossword, only to find that the sausages were exactly as before. They looked great, they smelled great but they still tasted awful. I am not by any means a quitter but I can recognise defeat when it stares me in the face, so I gave some to Hardy and then chopped up the rest for the chooks, who ate them with gusto. The other day, when I bumped into Constanza in the supermarket and she asked me how the sausages had turned out, I was able to say without blinking: 'As a matter of fact, I used them for lunch just the other day for a few friends and they finished the lot. In fact they practically fought over them.'

18 The Letter

I DO NOT KNOW where it all comes from but my in-tray overflows each and every day and I usually flick through it during what is supposed to be the lunch break. There is always a batch of letters and reports, but most of it is drug company rubbish which goes straight into the bin. I often wish the pharmaceutical multinationals would just leave the trees alone in the first place.

One day, there was a letter from England amongst my post. I put it to one side and decided to open it when I had dealt with the rest of the paperwork and grabbed a coffee. It turned out that the letter was from someone in Manchester. The handwriting was a bit shaky and hard to read, so it took me some time to realise that it was a 'thank you for looking after my wife' note from someone whose name I didn't recognise.

At first, I had no idea what the letter was referring to, and it was only later, during the afternoon surgery, that the penny suddenly dropped. The letter was about Eileen, who had passed away just a month or so before.

I had known Eileen for less than a year, but, a little like Teddy, I felt as if I had known her for a long time right from the start. I first met her when she came to live locally with her daughter Jenny and her family. Eileen said she made the move partly because she wanted to be close to Jenny but also because it was becoming increasingly difficult for her to manage on her own.

I am not sure whether Eileen already knew she was ill when she moved, but as soon as she arrived Jenny realised that there was something very wrong and asked me to have a look. It suited me to see her at home the next day, as I was doing a call on a neighbour a few doors up, so that is what happened.

Eileen was almost impossibly pale. Her arms looked the same colour as the covers as she lay in bed propped up on some pillows. She was a strikingly good-looking woman, and she turned and looked at me with clear, intelligent eyes. Her hand sparkled as the sun streamed through the window and touched the diamond on her fingers.

'Hi, I'm Paul,' I said, shaking her hand gently.

'And I'm Eileen,' she replied quietly in a broad Lancastrian accent. 'Would you like a cup of tea, pet? Kettle's on. And maybe you could be tempted by a piece of figgy pudding?'

'Ah'll av sum tea, thanks luv, but I doon't knoo what figgy puddin' is,' I said in my best *Creature Comforts* voice.

'Cheeky monkey!' she said, smiling, and handed me a slice to find out.

It was only after I had finished the tea and slice that we got down to business.

In addition to the pallor which was evident to one and all, examination unfortunately also showed that Eileen had a large lump in her tummy which shouldn't have been there. To find out what it was, Jenny chauffeured her mum here and there for a whole battery of tests and scans.

The answer was always going to be cancer and the tests all agreed it had started in the kidneys and then spread to the liver and the chest.

There were several councils of war held around Eileen's bed to decide on the best course to take; eventually, however, Eileen decided against treatment of any kind and simply asked that she be looked after at her daughter's home.

'So how long have I got?' she asked on my next visit.

'I have no idea,' I said.

'You must know something,' she persisted.

'All I know,' I replied, 'is that when I was at medical school a wise old professor said to us: "Whenever someone asks you: 'How long have I got?' never, never look at your watch."'

'Very funny,' said Eileen. 'But please give me some idea.'

'I simply can't,' I said, 'but I can tell you a story of someone I knew. A long time ago now I had a patient with a condition not too dissimilar from yours. She went down to one of the big Melbourne hospitals where she was poked and prodded and then told she had two weeks to live. She took her own discharge immediately.

'"Two weeks!" she said to me when I saw her. She was so angry. "Two weeks indeed! What do those pimply youths know? I'll give 'em two weeks. Right here and now I vow to make it two years."

'And against all odds, Eileen, she did.'

'I'm right with that woman,' said Eileen with a glint in her eye. 'So watch out and don't think you're getting rid of me any time soon.'

'Good,' I nodded.

There was a short pause, then Eileen looked up and said in a gruff voice: 'We shall fight on the beaches. We shall fight on the landing grounds. We shall never surrender.'

Over the following weeks, Eileen got wonderful support from both family and palliative care services. I visited on a regular basis, gradually broadening at the waist under the constant barrage of figgy pudding freshly made in honour of my every arrival.

I stayed on a little after each visit. I admired Eileen's courage but I also came to like her as a person. Although we became very friendly and the visits seemed as much like social occasions as clinical sessions, Eileen talked very little about either herself or her earlier life. All she ever said was that she had migrated many years ago as a result of some big family upheaval.

Despite her fighting spirit, Eileen gradually lost ground over the months that followed. Bit by bit her pain became worse and she required more and more medication to control it. She lost weight continuously, and as the tumour continued to grow she slowly but inexorably became exhausted. Towards the end she looked like a large lump with a little bit of woman round the edge of it.

As she grew iller I got into the habit of popping in on a daily basis. On one occasion, when I was closing my bag and preparing to go, Eileen put her hand on mine and said quietly: 'Are you in a hurry today, Paul?'

Not long before, Felix had left the practice altogether. Delphine never did recover and Felix had taken her to their beach house so that he could look after her full time.

He still came back and helped out from time to time, but my workload had jumped enormously.

I stood by Eileen's bed torn between knowing I should rush back to the surgery and knowing that Eileen had something to say.

'Not at all,' I lied and sat back on the chair by her bed.

'Would you mind if I told you a story?' she asked.

'I would feel privileged,' I said.

'I haven't told this story,' she said, 'in a very long time indeed.'

'The story begins,' she continued so quietly that I had to lean forward to hear, 'in Manchester where I grew up. We were poor at home so I left school at fourteen and joined the offices of a firm that made plumbing fittings. In those offices there was a young lad who had also just joined. He was tall and he was as handsome as anything. He was always real nice to me and he always smiled at me, even when some of the others got cross with me for making mistakes.

'I fell in love with him. Hook line and sinker. Right from the very start. We walked out for three years. Since his job with the company was going well we got engaged when I was seventeen and he bought me this ring.' Eileen looked down at her hand. 'He was promoted to junior salesman about that time and we were able to put a bit by each week. After a year or so we were able to buy a little house of our own. It was on the wrong side of town, of course, and it wasn't much to speak of really, but it was ours.

'We had a grand wedding and everybody came. We went to Morecombe for our honeymoon and just over a year later Jenny arrived. No woman was ever happier. I had a smashing fella, my own little house and a beautiful healthy baby girl. My cup was full.

'My husband had to travel around for the company quite a lot. First it was just round Lancashire, but later, when he got more promotions, it was over the whole of the north of England. He would stay away a night or two on the longer trips in hotels that the company paid for.

'Then one day everything changed. One day he just didn't come home from one of his trips. There were no notes or explanations. He just didn't come home.

'I thought at first that he must have been in an accident so I called the police. They checked everywhere, the hospitals and even the morgues, but found nothing. I called the company to find out what was going on, but they told me he had resigned the day or so before and thought he might have gone to another company. They didn't know where he was either. I tried everything I could think of—friends, family—but it was all a dead end. He just vanished.

'Days became weeks and weeks became months. Eventually months became years even. Night after night I would lay awake praying for him to come back. I didn't care what had happened. I didn't care what he had done. I didn't even care if he was with someone else. I didn't care if he made a success of his life or not. I just wanted him back so that I could hold him in my arms and tell him how much I loved him.

'I never knew what I had done wrong.' Eileen paused for a while and then continued.

'I have never so much as looked at another man in all those years. My husband is the only man I will ever love, but after several years on our own, the opportunity arose for Jenny and me to come to Australia and so we settled in Melbourne. I managed to get a good job as soon as I arrived and we have been very happy here ever since.

'And now here I am, lying in this bed, and I have told you this story because I know that my time is very near now and I wanted someone to know what happened. I wanted just one person outside of the family to know that I love him still, that . . . I wish beyond all other wishes that he was here by my side right now, so I could apologise for whatever I did that made him go away.'

Eileen turned to me with tears running down her face. 'I hope, Paul, that one day you may find the kind of love that has blessed my life, for it has been truly wonderful.'

I was very quiet on the way back to the surgery and subdued for the rest of the day. I just couldn't stop thinking that what made the love in Eileen's life so truly wonderful was that she gave of it so freely and had never asked for anything in return.

Eileen was right. Her time was drawing to a close and she died peacefully in her sleep, exactly a week after she told me her story.

It is always painful when such a special person passes away and I have been very grateful, on more than a few occasions, for the hurly-burly of my job, demanding, as it does, such complete focus on the living.

Eileen was certainly not forgotten, however. At the end of the day I would often sit by the fire with Hardy and think about how the real power of love is in the giving and not the taking.

'You're like that,' I would say to him as I stroked his head.

'Of course I am,' he'd reply as he licked my hand.

But in the daytime, thoughts of Eileen had to compete with a lot more pressing matters. Which is why, of course, I didn't immediately put two and two together when I opened the letter from her husband.

> Dear Dr Carter,
>
> I have just heard from a distant cousin that you looked after Eileen for the last few months of her life. I have been told that you looked after her very nicely.
>
> I thank you from the bottom of my heart.
>
> I would like to tell you a story.
>
> When I was a young man in Manchester I met Eileen at the place where I worked and fell head over heels in love with her. We had started at about the same time. She was pretty and she laughed a lot and I thought she was grand. We got engaged, saved what we could and bought a house. Not long after we got married we had a baby. No man was ever happier.

As I got promoted, my job started taking me all over the country and I had to stay nights away. I worked very long hours and over a period of a year or two became exhausted and got myself very down and depressed. You couldn't be depressed in those days. It was considered a weakness, so I hid it from everyone, including Eileen. Then one morning sitting in my hotel room I knew I just couldn't go on. I just couldn't face another customer. Right there and then I phoned in and resigned.

I felt a complete failure. In fact, I felt such a failure that I couldn't even face Eileen. My career had been such a success all the time she had known me that I couldn't let her see me as anything else. I decided not to go home that night.

Originally, I had only intended to stay in Barnsley for the one extra night and then go back and face Eileen the next day. But the next day I felt no better. Day by day my fear of her reaction, and that of family and friends, just grew and grew. I felt more and more down. In just a blink, or so it seemed, I realised I had been away a week. I was going to phone her on so many occasions but I just couldn't bring myself to even talk to her about the pathetic failure I was. As time went by, my exhaustion and depression never got any better and eventually weeks, then months and then even years went by.

There has never been anyone else and I have missed Eileen dreadfully over the years and often used to lie awake wondering if she would ever have been able to forgive me for what I did.

After some years I tried to get back in touch with her but she had moved to Australia and I couldn't find out where she was living.

Years later I got some good treatment and am now feeling much better. Since then I have come to realise what a terrible mistake I made all those years ago and bitterly regret what I did.

My only wish now is that our souls may be once more united in the world that follows this one where I will be able to ask her forgiveness at last.

Yours sincerely,
Harold

I put the letter down on my desk and went and stood by the window.

I felt overwhelmed with frustration at how opportunities are so easily lost, how misunderstandings are so easily taken as truths and how happiness can so easily slip away.

Without knocking Heather came into the room to collect my mail.

'Sorry, I didn't realise you were still in here,' she said when she saw me standing by the window. She picked up all the correspondence from my desk and then she looked over at me again.

'Are you OK?' she asked after a short pause.

'Yes. Yes, I'm fine,' I replied. 'Just got something in my eye.'

19 Isobel

ON THE WALL ABOVE the desk in my consulting room, amongst the memorabilia and certificates that have accumulated over the years, and next to the certificate stating that I braved an early morning ride in a hot-air balloon, is a picture of Mickey Mouse. He is holding a red tulip and smiling in that inimitable way of his from out of a simple black frame. Across the bottom of the picture, in a scrawly childish hand, is written: *All my love, Isobel.*

Mickey is beautifully drawn and coloured and is frequently admired by many of my younger patients. But what is not obvious to the casual observer is that Mickey is not only a nice drawing but also a miracle. Isobel was about ten when she drew him, and even by then she was so grossly disabled that just holding a pen required her complete dedication and concentration. Creating that flower-holding mouse as a Christmas present for me must have taken her a long time indeed.

Isobel was the fourth addition to the Hodgson family. Her arrival was an occasion for great joy and she was doted upon by both parents and elder siblings.

Harry and Wendy and their offspring lived on a small farm way out near Jackson's Crossing. It is hard country on that side of the highway, and the further you travel to the crossing the harder it gets. The ground is lighter out there and, being further from the hills, receives less rainfall than the rest of the district. Feeding a growing family from that land must have taken a lot of effort and a lot of skill.

For all the hardships, those first two years between Isobel being born and falling ill were happy ones. In the beginning it wasn't even recognised that Isobel was ill at all. She just started having difficulty doing things she had previously found easy. Even when she fell behind in her milestones the alarm bells didn't ring immediately. The changes came on so slowly that it was several months before it was recognised by anyone that Isobel had a major problem and, because of its rarity, it was several months again before the specialists at the hospital were able to put a name to it.

As Isobel's illness progressed, a dark cloud settled over the Hodgson household. Sadly, it never lifted and Harry was especially affected by it all. He started drinking heavily and little by little the farm got away from him. The paddocks gradually became overrun with thistles and serrated tussock, fences went unrepaired, and gradually all the usual maintenance and tidying jobs round the house and sheds were left undone.

I met Isobel for the first time when she was four, and by then her body was already badly distorted. Over the years the twisting gradually got worse and worse until she came to resemble a corkscrew.

For all the time I knew her, Isobel was attached to an oxygen cylinder and lay permanently on her side, withered arms and hands by her chest and withered legs twisted round one another. She always wore nappies, always endured great pain and frequently suffered chest infections and pneumonia. But the cloud that had settled over the rest of the household never appeared to affect Isobel in the slightest. If she noticed the water vapour, then she certainly never referred to it. She never stopped smiling and chatting. It was, in fact, impossible to shut her up. I don't believe there ever was a girl who talked as much. She would look up from her bed with that lovely clear face of hers that seemed way too big for her poor little body, sweep away the red curls of which she was so proud, blink her big blue eyes and chat and chat and chat. Usually about Whitney Houston.

'Good morning, Miss Corkscrew,' I would say.

'Good morning, Dr Baldilocks,' she would reply with a giggle.

Isobel was one of 'the Musketeers'. There were, by chance at that time, three profoundly disabled children in the district. They knew one another, of course, because they all went to the same school and all used the same taxi. The three of them took particular pride in living as normal a life as possible and in never missing a day of school if remotely possible. And if ever one of them did miss school, for whatever reason, then the other two would harangue the absentee mercilessly. 'The Three Musketeers' was what they called themselves.

The musketeers, in friendly rivalry, were also determined that they would outlive one another. They were the best of mates and when David passed away and then, later, Oliver, Isobel was devastated.

'Last man left standing,' I said, trying to cheer her up.

'Last girl, you mean,' she corrected me.

As she continued to deteriorate, asking Isobel to come all the way into the practice seemed an unnecessary complication, so I got into the habit of visiting the farm every week or so. It is a long way out to Jackson's Crossing, and with Felix having by then retired to look after Delphine it was difficult to fit everything in, but Wendy always had a cup of tea waiting for me and often a plate of food as well. I must have visited the farm many dozens of times over the years.

I initially starting driving out to the farm to check Isobel's chest for signs of infection, but over a period of time the visits became far more than that. Isobel and I had hit it off from the start and gradually our relationship deepened to something I valued very much indeed. After getting the clinical bits out of the way, I would help her with some homework or simply sit on the floor by her bed chatting with her about life, the universe and everything.

I had realised quite early on that whilst Amy and Isobel were not quite twins, they would have been of a very similar age. The one so strong and taken so inexplicably, the other so ill and yet so alive. I never told Isobel about Amy, but I often wondered to myself whether the same life force that had taken the one had somehow given me the other in some form of cosmic balancing act. I felt ridiculous for even thinking that, seeing that I don't believe in such things, still the thought kept recurring.

Isobel especially loved it when I took Hardy with me to visit her. Woongarra is not too far off a straight line between the surgery and the road out to Jackson's Crossing so, if time permitted, I would sometimes pick up Hardy on the way. He loved Isobel as I did, but eventually I had to stop taking him as his presence inevitably seemed to end in chaos. Wrestling matches with Isobel's dogs that led to tables and vases being knocked over was one thing, but a dog brawl that knocked out Isobel's oxygen line was quite another.

From time to time I 'borrowed' Isobel and brought her over to Woongarra for the day. From the vantage point of her stretcher tied to the back of the ute, she would watch me feed and move the animals and, of course, would chat to me as I checked the chooks, picked up fallen timber and fixed the electric fence. She enjoyed it all, but her favourites were the deer.

'What do their coats feel like, Paul ?' she asked once.

'I'm afraid to tell you that they're not really nice to feel at all. They're all bristly and spikey,' I replied.

'I still wish I could stroke them anyway, they look so beautiful,' she said wistfully.

Around this time, Isobel started to get another series of almost overwhelming chest infections requiring rapid dashes into Melbourne and prolonged periods in intensive care. Each time her parents were told that she wouldn't pull through; twice she was given the last rites.

I visited her at home shortly after one of these occasions and just for once she looked very down in the dumps.

'What's up?' I said.

She looked at me and simply said: 'Paul, I'm frightened.'

'Well by lucky coincidence then, you'll be cheered up by the award you've won.'

'What's that?' she said interestedly.

'You have now been appointed a life member of the Gong Club.'

'What on earth is that?' she asked with a puzzled look on her lovely face.

'The Gong Club,' I said, 'is very exclusive and only for very special people. Membership requirements are that you have to have been given the gong but then pulled through. I understand that you have been given the gong twice and that makes you a life member.'

'You're mad,' she said, laughing. 'Has anyone ever told you that you are completely nuts?'

'Many times,' I nodded in agreement.

And then I told her the story of John Paul Jones. I am not sure that my version was entirely historically accurate but I feel I got the gist of it. I told her how, during the revolutionary wars, the American had his ship battered to pieces in a battle with the English. How half his crew were dead and his ship was on fire and sinking. How the English had asked him to surrender and how he had sent them a message saying: 'I have not yet begun to fight.'

'You're my John Paul Jones,' I said to her.

She was uncharacteristically quiet for a while.

'I sure intend to be,' she replied.

Through all this time, apart from her stays in hospital, Isobel insisted on going to school and remained very creative. She wrote, she drew, she painted and she sang. She made all her own Christmas cards and I have a small leadlight parrot on the window of my office at home, which she gave to me as a present one year.

Isobel's birthday falls early in the new year. To mark the occasion of completing her sixteenth time round the sun, she planned a big party for all her school-friends. To my very pleasant surprise I also received an invitation, although I had no idea what to get her for a present. I hadn't a clue what music was in, and I knew even less about cosmetics or clothes, or anything else I thought a teenage girl might like.

But in the way that these things sometimes work themselves out, the solution presented itself just a few days before the great event.

One evening a wild deer was struck by a log truck in the Mullaways, north of Rushby. When the driver got out to check the damage, he found a small fawn standing on the road by its dead mother. The driver scooped up the fawn and, knowing that I had deer, brought it round to my place.

'What on earth do you want me to do with this?' I asked as he put it in my arms.

'I wouldn't know. You're the deer expert, doc,' he replied with a smile as he got back in his cab and drove off into the dark.

It was a cold night so I took the little fellow inside and put him by the fire. The fawn lay on the kitchen floor with the reflection of the fire making his coat come alive. He was shivering when he arrived but he quickly warmed up and seemed to enjoy Hardy fussing over him. He was very cute. He had big white spots and legs that were far too long for his body. Whilst I had no idea how I was going to find the time to look after him, I hadn't the heart to turn him away, so I put up some temporary fencing in the back of the wood shed and threw some straw onto the floor. He took to the bottle surprisingly well and, within a day or so, looked much better. He was also surprisingly easy to handle.

On the day of the party I tied a big bow round his neck, and curled him up on the front passenger seat, much to the disgust of Hardy, who was relegated to the back seat and made to wear a bow also.

I have been to many parties over the years but I have never again made quite the impact I did on this occasion, strolling nonchalantly in with a fawn in my arms and Hardy at my heels.

Isobel, as usual, lay on her side on her trolley, hooked up to her oxygen line. She looked absolutely stunning. Her beautiful red hair was held back with combs she had pinched from her elder sister and she was wearing a new dress. For the first time I had ever seen she was wearing makeup and had on wonderfully sparkly eye shadow and ultra gloss lipstick.

Her eyes doubled in size when she saw the fawn and her friends started screaming. When the noise died down a little, I held the fawn out. 'You always said you wanted to stroke one. His name's Jones,' I said. 'John Paul Jones.'

Isobel reached up and, in all that noise, the fawn quietly lay down beside her and allowed her, and all her girlfriends, to stroke him nonstop. Indeed, the fawn stayed by Isobel's side the entire party, except for one occasion when he stood up, stretched himself and peed all over the carpet.

'By the way, you look stunning,' I said after the fawn had settled.

'Yes, but you haven't seen the best bit,' she said, holding her nails up for inspection. 'Look at these.'

They were the most beautifully decorated nails I had ever seen. I looked in amazement at the ten different, tiny and intricately painted patterns, with lots and lots of miniature rings. They were sensational and I said so. In fact, only once did I ever see them more ornately decorated.

Something happened during that party. I am not sure why and I am not sure how. Perhaps it was simply that it was such a happy occasion, perhaps it was seeing Isobel and her girlfriends enjoying themselves, or perhaps it was just the right time. Whatever it was, I knew that something had lifted from me. I left the party feeling lighter.

I was halfway home when I heard a little voice in my head.

'You're ready, aren't you?'

'Ready for what?' I replied

'You know, to let go,' came back the voice.

I pulled the car off the road near the old wooden bridge at the bottom of the hill. The tyres scrunched on the gravel by the side of the road as I came to a stop and turned off the head lights.

'Ah!' I said, suddenly understanding. 'Is that really you?'

'Well of course it is,' came the simple reply. 'Who else would it be?'

I got out of the car and leaned against the front wheel arch, my breath making clouds in the cold night air. I pulled my coat around me and looked silently up at the Milky Way as it blazed back at me in its incomprehensible immensity.

'Yes, I think I'm ready,' I finally replied. And with that I let her go.

It was so simple, so painless. I had always imagined it would be horrid and complicated, but I simply looked up at the galaxy and let it happen. I raised my arms, opened my hands and let Amy float silently away to the stars.

I stayed there for a little while and then suddenly shivered with the cold and got back in my car. I pulled back onto the road and continued on my way home.

'What was that all about?' Hardy asked after we had been going again for a few minutes.

'Don't worry,' I said as I reached back and patted him. 'I'll explain when you're older.'

A few months after the party Isobel started to develop yet another series of chest infections. Perhaps it was the approach of the colder weather, or perhaps it only reflected her further deterioration.

Madge took a call one afternoon to say that Isobel was really unwell again. Rather than wait for me to do a home visit at the end of the afternoon, it was decided to bring her into the surgery.

It turned out that she had another bout of pneumonia. She was very poorly and looked exhausted. Listening to her chest was far from reassuring.

'You're off to hospital,' I told her.

'John Paul Jones is buggered this time,' she whispered as she held my hand and waited for the ambulance.

'But you know that in the end he always wins,' I replied, trying to keep the uncertainty out of my voice, and then I told her how well Jones was doing.

Against all the odds, the fawn had not only survived the birthday party but had also survived being landed with me as a wet nurse. He just grew and grew. A few months after Isobel's sixteenth, he started to lose interest in the bottle and was a bit too big and frisky to be kept in the shed. I put him out into the paddock and introduced him to the other deer. He's out there with them still and doing just fine.

'See you soon,' I said brightly to Isobel. 'Just you make sure that you come back as good as new.' The ambulance door closed with a bang.

But this time John Paul Jones didn't win. This time it was the turn of the English. Isobel, who had tapped on the pearly gates so many, many times, finally passed through them a few months before her seventeenth birthday.

I looked at her as she lay in her tiny casket. She wore the same dress she had worn at the party and someone had decorated her nails again. They were definitely the nails to have on your journey to the next world. They were wonderful. She would have loved them to bits.

It has been some years now since Isobel went to wherever we all go when we've finished this part. She was in my life for almost thirteen years, and I miss her dreadfully.

One evening, a few weeks after Isobel died, there was a particularly clear sky. Late, after we had both been fed and watered, and on the spur of the moment, Hardy and I drove back out to the old bridge. We stood by the car and looked up as that beautiful spiral blazed back at us.

'Look after her,' I said to Amy and then spread out my arms once more and let Isobel join her.

For a while we stayed motionless, then our concentration was broken by a passing car, and we got back in and headed for home.

'I still don't get what you were doing just then,' Hardy said on the way back.

'I'm not sure I do either, really,' I replied, 'but it sure felt good.'

I was going to finish by saying that what I miss most about not having Isobel around is her incredible life force, but then I decided that wasn't true at all, for I feel it with me every day.

20 The Swinging Arms

THERE ARE QUITE A number of pubs scattered around the district and when I first moved up to Woongarra I had high hopes of spending pleasant evenings in each of them. Over the years, however, I have tried them all and found them a rather disappointing bunch.

The Coach and Horses at Southdown, built for exactly that purpose, is a beautiful old bluestone building. It has an attractive bar and a ghost in the hallway, but it is always freezing cold and the indifferent food takes forever to arrive. The Weary Traveller in Lavenham has been unspeakable since it was jazzed up to accommodate hundreds of poker machines; the inn at Mt Oriole got closed down for licence infringements, and Jamieson's at Ellerstone, which has just undergone an extensive facelift, seems every bit as gloomy as it did before. Whilst the Guard's Van in New Lavenham is sort of OK and the Wirringa Hotel has some great deer heads on the wall, the pick of the bunch is the Broken Wheel at Castle Vale. But that's forty-five minutes away and a long way to go for an evening's entertainment by anyone's reckoning.

In the high street in Dixon's Bridge, on the corner above the old post office and across the road from the surgery, sits a large, squat, ugly brick building in urgent need of renovation. The name on the faded board proclaims it to be the Dixon's Bridge Hotel. I have never once heard it called by that name for it is universally known as the Swinging Arms and it is as rough as bags.

The Arms is exactly where you would not take your beloved for a Saturday night out. Not unless, that is, she had arms like hams and an ability to look after herself when the going got tough. I have never been out with anyone like that, although there would be plenty in the district to choose from, and this probably explains why almost all my contact with the Arms has been in the form of dispensing medical care to the customers.

Nevertheless, I have been a patron myself a couple of times over the years. The first time was a Christmas in July when I took my parents along. I can't remember exactly how I got talked into it, but I'm glad I did, for somewhere amongst all the laughing and merriment, I won Chaz in the raffle.

Over the years I must have spent thousands of dollars in hundreds of raffles and had never before won so much as a jar of homemade marmalade. But that Christmas in July at the Swinging Arms I scooped the pool.

Chaz was an impressive prize and my success was greatly envied by all. Not only does he stand around six feet five in his motorcycle boots, but he is a big boy with it. With his shaved head, voluminous red beard, black singlet and studs, he is very much my mind's eye picture of Thor, or possibly his dad, Odin. And, together with his spider-web tattoos and his great golden earrings, both he and his Harley were mine for a day to do with as I pleased.

I waited for the weather to warm up a bit before I claimed my prize. Then, after teeing it up with the Norse god himself, I spent a magical Saturday visiting every winery in the district: Chaz up front, and me, in leathers, sunnies and black helmet, clinging on for dear life behind.

At first I was worried that Chaz might not like having my arms round his waist, and he was worried that some of his bikey mates might see us. In the end, though, neither of us need have had any concerns: Chaz couldn't have cared less about my cuddling and we didn't see another bike all day.

It was a beautiful still spring day and we had a lot of fun. I had wondered, before we started, what we would find to talk about, but I needn't have worried. As the day unfolded, we discovered we had a surprising amount in common. Chaz had become single about the same time as I had, and our struggles with the domestic necessities of life had traversed almost identical lines. He had apparently lost a child too.

'So where to next, boss?' Chaz would say cheerfully at the end of each tasting.

I would peer at the map, stab at it with a finger and reply: 'Right there, Chaz.'

'Not a problem,' he would say. Then we would don our gear, hop on the bike and head off in a flurry of gravel and decibels.

Throughout the day, Chaz remained impressively professionally sober. I did not. I finished up tasting every wine made within a thirty-kilometre radius and by the end of the day could hardly sit on the pillion.

'Chaz,' I said, raising my glass late in the day. 'I toast you as a scholar and a gentleman.'

At least, that was what I intended to say. How it actually came out I have no idea. All I do know is that I spilt the wine and broke the glass. I also very nearly fell off the bike on the Ellerstone road. So for the rest of the trip home Chaz tied me firmly to him with baling twine to ensure there wasn't a repeat performance.

If I never win another raffle again in the rest of my life, I will die a happy man.

I have also been into the Arms in the company of a young woman. Just the once. Over the years the practice has hosted registrars who rotate every six months. On one occasion we were blessed with a very pleasant and capable young woman called Louise. Amongst the long list of hobbies and interests in her curriculum vitae she cited 'bushwalking'. I'm not sure we ever received a CV from a registrar that didn't list bushwalking amongst the list of hobbies, but in Louise's case the inclusion was genuine. Shortly after her arrival she insisted that we go walking together.

After discussing the various possibilities over a glass of wine the evening before, we decided on a walk in the Mullaways. The particular walk we had in mind starts just a few kilometres out of town so we decided to leave the car at the surgery and walk from there.

The Mullaways proved to be a good choice and the day turned out to be perfect for walking. The entire ramble was a delightful kaleidoscope of forest, views, birds and wallabies. We arrived back in town in the late afternoon, pleasantly tired and a little footsore. We were also very thirsty.

'I don't know about you, but I could murder a beer,' Louise said when we reached the car.

'I'm with you all the way,' I agreed, so we headed across the road to the Arms.

The placed was obviously packed and we could hear a lot of noisy chatter and laughter as we approached.

'Sounds great,' Louise said as I held the bar door open for her.

As my companion stepped through the doorway the noise stopped as abruptly as if it had been turned off by a switch. Everyone inside, to the last man, froze as we entered. People in the act of lifting glasses, playing pool and throwing darts became statues. No one gave me a second glance but fifty pairs of eyes were glued to Louise.

There was an awkward silence and then the barman pointed to his right. 'Down the corridor,' he said to Louise.

'What do you mean?' she replied, puzzled.

'Down the corridor, across the yard,' he continued as if the extra detail would somehow clarify matters.

'Sorry,' she said, 'what is?'

'The ladies,' he said in a loud whisper.

'What about the ladies?'

'Well, that's where it is.'

'And?'

There were a few moments of silence and then he said: 'Well, what other reason would you have for coming in here?'

I thought about suggesting that we were thirsty and that this was a pub, but the moment had passed and we retired back outside. As the door closed behind us, the party switch turned on again.

'I guess they're not too used to women in there,' I said.

'But it's certainly the best effect I've had on a bunch of blokes in a very long time,' Louise said.

Then, matching the noise coming from behind us, we laughed all the way back to the car.

Louise's stay in the practice was lovely and she was good at mucking in and helping around the farm as well. But if she did have a weakness it was her relationship with Hardy. She was ridiculously soppy with him and she would say to him that she thought it was tewwible that a howwid man made such a poor little doggy-woggy stay outside all day in the cold and the wet, while we are away, with nothing on but a thin furry-wurry coat to keep him warm.

'I completely agree,' said Hardy looking at her with adoration as she scratched his ears. 'It's so nice having you staying here, Louise. You're the only one who's ever really understood me.'

'Don't be ridiculous,' I said to him, 'I understand you much better than she does.'

But the upshot of it all was that the doggy-woggy spent a lot more time indoors than he had ever done before.

One evening, Louise let Hardy in while we were having an evening cuppa. As soon as she opened the door I knew she had made a bad mistake. A long-dead kangaroo had washed up on a bend in the creek a few days earlier and Hardy had clearly found it for himself. He had obviously not just rolled in it but had wallowed in it as well. He looked awful and he smelt disgusting.

'Out, out, out!' I yelled. 'And don't think you're coming back inside tonight,' I added as I slammed the door behind him.

'Ooohhh! What on earth had he been rolling in?' Louise said, holding a tissue over her nose.

'I could show you in the morning,' I offered as we headed off to our respective rooms, 'but it's probably best not to bother.'

Some hours later I dreamed of a phone ringing a very long way off. In the dream the ringing gradually grew louder and louder and more persistent. Suddenly I realised that it wasn't a dream after all, so I reached over, clicked on the bedside light and picked up the phone.

'Hello,' I said in a voice thick with sleep. 'Dr Carter here.'

'I'm so sorry,' said someone at the other end. 'Did I wake you?'

The bedside clock said three-thirty. I wondered for the thousandth time why people thought I did something different at night to everyone else. But instead of making a sarcastic comment I mumbled: 'How can I help?'

'Tyrone's got a high temperature.'

'And who is Tyrone?' I asked patiently.

'Tyrone's my little boy. You can't have forgotten him, you vaccinated him at the clinic only a few months ago.'

'Ah, yes, of course,' I said, pretending to remember.

'Well, he has a high temperature.'

I sat up in bed and said: 'And how long has he had this temperature?'

'Two days.'

'And what have you done about it?'

'Well, nothing.'

'Why?'

'Because you're the doctor and we're waiting for you to tell us what to do.'

'At three-thirty in the morning?' I asked a little incredulously.

'Well we've just got home from a bit of a do and we found that he was still unwell. So we would like you to look at him and tell us what to do.'

I gave the usual advice about fluids and Panadol and removing clothes, hoping that this would suffice at least until the morning.

'But if we take his clothes off, won't he get cold?' Tyrone's mother asked.

'That's the general idea,' I continued in a very patient voice.

'But what about pneumonia?'

I paused for a few moments. A large part of me was quite keen to tell Tyrone's mother what I *really* thought of the entire conversation thus far. Instead, however, I followed the advice I have so often given others: I took three slow deep breaths, letting myself relax more with each one. Tyrone is not well, transcendental Paul said soothingly to irritated Paul. All else is irrelevant.

'OK', I said. 'I'll meet you at the surgery in twenty minutes.'

'Couldn't you just come round to the house?'

'No. I would prefer to see you at the surgery.'

'And will he be OK in the night air?'

'Yes, he'll be fine.'

There was a short pause. 'But couldn't you make it a bit sooner, we're really tired and want to go to bed.'

'That is as soon as I can make it,' I said, and hung up.

I got up, pulled some clothes on and tapped on Louise's door to see if she wanted to come too. But she was dead to the world so I ventured out on my own. I hopped in the car and headed off down the driveway under a clear, still, moonlit sky.

'That deep breathing really works,' I acknowledged admiringly to myself as I crossed the front paddock. By the time I had reached the front gate grumpy Paul was in hibernation and transcendental Paul was in complete charge of the ship.

I was about to pull out onto the main road when I noticed that my letterbox was missing. By the lights of the car I could see there were long skid marks across the road, passing either side of where the letterbox had once stood. They continued across the grass and down the small embankment where the land falls away towards the creek. The two white indicator posts which had once marked the entrance were also conspicuous by their absence.

I backed the car up and swung it round to get some light to see by, and as I did so, I took in a sharp breath. Some forty or so metres away, near the bottom of the slope, balanced just above the bank of the creek, a car was lying on its roof. It was severely damaged and I could see that there were people inside.

Leaving the headlights on, I grabbed my bag, jumped out and ran down the slope. When I reached the crash I could see that there were four people inside, hanging upside down in their seat belts. They were all very still.

There was no smell of petrol so I cautiously approached the vehicle to turn off the ignition and begin what I imagined would be a fairly grizzly clinical assessment. But as I got close I heard a low rumbling noise coming from inside. I suddenly realised what it was and my tension immediately vanished into the darkness. For, as far as I am aware, corpses have never been known to snore.

I opened the driver's door and a strong smell of alcohol wafted out into the night. I took the keys out of the ignition and shook the driver's shoulder, gently at first and then, getting no response, rather more vigorously. Slowly he awoke. He looked around from his upside-down position, then he shook his head as if to clear it and looked at me. He stared at me for quite a while as his companions started stirring, then he rubbed his eyes and looked at me again.

'And who the fuck are you?' he said in a thick slurred voice.

'The Archangel Gabriel,' I smiled.

'That's funny,' came a sleepy voice from the back. 'I've always pictured him with more fucking hair than that,' and they all laughed.

'Anyone injured?' I asked and got four slurred negatives in reply.

'Well, this may be OK for fucking bats,' said the sleepy voice from the back, 'but I'd like to get the fuck out of here.'

So, with a fair bit of pushing and shoving, four lucky lads extricated themselves through the doors on the driver's side and the windows on the front passenger side. Then they all stood on my nature strip, swaying gently in the moonlight.

There was not a mark on any of them. Not so much as a cut or a scratch.

'Ah!' said the driver in sudden recognition. 'You're the fucking doc, aren't you?'

I nodded that I was.

'Yeah. I remember. Gave me a fucking jab a few months back. Hurt like fucking buggery,' he said. 'Well, doc, I have a fucking question for you, and it's fucking this: where the fuck are we?'

'On my fucking nature strip,' I said as a joke, but they didn't get it. They just looked around nodding their heads, saying: 'Yeah. Fucking right.'

'And I've got a question for all of you too,' I continued. 'What are you going to do now? I mean, how are you going to get home?'

There was a shaking of heads and someone muttered, 'Wouldn't have the faintest fucking idea.'

'Do you all live in town?' I enquired, and apparently they all did.

'Well,' I said, 'it so happens that I'm going into town right now, so I'll give you a lift in. You can get your car picked up in the morning. But I want one thing really, really clear. Nobody, and I mean nobody, chucks in my car.'

There was a lot of nodding of heads.

'That's real fucking good of you, doc,' said a tall lad with curly red hair. 'We'll put this one on the slate.'

So the boys piled into my car and we drove into town. To my pleasant surprise no one vomited on the upholstery and I managed to get them delivered to their respective homes without any further incident.

When I got home some while later, I found to my distress that I hadn't shut the back door properly when I left. The door had swung open and Hardy, like the cheeky opportunist that he was, had sneaked in and camped on my bed.

For the second time that night he was evicted, but the damage was done. I couldn't be bothered to make up a clean bed so decided to sleep in the guestroom instead. I was about to get into the bed when I suddenly realised that it was already occupied, so I spent the rest of the night on the couch.

The next morning at work I felt a bit seedy. Not only had I had been up a fair bit of the night, but there was a large ridge running down the middle of the couch which did nothing to help me get the best out of my rest. I was just about to start the day's surgery when Heather let me know that Tyrone's mum was on the line.

'Oh my God!' I exclaimed. 'I forgot all about him!'

'And she's not a happy camper,' Heather added.

'I can well imagine,' I replied. 'You'd better put her through,' I added as I moved the hand-piece a little further away from my ear.

'Have you any idea how long you kept us waiting?' she shouted. 'Do you realise that we waited for you for nearly an hour? How could you stand us up in the cold and the dark like that? Did you forget about us or just ignore us deliberately? What sort of a doctor does that?'

'I'm very, very sorry,' I replied, and decided that the best strategy was to answer her questions with one of my own: 'So how's Tyrone?'

'Oh, he's fine,' she dismissed. 'We gave him some fluids and Panadol and took his clothes off and he was as right as rain this morning. But that's not the point,' she said angrily and then continued to list my shortcomings for quite some time. When she had finished I apologised once more, and although I could not tell at the time whether she was satisfied with that, I am happy to report that she still brings Tyrone to see me.

Over the years, the Arms has proved to be a regular, if tiresome, source of income. Regular in that it occurred every weekend, and tiresome in that it occurred every weekend. The calls for help usually started late in the evening and would sometimes continue right through to early the following morning. Not only did the boys seem keen to settle differences by direct means, but they sometimes resorted to billiard cues as well. In addition, there was a short flight of steps outside the bar door which the regulars seemed to misjudge with surprising frequency.

The big day at the Arms is Saturday. The week's work over, the boys start congregating from midmorning onwards. By lunchtime the place is half full and backslappingly good-natured. By the end of the racing and football it is crowded and cranky. By ten o'clock at night it is bursting at the seams and explosive.

A few months after forgetting all about Tyrone, I got a call for assistance from the Arms. Normally whoever was on bar duty would simply phone and say they were sending someone over to the surgery for stitching or X-raying or whatever. This time, however, the barman asked me to come round straight away because some geezer had been knocked cold. At least I thought that was what he had said, for it was a little difficult to hear against all the background noise.

'Have you called the police?' I asked, but the phone had gone dead.

Having taken the call at home, I threw my gear in the car and drew up outside the pub less than ten minutes later. From the audible commotion inside, it was obvious that it was on for young and old.

I looked around but there was not so much as a police dog in sight. Feeling rather apprehensive, I cautiously opened the door and slipped in.

The whole place was a seething mass of struggling men. Chairs were flying and glasses were airborne. It looked like something out of a Wild West movie. Through all the chaos I glimpsed the feet of someone lying on the floor in the far corner. I presumed that this was my patient, so I ducked under the nearest table and started to crawl round to him.

I was about halfway to my target when a great hairy paw the size of a dinner plate grabbed me by the shoulder and jerked me to a standing position. The paw belonged to Bluey, a local bricklayer. He was a giant of a man with a great curly mop of salt and pepper hair and a reputation for resolving issues physically.

He held me tightly by the front of my jacket with one hand and then slowly raised the other. I thought my time had come but, to my intense relief, instead of dispatching me into next week, he called out to the assembled throng.

'Boys!' he boomed in a voice like a ship's foghorn.

Instantly the whole place went quiet and still. Everyone stopped in mid-combat and into the silence he boomed again: 'Boys! I want to make it real clear that nobody, and I do mean nobody, hits the doc!'

I nearly fainted with relief.

There was a chorus of assent, which I acknowledged with a small wave to various parts of the room. Then, after the briefest of pauses, the entire place plunged itself back into turmoil.

As he let go of my jacket, Bluey bent down and said: 'Thanks for pulling the boys out of their car, doc. And thanks for running them home afterwards. That was real nice.'

Bluey escorted me to the corner where Max, the injured man, was lying. As far as I could tell he was still alive but deeply unconscious. Whether he had a head injury or was simply in the advanced stages of inebriation was not possible for me to determine. Bluey got the barman to phone for an ambulance and then he and I carried Max between the combatants and out onto the pavement.

Even in the cool evening air, Max remained unconscious. It was obvious that he would be much better off in a hospital, so when the ambulance arrived we organised a helicopter. Luckily, there was one available. It was dispatched immediately and we were told it would arrive at the football ground fifteen or twenty minutes later.

A couple of the lads were hauled out of the fray by Bluey and sent to go and turn on the training lights so that the pilot could see where to land, and Max was taken to the ground to await the arrival of his airborne transport.

Even after all these years, I am still surprised by the speed of the bush telegraph. By the time the helicopter touched down, there was a bigger crowd than there had been for the game earlier that day.

The transfer was simple and in just a few minutes Max disappeared noisily into the night sky. As the crowd started to disperse I turned to Bluey and said: 'By the way, what was the fight about?'

He stood still for a while, clearly thinking hard. 'Buggered if I know,' he finally said, shaking his head.

'Well what started it?' I persisted.

'I'm buggered if I know that either,' he replied. There was a moment's silence and then he continued: 'I don't think it was about anything in particular. I think the boys were just letting off a bit of steam.'

'Well, there you go then,' I said as I got into the ambulance for a lift back to my car. Oh and by the way, Bluey, thanks for the new letterbox. It's great. Better than the old one.'

'Not a problem in the world, doc. Least the boys could do,' and he walked off into the darkness.

I drove home, thinking how tame were the ways in which I chose to let off steam, until I got back home and found that Hardy had revisited the kangaroo and I had left the back door open again.

21 Beck

WITH A LOUD CRASH, all six of us fell onto the bed together. There was Beck, of course, her husband Tom, the nurse, the constable, the sergeant and myself. For a brief moment we all lay there exhausted. Then, from the bottom of the pile, Beck, unnoticed by the rest of us, quietly stretched out her arm, flicked on the lighter she had in her hand and set fire to the bedroom curtains.

'I can smell burning,' said the nurse in alarm, and pandemonium broke out once more. The lighter was eventually confiscated and the curtains extinguished, but only after a great deal of pushing and shoving.

Everyone except Beck got off the bed. She remained pinned face down in the pillows with her hands held tightly behind her back by the sergeant.

'Quick, doc, give her something,' he said to me.

With hands shaking slightly from all the excitement, I drew up an ampoule and gave Beck a shot in the arm.

I had known Beck for some time. Not only was she a regular at the surgery but I had also been out for tea at their place in the Mullaways. Their property was very pretty and the house, which they had built themselves, was set on the highest point. Below the house, the farm ran gently down to the creek in the gully below. It was good dirt but the only animals on the place, apart from a couple of steers they kept for their freezer, were a few ancient ponies and some geriatric sheep.

Beck was in her late forties when I first met her. She had a kind, open face which was covered in freckles and framed by a mass of curly blonde hair. She was a petite, mild-mannered woman who was very popular in the area.

About a year or so before that morning on the bed, Beck presented to the surgery feeling very down in the dumps. It had all started with a family row, and the upshot was that Beck and Tom hadn't seen their nephew and niece since then.

She had all the signs of depression but wouldn't accept any treatment. Over some months she became increasingly unwell. I suggested we involve local psych services but she wouldn't have a bar of that either.

Early on the morning that Beck set the curtains on fire, Tom had phoned the surgery and asked to speak to me urgently. Beck had been acting very strangely since first thing. When he'd asked whether she was OK, she had responded by throwing things around the house. After emptying the kitchen drawers onto the floor, Tom continued, she had gone out for a walk on her own and had seemed a bit calmer on her return.

I explained to him that I was fully booked but would be happy to do a house call at lunchtime. At first Tom said that would be fine but then, to the accompaniment of a great deal of banging and crashing in the background, he calmly told me she was throwing things around again and could I come right now.

I got Madge to reschedule the rest of my morning and arrived at Beck and Tom's place only ten or fifteen minutes later. Everything seemed fine as I got out of the car. I found the front door open, so I just called out, 'Hi', and went in.

By lucky chance I caught a flash of light and movement out of the corner of my eye and was able to duck just in time to avoid the glass ashtray that had been aimed at my head. It sailed through the doorway and exploded into a thousand pieces on the front path.

'And you can fuck off for a start,' Beck screamed at me, appearing from the kitchen with a glass sugar bowl in her hand.

The house looked as if it had been hit by a whirlwind.

Beck threw the sugar bowl at the TV, narrowly missed it, and then sat on the couch, clicking her fingers and spitting at me. Tom, who had been quietly sitting in the corner, folded his paper, got up and came over to greet me.

'Thank you so much for coming,' he said quietly, and shook my hand.

I carefully sat down on the chair nearest to the door, in case a rapid exit was in order, and looked at Beck. She was very agitated indeed and did not look at all well. The dark rings under her eyes gave her a hunted look and there were scratches on both forearms.

'Hello, Beck,' I said.

'I don't want you here, so fuck off,' she shouted at me.

'How can I help?' I persisted.

'You can't. I don't want your fucking help,' she screamed. 'So just fuck off and leave me alone.'

'As you are aware, doctor, Beck has not been well for some time,' Tom said quietly and slowly. 'She has been getting worse over the last week or so and today things are quite out of control, as you can see.'

'I will not have you discussing me like I am not here,' Beck screamed at the top of her voice.

'For the last month,' Tom continued calmly, 'Beck has been hearing voices, haven't you, darling?'

'Yes, and they're telling me to kill everyone here, right now,' Beck shouted. 'First you, then him,' she pointed at me, 'and then myself.'

'I guess you would have to be last,' I said, trying to lighten up the situation.

Beck got up, crossed the room and leaned forward until her face was very close to mine. 'But you will be first,' she screamed, 'if you don't stop trying to make fucking fun of this.'

There was a fairly long pause and then I asked: 'Beck, do you think you would be better off in hospital?'

The response was instantaneous: 'I'm not going to any fucking loony bin and you can't make me. So don't even think about it. We live in a country where it's against the law to force people to do things they don't want to do.'

There was a longer pause this time.

'You would be best off in hospital,' I said.

'How dare you say that to me? How dare you suggest I would need that? I'll sue you for every penny you have, you pompous opinionated prick,' she said.

'You should listen to the doctor, darling,' interjected Tom quietly.

'I have,' she shouted back at him, 'and he's nothing but a pompous opinionated prick. And I don't like him either,' she added as an afterthought.

There was yet another pause.

'Tom,' I said, 'if it's OK with you, I'll go and rustle up some help, get the necessary paperwork signed and hopefully be back here within the hour. Right?'

'Yes,' said Tom as calmly as ever. 'That's exactly what I hoped you would say.'

I left the house and drove to the neighbours just a little way down the road, where they kindly let me use their phone. I organised for the police and a psych nurse to meet me at Beck's and was lucky enough to find a suitable hospital bed. I passed the time waiting for everyone to arrive by filling out all the various forms that allow the system to override an individual's wishes in situations such as this. In a little over half an hour I was once more standing at Beck's front door, but this time accompanied by Sergeant Hogan, a young constable and a nurse.

'Everyone ready?' I asked, looking around.

They nodded and we were about to go in when a thought struck me. I turned to the police. 'How about you boys leave your hardware in the car? The last thing we want here is to add any complications to the equation,' I said, indicating their holsters.

There was a moment's reluctance, but then they unbuckled their guns and put them back in the divvy van.

'Everyone ready?' I asked again, and was about to knock on the door when the constable pulled out his nightstick and held it at the ready.

'What in God's name do you think you're doing?' hissed the nurse.

'I've got to have something to defend myself with,' he replied defensively.

'Don't be ridiculous,' she blazed at him in a whisper. 'We're going in there to help a sick person, you idiot, not arrest some hardened criminal!'

The lad went bright red and the stick followed the guns into the van.

On the third try, I knocked on the door, called out Beck's name and we all entered the house.

It certainly couldn't be said that Beck was happy to see us. Household items and invective flew thick and fast. In the uneasy truce that followed the first barrage, Beck reached over and grabbed the lighter from the breakfast bar.

'I'll torch the whole place if you don't all leave immediately,' she screamed at us, flicking the lighter on and holding it in front of her.

Very calmly the nurse explained to Beck that she was going to hospital.

'No!' Beck shouted at the top of her voice. 'I am *not* going and you cannot make me.'

'Well, actually, we can,' the nurse replied.

Beck immediately turned and disappeared at high speed into the bedroom. She tried to slam the door behind her but she was not quick enough and the sergeant got his foot in the way. The police forced their way through the door and the rest of us followed behind. In the confined space of the bedroom, the six of us tussled for quite some time. Then we all seemed to become intertwined, collectively lost our balance and fell onto the bed.

Eventually we all got up except Beck and I gave her an injection. Beck, held down firmly by the sergeant, lay motionless on the bed whilst the rest of us caught our breath and the curtains were rendered safe once more. The effects of my injection appeared miraculous to say the least. At the very instant the needle went in, and even before I had given the medication, every muscle suddenly relaxed and Beck looked like nothing so much as a rag doll.

'Thank the Lord for that,' said the sergeant and started to release his grip on her.

'No!' I cried out 'Keep a hold, the injection doesn't work that fast.'

'It obviously has for her,' he said, and let go.

'I very much doubt it,' the nurse warned, but for a few seconds nothing happened and Beck lay still.

'See?' Hogan was in the middle of saying when Beck suddenly sprang into life. Showing remarkable speed and agility, she spun round and bit him hard on the hand.

'Jesus Christ!' he roared. 'She's bitten me. God almighty,' he cried looking down at his hand. 'She's made it bleed. Bloody hell, doc, you could have warned me.'

'I thought I had,' I was going to say but was beaten to the punch by another attempt by Beck on the sergeant. He was ready for her this time, though, and she finished up face down on the bed with her hands handcuffed behind her back.

'I am so sorry we had to do this,' I said to Beck.

'Fuck off,' she hissed. 'You pompous opinionated prick.'

'I can see she likes you,' the nurse smiled at me.

Eventually the injection really did take effect and Beck made the journey from the bedroom to the back of the divvy van with remarkably little fuss. Then, in the company of the nurse and the paperwork I had completed earlier, she was driven quietly down the rutted driveway to the road and then on to the hospital in Lockridge.

I stayed, had a cup of tea with Tom and then drove back to the shattered remains of my morning surgery, which seemed very tame by comparison.

Beck turned out to be the star of the hospital. Once she started on medication she never looked back and the voices disappeared almost immediately. Just a short time later she was happily back at the farm with Tom. Apart from a few natural misgivings about the need for life-long treatment and some annoying side effects, she was as right as rain.

Over the years, sadly, I have been involved in many similar situations. They may often be humorous in hindsight, but it is sad indeed for people to be doubly robbed of their freedom and dignity by both disease and treatment. Forcing people against their will into secure settings was not exactly what I had in mind when, all those years ago, I walked through the gates of medical school for the first time. Nevertheless, it is sometimes the only option available if we are to protect patients from hurting themselves or other people.

Each and every one of these situations has left me with indelible memories, but a couple stand out even more brightly than the rest.

The first of these involved Bernard, who had the unfortunate combination of unstable thinking and an overwhelming passion for keeping venomous snakes. He had all the appropriate licences to collect and breed the reptiles and he kept them throughout his house in hundreds of glass tanks of every shape and size.

There was a time when Bernard didn't realise that he had fallen ill again and was therefore, understandably, extremely resistant to the ridiculous suggestion, as he saw it, that he go should go back to hospital once more. When being pressured to accept this course of action by the team who had gathered at his house for that express purpose, Bernard decided to protect his freedom by setting upon us his 'only true friends in the world'.

Lids were thrown everywhere and Bernard started smashing tanks open with a golf putter, but I am delighted to report that, despite all this encouragement, not a single beast chose to leave the warmth and safety of its nest.

I did not escape personal injury, however, sustaining a small cut on the back of my hand from a flying splinter of glass. For weeks afterwards I attempted to sell the faint mark as a snakebite to anyone who would listen. Eventually everyone got fed up with the story and told me to bugger off.

The other particularly vivid occasion occurred in the small hours of the morning. It had been a long, cold, wet winter that year but on that night the weather was particularly evil. The wind cut straight through to the bone and the icy rain was horizontal.

On the road to Hanover, on a small farm that backs up to the ranges, live a retired vet and his wife. They were awoken around two in the morning by a persistent banging on the front door. When they got up to see who it was they found Evelyn, their next-door neighbour, collapsed on the doorstep. She was wearing only a nightie which was spattered in mud from neck to knee. She was drenched to the bone and her teeth were chattering with cold.

They brought her inside, wrapped her in blankets, gave her a cup of hot tea and lit the fire.

When Evelyn had recovered enough to talk, they asked her what on earth had happened.

'It's just terrible,' she cried out, bursting into tears. 'Douglas has murdered the children.'

The vet and his wife were profoundly shocked, of course, since they knew Evelyn's husband as well as they knew Evelyn herself. They immediately phoned the police and related what had happened. In hardly any time at all the house had been turned into an operations headquarters and a large squad of heavily armed police had set off into the storm for the farm next door.

When the squad reached Evelyn's farm they took up their positions around the house and an officer knocked on the door. He had to knock for a long time, but eventually the lights went on and the door was opened by a very sleepy Douglas in pyjamas.

Douglas was naturally a bit stunned at being held at gunpoint whilst a great body of police surged into his house. They searched it from end to end but all they found were four peacefully sleeping children.

'What the hell is going on?' exclaimed Douglas when the guns had been put away. 'And where's my wife?'

The police told Douglas where his wife was but suggested that he stay with the children while they went back to the vet's and sorted things out. Recognising that things were not quite as they had at first seemed, the police called in an experienced policewoman to go through the story with Evelyn in a little more detail.

'Tell me exactly what happened tonight,' the officer said gently.

'It's so sad, it's just so sad,' Evelyn replied.

'Yes, I'm sure, but what exactly is it that's so sad?' she coaxed.

There was a long pause, then Evelyn looked up at her.

'Douglas murdered all the children,' she sobbed. 'But that's not the worst of it,' she added. 'The really sad part is that it's not the first time he's done it.'

'Ah,' said the officer, who got hold of my number and woke me from my slumbers.

'I think I need your help,' she said.

'I think you do too,' I replied when I heard the story, and got out of bed.

The policewoman and I talked with Evelyn until dawn and by six o'clock Evelyn agreed to have hospitalisation on a voluntary basis. She had been very resistant to the idea at first, but as the hours went by she was gradually persuaded that this was for the best. Not that she had been persuaded by us, she hastened to let us know. Rather, during the course of the discussion she had asked God for guidance and this was what the Almighty had advised her to do.

The police were very gentle with Evelyn. They did not hurry or hassle her and neither did they handcuff her. They just quietly took her to the hospital in the back of a patrol car with the policewoman holding her hand to keep her company.

'I think, Lord, you gave her exactly the right advice,' I said as they pulled away.

Happily, although not everyone who spends time in a psychiatric hospital makes a miraculous recovery, Evelyn's health has gone from strength to strength since then. Every day she thanks her maker and her medication for restoring her to wellness.

Beck, too, has been happy and well since she was hospitalised. These days I get a smile and a chat whenever our paths cross and she often apologises about the ashtray.

'And I'm sorry about all those 'fucks',' she said to me once when we happened to be standing in line together at the supermarket checkout.

'For Gawd's sake!' I hushed her. 'Keep your voice down. You'll be overheard and you know what the gossips are like in this town.'

The sixteen year old behind the cashier tut-tutted in disapproval at two embarrassing middle-aged farts leaning on one another's shoulders and screaming with laughter.

A few months later, Charlie, my registrar at the time, was preparing for his fellowship examinations. Charlie is a really nice bloke, a little on the serious side perhaps, but he will make an excellent family doctor. He was planning to get married shortly after the exams, so he was keen to pass first time and had studied hard.

Charlie asked me if I would organise some cases for a trial clinical examination. I was very happy to help out and accordingly set aside a

Saturday afternoon. I contacted people who exemplified various clinical issues and who I knew would be happy to participate.

In the literature that Charlie showed me about his examination, it indicated that one type of patient with which the candidate might be presented was: 'the difficult case'.

Accordingly, I phoned Beck and asked if she would be happy to come along and be difficult.

'Of course I will,' she said over the phone. 'Be delighted to. Do you want me a just little difficult or very?' she added.

'Oh, I don't know. Perhaps just like you were that day at your house,' I replied and thought no more about it.

The practice examination was a great success. I had organised four patients for the afternoon and the first three went really well. Charlie had handled everything I had thrown at him and had dealt with the cases efficiently and competently.

We had a quick break for a cup of tea before the last case and then went into the room where Beck was waiting for us.

She was sitting hunched in a chair in the far corner of the consulting room and I instantly knew that there was something very wrong. She had a hunted look on her face and was clicking her fingers incessantly

'Oh God,' I thought with a sharp in-drawing of breath, 'please don't say that coming here today has triggered anything.'

I was about to abort the whole thing when she turned to Charlie.

'And you can fuck off for a start,' she screamed at him.

Charlie was visibly taken aback. After a brief pause he regrouped and said, in a slightly strained voice: 'How can I help?'

'You can't fucking help and I don't want your fucking help, you pompous opinionated prick,' she screamed at him.

Charlie tried hard to maintain a professional, clinical approach even when Beck starting knocking things off the edge of his desk. He even asked another question or two but finally lost his cool when she produced a cigarette lighter from her pocket and kept clicking it on and off. He picked up the phone and said to the receptionist on duty: 'Get the police here, quick.'

I felt sick in the stomach, worried that I had endangered both Beck's health and Charlie's confidence by bringing her to the exam.

I got out of my chair in order to intervene and repair the damage I had caused, when Beck put the cigarette lighter back in her pocket, settled back in her chair and said with a smile, 'Was that the sort of thing you wanted me to do, Paul ?'

Charlie and I slumped back in our chairs, both feeling rather pale and sweaty.

'Was that all put on?' Charlie asked in amazement.

'My God, Beck,' I said with a nervous laugh, 'that was brilliant. You deserve an Oscar.'

'Just because I'm better, Paul, doesn't mean I've forgotten what happened,' she said. 'I remember every little bit of it. So anytime you want a 'difficult patient' to practice on, just let me know. OK?' she added with a smile.

We eventually bade Beck farewell, sat down and looked at one another.

'Wow,' said Charlie.

'Wow, indeed,' I agreed. 'Do you reckon you got anything out of it?' I asked.

'Yeah, heaps, but I don't know if any of it will be of any use in the exam,' he replied.

We were having a quiet chuckle when the phone rang and Meaghan informed me that there were two policemen in the waiting room.

'Oh, God,' I said. 'We forgot to cancel them.' And I went out to apologise.

I saw Beck just a week or two after the trial exam and apologised in case the afternoon had stirred up any unpleasant memories for her.

'None that weren't already there,' she said. 'And I still remember all the best bits, which, just for the record, were the ashtray, the curtains and biting the sergeant on the hand.'

Since that time there have been many more practice clinical exams for many more registrars. I have thought about it occasionally but have never again had the courage to ask Beck to be difficult.

22 Walnuts

HANGING IN THE KITCHEN, above my car keys, is a pen-and-wash drawing of Hardy mounted in a stylish wooden frame. It's an attractive and elegant portrait and over the years I have had a great deal of pleasure from it. Even now, I look at it most days. It's not a portrait of Hardy himself of course, just some Large Munsterlander or other, but it does look an awful lot like him.

One weekend, at a medical conference in Hobart, I had found the afternoon session rather tedious and decided to wander out for a walk around the town. Down by the harbour, I chanced upon an art gallery so I went in to have a look.

By coincidence an auction was about to start and the place was packed. I found a seat towards the back of the gallery and settled in for some entertainment. Not having even sighted the catalogue, I had no idea what was on offer so I simply sat there, quietly enjoying the noise and excitement associated with each new lot. Suddenly, to my amazement, a pen-and-wash drawing of Hardy was placed onto the easel and the auctioneer began waffling on about it.

There was never any question in my mind whether I should own the work, so I borrowed my next-door neighbour's number card and just kept sticking my hand up until I did. I had no idea how much the picture had been valued at and I can't even remember how much I paid for it. I simply bid until there was no one else left and then carefully brought it back to the mainland in a cocoon of bubble wrap.

As I have said before, Saturday mornings were always busy. The surgery was often fully booked by nine o'clock and then there were always walk-ins and accidents as well.

There are so many accidents that I am no longer surprised it is considered OK to angle grind or chainsaw without safety goggles. I am no longer surprised that it is considered OK to ride horses and motorbikes with neither experience nor helmets, and I am no longer surprised that it is considered OK to let two year olds near hot things.

But I am still a bit surprised that it is considered OK to keep doing it, over and over again. It all seems so annoyingly predictable, especially when you are keen to go home and watch the cricket.

Eventually, however, the waiting room finally cleared. I thanked Meaghan yet again for running the surgery so efficiently and headed back to the farm.

Once at home I quickly made a sandwich, poured a beer and slumped in front of the TV just in time to catch the beginning of a day-night against the old enemy. I had watched a few overs when I realised that I hadn't seen Hardy since I'd got home. He hadn't jumped up and annoyingly put his feet on the car; he hadn't squeezed past me when I came in the back door, and he wasn't lying next to me watching the cricket. In fact, I hadn't seen him at all.

'He'll be around somewhere,' I thought as I poured myself another beer and turned back to the game. But he still hadn't put in an appearance by the drinks break.

'Silly idiot's got himself locked in somewhere,' I said, so I got up, stretched and went to have a look for him.

After a few minutes of calling around the place and opening doors, I realised he wasn't in the house, so I wandered over to the farmyard. I called his name as I went, but he still didn't appear. I checked the stables and workshop and opened every shed door that was closed.

I still wasn't concerned, only mildly puzzled. I thought that he'd probably gone down to the creek or found a fox to chase.

'Lovely,' I thought. 'He'll probably come back stinking and mangy again.'

I was keen to get back to the cricket so I decided to shout his name a few more times and then call off the search. As I turned to go back to the house I thought that I heard the faintest of responses from the hay barn down by the shearing shed. I went over to the barn and there he was, wedged between the stack and the side wall of the shed. He lifted his head and looked at me.

'Hello, you silly bugger,' I said. 'You had me a bit worried there for a while. Stop playing around and come and watch the cricket with me.'

He gave a few desultory wags of his tail but otherwise didn't move. This was so unlike him that for the first time I felt some concern.

With great difficulty, I squeezed into Hardy's tight hidey-hole and then, with even greater difficulty, lifted him out into the sunshine. It was immediately obvious that he was very ill: he was hardly moving, he was panting and he felt cold.

I left him where he was and went back to the house to see if the vet's surgery was still open. It was, so I drove back round to the hay barn, put Hardy on the back seat with a blanket over him and headed back into Dixon's Bridge at high speed.

Simon is a lovely man whom I have known pretty much since I moved up from town. He had just returned from a calving and, by lucky chance, was at the surgery cleaning up.

Unlike me, Hardy didn't like Simon. It may have been because of the needles Simon has given him over the years, or it may simply be the vet smell of disinfectant on Simon's overalls. Whatever the reason, Hardy always tried to slink away whenever he saw him. Today, however, he didn't care. He just lay on the stainless-steel trolley, looking at us, trusting us to help him. Simon examined him and agreed he was gravely ill.

'Could be snail bait,' he said.

'No,' I replied with a shake of my head, 'we don't use it anywhere on the property.'

'Any other poisons?' Simon asked. 'He just looks like he has been poisoned.'

'The Ratsac is inaccessible; we haven't used fox bait all season, and all the sprays are carefully locked away,' I replied.

'There is one other possibility,' Simon said.

'Internal haemorrhage?' I asked. 'That's what I was thinking.'

Simon nodded. 'Could he have been hit by a car?'

'Not as far as I know,' I said, 'but I was at work, so I can't be certain.'

Simon examined Hardy again, then shaved a small area on his tummy and popped in a large needle. When the trocar was removed, we both stood and watched in silence as blood dripped out freely.

'He's done his spleen,' Simon said decisively. 'He needs a blood transfusion and a splenectomy. We don't have much time, so how about you put up the drip while I go and organise things?'

'Where do I put it?' I asked.

'Wherever you can get it in,' Simon replied from the other room.

The drip trolley was much the same as my own, so I set to. I shaved a leg, found a vein and got in first time. The only difference from what I did most days was having to shave the fur off first. But then, I thought with a brief smile, I had a few patients who needed that anyway.

The drip ran well but Hardy looked very sick and it was obvious that time was running out.

Simon organised the hospital and let them know that a transfusion would be needed as soon as we got there. He helped me carry Hardy out to my car, tied the drip to the hook above the door and told me how to find the place.

I was about to drive off when a thought occurred to me. 'How can the blood be ready when we haven't cross-matched him?'

'No need to, dogs all have the same blood group,' he replied.

In a spray of gravel, I launched myself onto the main road and headed off at breakneck speed.

I don't remember much of the journey to the animal hospital, but I do know that I did it in just a little over forty minutes. I have travelled the same road many times since, for other reasons, and I have never managed anything much under an hour.

Over the years, usually for sound clinical reasons, I seem to have spent quite a lot of my life attempting to break the land speed records for getting from A to B, C to D and also E to F. Along the way I have had a tilt at the rest of the alphabet and then done it all in reverse as well. Although my speedometer often indicates a figure higher than the authorities would approve of, I have never been involved in an accident or even a near miss, unless you count wandering livestock or kangaroos.

Surprisingly, I have only been booked for speeding once, but it really sticks in my throat because it was probably the most justified occasion of all.

Roger was a keen member of the local tennis club and in the annual club competition had reached the finals of the mixed doubles. I understand that the game was tense due to some personal issues between the two couples involved and that there was consequently a lot at stake.

It was a tight game but, little by little, Roger and his partner had gradually gained the upper hand. At five four up in the third set it was Roger's turn to serve for the match. Roger threw the ball up into the air but instead of swinging his racquet and serving an ace, he blocked off one of his coronary arteries and fell to the ground. Someone phoned the surgery and less than three minutes later I was thumping his chest and giving him mouth to mouth by the service line. Unfortunately my efforts were to no avail and it seems likely that Roger had passed through those famous gates even before he reached the ground.

I waited until the body had been removed by the local funeral director and then went sadly back to the surgery for Roger had been a popular member of the community.

My speeding fine arrived exactly two weeks later. Despite lots of impassioned letters fired off to all points of the compass, the powers that be made it clear that the fine stood. I took the matter to court, but all that achieved was a much bigger fine for losing my temper and informing the magistrate that when his wife had her heart attack I would make sure I stuck carefully to the speed limit.

And on the way to the hospital I thought of all the things Hardy would rather be doing right now. He loved running and swimming, of course, and he loved lying on his back on my bed since I was weak enough to let him get away with it, but his favourite thing in all the world was fighting with the dogs at the sawmill.

I often went over to the sawmill to pick up timber or fence posts and Hardy always insisted on coming with me. In fact, if he got so much as a whiff that the sawmill was on the agenda, he would be in the back of the truck already waiting for me.

When we arrived at the mill I would go to the office to let them know what I wanted and Hardy would jump down to see what other dogs were around. The mill was run by four brothers and, since they all had a dog or two each, there were usually at least half-a-dozen animals wandering round the yard at any given time.

When Hardy had sussed out who was there and the yard dogs had realised they had a visitor, they would all start circling one another, hackles up and growling. This would usually go on for some time. Inevitably one of them would cross some boundary invisible to humans and the whole cluster of dogs would erupt into noisy, furry warfare.

No one ever took any notice of the fights and certainly nobody ever tried to intervene. We just left them to it and got on with our own business. Not once did any of them ever get injured.

When it was time to leave, Hardy would simply disengage from the fray and jump up onto the back of the truck.

'Now that,' he would pant when we got back home, 'was really good fun.'

'Yes,' I would agree, 'that's exactly what it looked like. But now make yourself useful and give us a hand getting this timber off.'

He wasn't good all the time, though, like the time he killed a lamb. At first, I couldn't believe he'd done it. He was so well-behaved with the sheep normally and so gentle with the little ones. But I'd been out all day and I suspect he had grown bored and got himself into mischief. When I got back I found a mauled lamb near the front drive and Hardy turned up at the house later with blood and wool round his mouth.

'Hello,' he smiled nervously at me.

For the second and last time in his life I gave him a whacking. He also spent the next week with the dead lamb tied around his neck.

'What on earth is that tied around your dog's neck?' my mother asked.

'A lamb,' I said simply.

'Do you know,' she continued, 'I was afraid you were going to say that.'

I screeched to a halt outside the casualty entrance and someone came out to the car with a trolley. Hardy was loaded onto it and taken straight into emergency. Within a few minutes he had a transfusion running and then it was a matter of waiting and seeing how he went.

After twenty minutes or so it was obvious that he was still deteriorating.

'The drip's just not holding him,' the duty vet said. 'I think we should take him to theatre.'

'When?' I asked.

'Right now,' she replied.

So Hardy was wheeled out of emergency and down the corridor to the theatre suite. Somehow he managed to lift his head and look at me for several moments before he was taken through a doorway and the plastic swing doors closed behind him.

I went off and found myself a coffee. I then went for a long walk outside, but eventually it grew too dark so I came in and tried to read the paper. I have no idea how long Hardy was in theatre but it seemed like a long time indeed.

I sat with the paper on my lap, looking out of the window, and for some reason thought of the Woongarra Dog Club. Membership of this exclusive club was only granted if you ran over a dog on the farm. A bit macabre I know, but it helped to laugh about these things. There had been a few such memberships granted over the years and I wondered if there was now a new member who perhaps didn't even know it.

A couple of years previously my parents had gone on a holiday back to England and left me dog-sitting their rather twitchy sheltie, Biggles. Everything went well to begin with but then he made a poor decision and decided to attempt biting Susie's tyres as she drove off one day. When it became obvious that Biggles had misjudged his attack, I comforted Susie with a cup of tea and then peeled Biggles off the driveway. I put him on a sack near the front door, intending to bury him later, and then promptly forgot about him.

Heather and Rob happened to come to dinner that night and after the main course Rob shared a concern with me.

'I hope you don't think I'm interfering, doctor, but that dog by the front door doesn't look too good at all,' he said.

I played the innocent and we all trooped outside. Biggles was lying on his back with his legs stiffly raised to the heavens.

'Quick, Heather,' I said, 'he needs mouth to mouth.'

'Why me?' she asked in horror.

'Because you're the one used to having dog hairs around your mouth,' I replied as Rob doubled-up laughing and Heather punched me in the ribs.

'I'm sorry,' I said when Rob and I had recovered somewhat. 'I completely forgot he was there. I meant to chuck him on the bonfire before you arrived,' I joked.

I phoned my parents later that evening and let them know that Biggles had gone to the big kennel in the sky. They were understanding about it at the time but my mother has changed her tune since. She must have been told what I had said for, to this day, she is suspicious that instead of giving Biggles a proper Christian burial I disposed of him in a way more suited to a heretic.

The vet, now dressed in a theatre gown, suddenly reappeared and sat down opposite me. I looked up at her face and knew what she was going to say.

'I'm really sorry,' she said quietly, 'we lost him.' Then, after a long pause, she continued: 'His spleen was so badly damaged we just couldn't control the bleeding. We tried everything. It just didn't work.'

For a while, we just sat there in silence.

'Would you like us to dispose of the body?' she asked gently.

'No,' I said shaking my head. 'I'll take my friend home with me.'

So he was brought out to me, lying on a trolley. I thanked the staff for everything they had done, picked him up in my arms, carried him back out to the car and gently laid him down on the back seat.

I remember nothing about the journey home except that it was night-time.

I lay Hardy by the kennel he had hardly ever used and went inside to a house that suddenly seemed very quiet and very dark.

I poured myself a large Scotch and went and sat by the lake under the stars.

In the morning I dug a hole in the orchard next to the walnut tree, exactly where he liked to charge through on his way back and forth to the farmyard. He was a big dog and he needed a big hole. It took a lot of digging to get it done, but when I was eventually satisfied, I gently lowered him into the ground with full reverence and stood back.

There the silly devil lay with his legs poking out. The hole wasn't nearly big enough.

My parents, who had come up from town for the occasion, started to giggle. 'That dog of yours was always a clown,' my father said. 'There he is, stiff and cold, and he's still playing the fool,' and we all laughed.

The hole was enlarged and Hardy eventually went to his eternal rest together with a bag of sandwiches and a few of the chook eggs he so liked to steal whenever he got the chance. I had difficulty seeing what I was doing as I closed the soil over his gentle head.

'He was a lovely dog,' my mother said as she dabbed her eyes. 'He made me feel as if I was the most special person in the world, and I swear he understood every word your father said to him.'

'We'll be lucky to see the likes of him again,' my father added.

'We will indeed,' I agreed.

When I had raked everything smooth, we went back to the house and sat in the kitchen having a cup of tea.

'Thanks for coming,' I said.

'Will you be OK?' they asked.

'Of course I will,' I reassured them. But that evening I didn't just feel sad. I felt something else too. Something I hadn't felt since Linda had left all those years before.

For the first time in ages I felt lonely. All of a sudden the house seemed too big for one person. All of a sudden it seemed far too quiet.

'Sorry to hear about your dog,' Brian said to me at the sawmill the next time I was there. 'Every time they see that ute of yours, the dogs go crazy. I think they really miss him.'

'Yes,' I said a trifle wistfully, 'I do too.'

'What do you think happened to him?'

'I have no idea,' I replied. 'No idea whatsoever.' And to this day I still don't know.

It would be nice to say that the grass in Hardy's part of the orchard took on a specially rich green, but in all truth it didn't. It would be nice to say that the trees in that part of the orchard became brighter and glossier, but they didn't look any different either. There is not even anything to see any more, for the mound has completely flattened out with the continuous back and forth of the ride-on.

It is as if Hardy quietly slipped away into the next world without leaving any traces in this one.

We have been getting more walnuts recently, come to think of it. So perhaps that's what he is now: walnuts.

23 Helen

I DROVE DOWN THE freeway through pouring rain. The traffic was heavy and the travelling was slow.

'I'll be late,' I thought.

But there was nothing to be done about it. I had cut short the afternoon surgery in the hope that, just for once, I might be on time for something, but it didn't look like it was going to work. I had been really nervous about the whole matter right from the start, and now the certainty that I was going to be late made it even worse.

'Fancy going on a blind date at your age,' I muttered to myself. 'You silly fool, turn around, don't do it. She'll be dull and plain and opinionated. She'll smoke all the time. She'll . . .' and so it went on and on as I slowly threaded my way to Melbourne, falling ever further behind schedule.

I don't know whether Hardy's death, just over a year before, had been the starting point, but after he died I started feeling lonely. I had been on my own for quite some years and it had never bothered me. I still loved my work and I still loved the farm, but I just didn't feel as complete as I had before.

There had been many losses over the years. Teddy's death had upset me greatly at the time, and I often thought of Dave and Russell and Eileen and Isobel. And Amy, of course. But, despite it all, life had gone on and I always responded by throwing myself into the here and now, working ever harder at both practice and farm. I was grateful that there was always so much to do and that the doing of it always felt so healing. And the system worked.

After all, I had even let Amy go to float amongst the Milky Way hand in hand with Isobel.

And when Delphine never got better and Felix had to leave with hardly a 'goodbye', the increased work load was, in some ways, quite therapeutic.

But it was as if Hardy was a straw too many. For now I no longer felt completely happy and contented on my own, and just being busy no longer seemed enough. It felt as if the heavy lid on all the memories could unhinge itself at any moment and the contents spill out and overwhelm me.

I no longer wanted to deal with that sort of stuff on my own. Despite all the support I received from those around me, I was lonely.

The loneliness hadn't come on all at once or in a rush. Rather, it had crept up slowly and stealthily. Little by little, over the weeks and months after Hardy went to the orchard, I became increasingly aware that the house seemed dark and cold and empty when I got home from work, and I felt a sense of emptiness spending evenings on my own. I missed talking to him about all the cases I had seen that day. I missed ruffling his ears as we sat gazing into the dying embers of the fire, and I missed talking to him about all our friends amongst the stars.

I started finding excuses for staying at work, leaving the surgery later and later. On getting home I would turn on all the lights, fill the house with opera and pour myself a drink. For a while I had some regular and intimate conversations with Messrs Walker and Daniels. They're pleasant enough fellows, but they only have one point of view, and I knew that in the end they didn't have the solution to anyone's problems, let alone mine.

One evening I was idly flicking along the book-shelf when I came across *Becoming Single*. It had been a present from Andrew and Margot. 'Thanks very much,' I had said at the time but then put it largely unread on the shelf.

But from some acorns, just occasionally, do mighty oak trees grow. I took *Becoming Single* off the shelf and started to flick through it. I had already thumbed my way through the first few chapters in a desultory way, feeling that the book had little to offer me when I found, at the end of chapter three, a statement that really caught my attention. 'There are always advantages to your present situation,' it stated. 'So why not list them?'

'Bullshit,' I said, but I went and got paper, pencil and a bottle of Red Label and sat down at the kitchen table.

I sat for quite a while, completely stuck. Then, after a glass or two, the ideas began to flow as if a veil had lifted and, as I was supping my fourth, or perhaps it was my sixth glass, I experienced a major breakthrough. My sense of relief was overwhelming, for I felt as if I had found the answer to everything. The solution to all my woes. I carefully and comprehensively wrote down my thoughts, read through what I had written, nodded to myself in agreement and then staggered off to bed content that a difficult job had been well done.

I woke the next morning knowing exactly what the bottom of parrots' cages taste like and experiencing the kind of headache that swells the membership of temperance unions. I had also slept through the alarm.

I was hurrying through a rapid shave and a glass of soluble aspirin when I suddenly recalled my literary efforts of the previous evening. That is, I remembered having written something very important, but, for the life of me, couldn't remember what it was.

My ablutions completed, I went in search of the thesis and found it on the island bench in the kitchen. I confess I was surprised by what I found.

It was brief and to the point:

'Don't forget you have an early appointment.'

'Fuck,' I said as I looked at my watch and then shot out the door.

I thought of getting another dog, but in my heart I knew that wasn't the answer. People, that's what I needed. So I became a lot more attentive to my network of friends than I had been for a while. I phoned people up and I wrote to them; I lunched with them and remembered birthdays.

I even held some dinner parties.

I would like to say that over the years I have converted myself into someone who would turn Jamie Oliver green with jealousy, but I haven't. Despite all Archie's educational efforts, I am as hopeless a cook today as I was when I shared an undergraduate flat in North London with four wild trainee Jesuits many years ago. I think the secret is that I simply don't enjoy it. It seems so nerve-wracking trying to work out how to get everything to boil at the same time.

So I did what all sensible, right-thinking people with no skill and a large farm kitchen do when they wish to entertain: I organised for Pamela and Carmen, the identical twins, to do the catering and for Phill to do the waiting. The twins were always happy to oblige so long as they could play Don Giovanni whilst cooking, and Phill was always happy to help so long as he could wear his Carmen Miranda outfit.

Those dinner parties were wonderful. I am sure the food was fabulous but I can't for the life of me remember what any of it tasted like because Phill always stole the show, and by dessert everyone had cottoned on to the fact that there were twins in the kitchen. My only memories are of the fun and laughter.

I also started to receive invitations out. I had been fairly reclusive for a long time, so when I finally dragged myself away from the farm and the surgery to participate in the dazzling glare of the local social scene, word went round at the speed of light. The bush telegraph fairly hummed with the message that a single doctor was on the loose. Native bearers ran in all directions and the jungle drums could be heard all night.

I was deluged with offers of lunches, teas and dinners and even, on one occasion, to 'join a group of liberal like-minded adults for an evening of erotic fun', which I hasten to add I didn't attend.

I politely declined all offers from single females for 'tea for two' and stuck to groups (apart from the liberal like-minded ones). I had thought that sticking to groups would be a safe option, but found that this policy by no means guaranteed me protection. Inevitably my hostess would thoughtfully also invite, and then seat next to me, her single sister, her single sister-in-law, her single cousin, her recently divorced best friend or her recently bereaved next-door neighbour. They were all lovely women but sparks were noticeable by their absence.

Through this exercise, however, I came to realise what I was doing: I was on the prowl. I had enjoyed being on my own for a long time but now I wanted someone in my life again. I wanted a mate.

During this time, Jack, an old farmer who I knew quite well, came to see me for a repeat prescription of his blood pressure pills. He was a great character who lived on his own on a small farm about halfway up Mt Miranda beyond Rushby, on the way to Cowley. The local legend was that he had been engaged once, but that she had cheated on him whilst he was away at the war and he had never looked at another woman since.

When the consultation ended he didn't move. He simply sat there in his dirty overalls and the battered hat with all the cigarette burns.

'Is there something else?' I asked.

He leaned forward a little and looked at me with a serious expression on his face.

'I hear you were married once,' he said.

'Yes, as a matter of fact I was,' I replied cautiously, not quite clear where the conversation was heading.

'I also hear around that you're looking for a woman again.'

'Goodness,' I said, startled to find I was public gossip yet again.

'At the risk of being personal,' Jack said, 'there's something I'd like to ask you.'

'And what might that be?'

He leaned further forward in his chair until our faces were almost touching.

'Are you a slow learner or what?' he asked with a wry grin that showed every one of his rotten teeth.

'Twenty deep at the tip is what they should be,' he muttered darkly as he got up and left the room. 'Twenty bloody deep.'

Worried about the fact I was living in a goldfish bowl, I started spending weekends in Melbourne where I could be more anonymous in my social life. I took to dining and staying with friends, especially David, a surgeon I had known for many years, and his wife Janice, who took me on as her personal project to be sorted out.

Like their country cousins, everyone in Melbourne was sympathetic to my cause and arranged many pleasant evenings on my behalf. Over the next few months I met thin girls, stout girls, tall girls, short girls, motivational speakers, golfers, lecturers, scientists, musicians and weavers. There were many lovely evenings; there was lots of fun and laughter, and there was also, from time to time, you will be relieved to hear, even a bit of slap and tickle. They were all lovely women but none of them was for me.

The difficulty in satisfying me gradually had a dampening effect on everyone. A little like the real estate agents all those years before, the maidens and matrons eventually lost interest in me. The dinner party invitations gradually dried up and my friends ran out of eligible introductions.

Meanwhile, life in the country continued on much the same. The farm was busy and the practice busier, so I reverted to type and took the easy option of simply throwing myself back into it all again.

On one occasion, feeling a bit jaded, I organised a locum and took some time off to go to Melbourne for a few days of shopping, eating, drinking and generally mucking about. I was strolling along Collins Street looking for something really exciting like socks or something, when I was nearly knocked off my feet by a whirlwind of raven hair and pinstriped power suit which wrapped its arms around me and gave me a huge kiss on the cheek.

'Paul!' she screeched. 'You old bastard. Haven't seen you in ages. God you look good. Come and have a coffee with me, no excuses mind. I insist and I want to hear all the goss from the country too.'

'Why, Sheila!' I exclaimed when I realised who it was.

I recovered from the onslaught, disentangled myself and wiped away the lipstick. 'How wonderful to see you,' I said. 'Coffee would be great.'

It had been some years since I had last seen her and we had not parted in exactly pleasant circumstances.

We found a place nearby in the Block Arcade where it is possible to sit in a fashionable pedestrian thoroughfare and drink really expensive coffee whilst being constantly banged in the back by the shopping bags of passers-by.

I looked across the table at her. She had always been a snappy dresser and today was no exception. She was a stunner and, if anything, her hair was even blacker than I remembered.

'Gosh you look well,' I smiled at her.

Sheila had been a receptionist at the surgery for a while. Meaghan was about to leave to have her baby and we had advertised in the local paper for a replacement to fill the vacancy. Madge had dealt with all the responses, had sorted out half-a-dozen or so of the more likely-looking applicants for interview and then arranged times for them. For some reason I was handed the job of interviewing.

It did not start out as an exciting morning. I sat through a number of interviews with pleasant but dull women and became progressively more despondent at the frequent discrepancy between application letters and real life. None of them was suitable in the slightest. I sighed as I looked at the last resumé: some office experience, married with two children. She sounded much like the others but I called for her anyway and into my life walked Sheila.

She had a huge shock of the blackest hair I had ever seen and wore eye-catching makeup, a tight suit and the sort of stilettos that are definitely not allowed on aeroplanes. She was engaging and intelligent. She was loud and funny. She was good looking and curvaceous. She oozed pizzazz and I hired her on the spot.

From Sheila's very first morning duty it was obvious that I'd made a big mistake. Madge and Meaghan hated her. They hated everything about her. They hated her looks, her makeup, her curves, her clothes and they especially hated her high-heeled shoes. They hated both her ability to be decisive on the phone and the efficient way in which she ran the front desk. They hated the way she fluttered her eyelids at the patients and they hated the way the entire male population of the practice immediately gravitated to her.

Over the weeks following Sheila's appointment a few people expressed surprise that I had taken her on. But when I asked what they meant they simply raised their eyebrows knowingly and shook their heads.

At the practice, though, Sheila performed well and gave not the slightest reason for comment or criticism. The front desk remained in a state of undeclared war. There was nothing obvious, of course, everything was very polite. Just a dig here, a look there, a pointed 'I am sure Sheila would be only too happy to do that for you, doctor' and an atmosphere you could cut with a knife.

In fact, the only thing Madge and Meaghan ever liked about Sheila were the twins, who came to the surgery every day after school. They would sit quietly in the staff room and beaver away at their homework in a very mature manner, waiting for Mum to finish her shift.

Despite the twins, the cold war on the reception desk not only dragged on but got worse after Meaghan left. It was quite awful but I really couldn't see any solution. Then one day, out of the blue, the situation suddenly resolved itself. A pleasant woman of thirty-something, whose husband worked for a company based in Holland, asked to see me at the end of a Saturday surgery.

'When you have a little time I would like to discuss a personal matter with you,' she said. It sounded a bit ominous so I made sure I had plenty of time to see her.

'How can I help?' I asked as we sat down.

'I have always been very happy with this service but I now wish to lodge a complaint.'

'Oh dear,' I said, getting out some paper and a pen. 'You had better tell me what the problem is.'

'You'll remember that I came to see you three weeks ago?'

'Of course.'

'And you will remember the reason for my visit?'

'Of course.'

Indeed it would have been hard to forget. She had told me she had accidentally fallen pregnant whilst her husband had been away in Holland. She had asked for my help in resolving the matter swiftly and discreetly and that is exactly what I had done.

'Well, I would like you to know that the story is now all round the town. One of your staff has looked at my file and talked. Someone has now thoughtfully informed my husband, of course, and there will be hell to pay when he returns.'

I expressed great regret and then defended the staff. 'But no one here would do anything like that. They just couldn't have done it. I'm sure this is a mistake, I have full trust in them.' I carried on defending my staff for a while but eventually had to give in. Apparently there had been witnesses to the transgression and it became obvious that the story was true.

'Do you know which staff member it was?' I asked quietly.

'I certainly do,' she replied. 'It was Sheila.'

I was speechless with shock. When I finally got my voice back I profoundly apologised to the woman and assured her that the matter would be dealt with immediately. A short time later I showed her from the surgery and organised to see Sheila the following morning. I felt sick, knowing that for the first time in my life I would have to play the tough employer, and I didn't sleep much that night.

Sheila looked a little flustered when she arrived the next morning.

'I know what this is about,' she said, looking like a ghost, suggesting that indeed she did.

I had been rehearsing all night what I was going to say and had called in Madge to help give me the courage to say it.

'Sheila, I have just one word to say to you,' I said. 'Goodbye.'

'What!' she screamed.

'Effective as from now.'

'Please, please, Paul give me another chance,' Sheila cried. 'My husband will kill me when he finds out.'

'Well that will make two of you then,' I said sarcastically. 'Sheila, what you did was unforgivable. Please go. Right now.'

And Madge handed Sheila her dues and off she went.

And I hadn't seen her again until that day on Collins Street when she wrapped her arms around me and covered me in lipstick.

'So how's everyone at the practice?' she asked when the coffees arrived.

I gave her all the local tittle-tattle and then asked after her family. The twins were doing well at school, but Sheila had parted company from her husband a year or so before.

'So what are you up to yourself, these days, Sheila?' I asked.

'I'm glad you asked,' she said. 'Because I'm having the most fantastic time. My life has really turned around since I got rid of his Highness. I landed this fabulous job and I'm really enjoying it.'

'Great. What's the job?'

'You are looking at the office supervisor for Derivatives Trading,' she said, showing herself off.

'But that's wonderful.'

'And I've got sixteen people working under me.'

'Fantastic.'

'Now, how about you? Still on your own? Have to fix that,' she said when I nodded.

'Let me see, who do I know . . . Got it,' she said with a smile and a tilt of the head. 'How about me?'

'Well that's the best offer I've had today,' I laughed, 'but I'm afraid I'm going to have to disappoint you.'

She drank the last of her coffee, looked at her watch and stood up. 'It was lovely to see you, Paul, but I have to dash, especially since you don't want to marry me,' she laughed.

We made our goodbyes and she picked up her bag. She had already turned away from the table when she suddenly turned back.

'It was really lovely bumping into you today, Paul, because, of course, it's really you that I have to thank for my new job.'

'How come?' I asked, a little surprised.

'You know, the letter.'

'What letter?'

'The letter you wrote to Derivatives.'

'But I . . .'

'You can't have forgotten,' she said with a twinkle. 'You must remember how you wrote me the most glowing reference and were even kind enough to say how sad you were that I had had to leave the surgery to look after my sick mother.'

'But Sheila!' I exploded. 'You're crazy. What if they had given me a call?'

'No chance of that,' she said with a laugh. 'I put the wrong phone number down.'

And with that, she turned and was swallowed up by the throng of shoppers.

I shook my head and smiled as I went to the counter for another coffee. Sheila might be a naughty fairy but I liked her very much. Just for the occasional coffee, mind you, definitely not for life.

I haven't seen her since and I certainly haven't been asked for any references, but from time to time I wonder if she still signs my name at the bottom of applications.

I was still smiling and shaking my head when I returned with my coffee. I was enjoying Sheila's naughtiness so much that it was some moments before I became aware I was no longer alone at my table. I looked up and realised there was a woman sitting opposite me. She was surrounded by a mountain of shopping bags and she was simply the most beautiful woman I had ever seen. She looked up at me out of deep brown eyes the size of saucers and said: 'I'm sorry to gatecrash, but all the other tables were crowded.'

'Not a problem,' I said a little breathlessly. 'Be my guest.'

'I hate shopping,' she said with a smile and waved her hands at the bag mountain.

'Yes,' I replied, 'I can tell.'

She laughed politely at my rather lame jest. I drank my coffee as fast as the heat would allow and made to go.

'I officially pass the table over to you,' I said with a little bow.

'You're too kind,' she replied with a smile and a small bow in return.

With my shopping completed and my credit card loaded, I headed back to the country that very evening. Sitting in a queue at traffic lights and gradually inching forward, I did not give Sheila so much as a thought. All I could see was a beautiful face with great big eyes and a mop of dark curls.

'One of those,' I said to myself with a sigh, 'would suit me just fine.'

Back on the ranch things went on much as before, with surgeries, house calls, broken fences and animals to look after. I hardly had time to think of anything other than getting through each day.

Then a few weeks after the trip to Melbourne, I was sorting out some paperwork before heading off home when my phone rang and Heather said: 'It's a friend of yours, would you like me to put her through?'

'How are you travelling, you old bugger?' Janice asked in that bright and breezy way of hers. 'Still working too hard?'

'What's the problem?' I joked. 'Not referring enough patients to that husband of yours?'

'David's busy enough, thank you,' she said. 'What you can do for me, however, is write down a telephone number.'

So I did.

'And is this number the gateway to everlasting happiness?' I added a little sarcastically.

'It sure is, you old cynic,' she replied. 'I know you've had a few false starts. I know you've had your hopes raised a few times. But this is it.'

'So, dear Janice, why in hell haven't you given me this number before, then?'

'Because you haven't been ready, you great schmook,' she said, 'and nor, for that matter, has she.'

'Is that it?' I asked.

'Sure is, buster,' she said. 'The name is Helen and the rest is up to you.'

Over the next few days I started to dial the number on a few occasions. Somehow my fingers always got clumsy or I found a reason not to complete the connection. I took the number home every night and I took it to work every day. I think it sat variously on my desk at home and at work for a full two weeks before I dialled it in its entirety.

'Hello?' said a young girl.

'Oh, hi!' I said, trying to sound relaxed. 'Could I speak to Helen, please?'

The phone was put down with a clank and in the distance I heard the girl say: 'Aunty, there's some bloke on the phone for you. He said, "Oh, hi!",' she added with a giggle.

'Thanks, Lucy, tell him I'm coming.'

'She's coming.'

'Thanks.'

There was a long pause, then: 'Hello.'

I tried to swallow but my mouth was dry. In a somewhat cracked voice I said: 'Ah, hello. My name is Paul. I hope you don't mind me calling. I was given your number by Janice.'

'Yes?'

'I hope you know she has given me your number.'

'Yes. She did mention something.'

'Good. Well, I was wondering if you would like to go out to dinner one night.'

There was a much longer pause.

'I'm afraid that I couldn't possibly manage anything before a week next Thursday at the very earliest.'

'That would suit me just fine,' I said quickly. 'Where would you like to meet?'

'Well . . . why not surprise me.'

'So would you like me to organise something and get back to you?'

'That's exactly what I would like you to do.'

So I did.

I do so many house calls round the district and have come to know it so well that it often seems that my ute can find its own way around by autopilot. A week later, on the Thursday of the date, I pulled up in the rain outside Jonathon's house, realising that I had been aware of nothing of the journey there.

'There's preoccupation for you,' I thought as I got out.

Carol let me in and I found Jonathon sitting in his wheelchair by the huge picture window that looked out over the valley. There was a rug on his knees. The normally stunning view was obscured by mist and rain but cattle could just be seen grazing in the paddock below the house. As Carol announced my presence Jonathon turned to say hello.

I visited Jonathon often, making the journey out to his farm a couple of times a week. He was dying of cancer and although his pain management was difficult to stabilise, he had come to peace with his condition. His only regret, he used to say, was that having lost his taste for red wine, some other bugger would get the benefit of his cellar.

Over the eighteen months since he had been diagnosed we had become good friends. He was a witty, amusing man with a keen intellect and, despite my reason for being there, I enjoyed visiting him very much indeed.

I opened my bag, got out my bits and pieces and asked him how things were going.

'Fine, fine,' he lied as usual.

I checked him over, discussed his medication and wrote out some prescriptions.

'Would you like a cup of tea with us before you brave the elements?' Carol asked.

'I certainly would,' I replied. 'But I can't be too long. I've got to be in Melbourne at seven-thirty, and for once I can't be late.'

Jonathon turned to look at me. 'A doctor, wanting to be on time?' he said in mock surprise. 'Anything interesting? I notice you have your glad rags on and I imagine it isn't solely for my benefit.'

I blushed. 'Well actually, I'm going on a date.'

'Good for you,' Carol said. 'What's she like?'

'Well,' I said as I sipped my tea and bit the end of my biscuit, 'she's beautiful, she's intelligent and sexy, has a lovely figure and a wonderful sense of humour.'

'Sounds perfect,' said Jonathon. 'How long have you known her?'

'I haven't actually met her as yet,' I admitted. 'In fact, tonight's the night.'

'Oh!' Carol and Jonathon said together, and there was a gap in the conversation for a while.

'Then how do you know what she's like?' Carol asked, eventually.

'I don't. I'm just hoping and dreaming.'

'They definitely sound the sort of hopes and dreams to have,' nodded Jonathon. 'But what's the connection?'

'A mutual friend in Melbourne gave me her telephone number.'

'So let me get this straight,' persisted Jonathon. 'Is this a blind date?'

'It certainly is,' I replied. 'I've never been on one before and I am somewhere between really excited and absolutely petrified.'

'But Paul, this is wonderful,' Jonathon said. 'Endings and beginnings,' he murmured after a few moments' silence. 'Here I am, close to the end, and there you are, Paul, going out on a blind date full of exciting possibilities. Here's to both our futures,' and he lifted his cup high.

I finished my tea, packed my things and headed out to the ute into the worsening rain. As I was giving my farewells, Jonathon touched my sleeve.

'Perhaps I'll meet her one day,' he said.

'That would be really nice,' I replied, but, sadly, he never did.

I pulled off the end of the freeway and found my way into the city using every trick and sleight of hand I knew. Even so, every light was against me and I got further and further behind schedule as the Melbourne rain teemed endlessly down.

The restaurant I had organised was near the top end of the city and when I finally reached my destination it was almost impossible to find a park. I eventually found a few square metres on a rooftop and then had to run for cover with my coat over my head.

I did make it to the restaurant eventually and, considering everything, thirty minutes late didn't seem too bad at all. She was bound to keep me waiting for at least an hour anyway.

'Table for two on the balcony, booked a week ago,' I said brightly to the waiter as he approached me.

'Yes, sir,' he said with the slightest hint of reprimand in his voice. 'Your companion has been here for quite some time already.'

'Oops!' I said, as he led me across the room.

The restaurant was crowded and it took us a little while to negotiate a route through the main dining room to the archway that led out onto the balcony. As we passed under the archway, I stopped in my stride and drew in a breath. There, sitting at the table in front of us, was my beautiful shopper. The waiter held a chair back as I approached the table. I stared in amazement as she looked up at me with those deep brown eyes.

She offered me her hand and said: 'You must be Paul.'

'Sorry, sir, my mistake. This is the wrong table. You're actually with the large plain girl with the greasy hair and a cigarette in her mouth over there in the corner,' I expected the waiter to say. But he didn't. He merely held my seat for me, folded the napkin on my lap and asked if I would like a pre-dinner drink.

I sat down very slowly, still expecting someone to rush across at any moment and ask why on earth I was sitting with their wife/partner/lover and would I please move on promptly. But no one did.

Suddenly my date frowned slightly and leaned forward. 'Haven't we met before?'

'We certainly have,' I nodded in reply. 'You told me you don't like shopping.'

She concentrated for a few seconds and then gradually her brow cleared. 'Ah, yes,' she said, 'and you gulp hot coffee, pretending it's not uncomfortable.'

And, as she smiled at me across the table, every atom of my DNA swooned and I knew that my life would never be the same again.

24 Maggie

'YOU'RE LOOKING VERY TIRED, Paul,' Maggie said in her soft highland accent. 'You've got great dark rings under your eyes and you look like a ghost. You've obviously been working much too hard since Felix left and you're going to make yourself ill unless you do something about it immediately.'

I sat down on the edge of the bed and Duncan sat on the other side. Maggie was propped up between us on a great pile of pillows. She had a dressing gown pulled tightly round her and she wore a scarf on her head. She was very pale and she was very, very thin.

'I know, I know,' I replied, nodding my head.

'Well don't just "know",' she said in mock fierceness. 'Do something about it.'

'I will, I promise,' I said.

'And I hear you're travelling down to town a fair bit these days,' she added.

'Is there anything about my life that's not public knowledge?' I asked.

'I wouldn't think so,' Maggie replied with a grin. 'So, come on. What's she like? Is she nice?'

'Yes, she's really lovely,' I smiled. 'Name's Helen. We've been out a few times. Gone to concerts and things. I really like her.'

'Good,' she smiled back. 'I am so glad for you.'

I gazed out of the window. It was a bright sunny day and the garden was a riot of flowering shrubs and trees. In the middle of the lawn, not ten metres from the house, a bird feeder hung from the lowest branch of a gum tree. The feeder was a noisy, seething mass of red and blue as a great flock of rosellas squabbled over their food. I loved looking at the birds and Duncan topped up the feeder especially when he knew I was coming to visit.

How typical of Maggie to be thinking of others, I thought. 'Stop worrying about me,' I said. 'Let's just worry about you for a while.'

Just two and a half years before, Maggie had found a lump in her breast. She had gone through all the usual tests and, unfortunately, they had confirmed everyone's worst fears. She'd had a mastectomy as soon as it could be arranged, but lymph nodes taken out at the time of the operation had already shown traces of cancer. Over the following months Maggie received both chemotherapy and radiation and, for a while, everything seemed to go well. Then, one night, she turned over in bed and broke a rib. There were lots more tests, of course, and it became obvious that the cancer was on the move again. Within a short while she became too ill to come to the surgery and I started visiting her at home.

Duncan and Maggie were wonderful people, and it was a very pretty drive up to their house, perched on the hill opposite the cemetery. They had been on their own since the boys had grown up and moved away and they lived very much for one another. Maggie's illness had been a devastating blow to both of them. My initial visits had been rather sad and gloomy episodes so, believing that laughter is often much better than a handful of pills, I took it upon myself to cheer them both up and made it a rule to bring at least one new joke along to each visit.

Maggie responded immediately to the new treatment and, although she didn't contribute herself, she made sure Duncan always had a joke waiting for me in return. However, where my jokes were quite tame, Duncan's were often quite raunchy. Over time I did learn to loosen up, though, and eventually even made Duncan blush on occasions.

When I arrived for my weekly visit, Duncan would bring in a tray and we would all sit and admire the birds on the feeder whilst we had our tea and biscuits. When we had cleared the clinical necessities out of the way, Maggie would look at us and say: 'Well, come on, boys,' and the stories would begin. The visits were oases of laughter. Duncan always laughed loudly at whatever offerings I brought, but reserved his loudest screams of appreciation for his own jokes. I often left with my face aching from laughter and I always left feeling much better in myself.

One day Duncan's contribution was about how things are not always what they seem. I was ready with a joke of my own, but Duncan's story so reminded me of something that had happened in the surgery only a few weeks before, I decided to tell them about that instead.

'Would you like to hear a real story?' I said.

'Of course,' they replied.

'At medical school, I was taught never to take anything at face value. A good idea in theory, of course, but, like everyone else, I often do.

'As you know, up past Rushby, in the Mullaways, there's an army training ground. Often, when they are up there on manoeuvres, the soldiers don't take medics with them. We're the nearest medical practice and so, if there are any problems, they bring their casualties to us.

'They were running some orientation exercises a month or two back. I felt quite sorry for the poor buggers really, because, as you know, the weather was quite horrid. During one of the exercises a young and inexperienced lieutenant got separated from the rest of the platoon in extremely heavy weather and spent a very cold, wet and miserable night out in the bush alone. A search party, sent out at first light, found the missing officer quite quickly, but the lieutenant's condition was worrying, so it was decided to bring the officer down to the surgery for a check-over.

'A large camouflaged personnel carrier appeared around ten o'clock and took up half the car park. A stretcher was unloaded from the back of it and a soldier, covered in mud from head to toe, was carried into the treatment room.

'"Sergeant Smith, bringing in Lieutenant Hobson, J, 142793, sah," said the leader of the stretcher party as he snapped his heels, saluted and handed me some paperwork.

'"Put Hobson over there," I said, indicating one of the examination couches. "And by the way, you don't need to salute or call me sir."

'"Very good, sah," said Smith as he saluted again.

'Even a cursory glance showed that Hobson was ill. The temperature was so low that we couldn't get the thermometer to register at all, and the top blood pressure reading was below where the bottom one should have been. We wrapped Hobson up in a space blanket and turned on some heaters. I cleaned the mud off an arm as best I could, put up a drip and started to give some warmed saline. Bit by bit, over the next hour, Hobson's condition improved and the temperature and blood pressure gradually rose back to where they should have been in the first place.

'"How are you feeling now?" I asked.

'"Much better, thank you, sah," Hobson whispered weakly.

'"Please don't salute," I said quickly, putting a hand across to prevent it. "You've got a drip in your arm."'

'Once the immediate and urgent clinical needs were under control, it was time to do a full examination to see if there were any other problems in addition to the hypothermia.

'I opened the space blanket, unbuttoned the jacket and, without even thinking about it, pulled up Hobson's singlet to listen to the heart and lungs.

'When I did this I'm not sure that I was expecting to see anything other than a hairy chest and a dog-tag. But I was stopped dead in my tracks. What I was *not* expecting to see was a hot pink silk bra filled with a very ample bosom.

'"I beg your pardon, ma'am," I said as I hurriedly pushed the singlet down again."I had no idea . . ."

'"Don't worry," Hobson replied faintly."I'm just a soldier, exactly like all the rest. Oh, and by the way," she smiled, "you don't have to call me ma'am.'"

'Well,' Maggie smiled at me when I finished, 'perhaps not *exactly* like all the rest.'

A couple of years before I started visiting Maggie, I met a delightful lady called Bronwyn who worked as a cook at Our Lady's College, over at Heddington. She came to see me one day because she had started dropping things in the kitchen.

At first, I admit, I didn't take it all that seriously and thought she was probably just rushing and being clumsy. But when she came back a few weeks later and told me that the dropping was getting worse, I listened to her more carefully. Examination showed that she did indeed have a problem and Bronwyn was sent off to a specialist who confirmed that she had multiple sclerosis.

At first things weren't much different for her, but over the months the dropping got worse and eventually she had to give up her job.

Bronwyn was started on a whole host of treatments that made little difference and, watching her gradual decline, I felt particularly helpless. After examining her one day and finding yet more evidence of worsening disease, I said: 'If only I had a magic wand.'

Things went much the same for a while and then, at the end of one of our regular visits just a few days before Christmas, Bronwyn handed me a package.

'I thought I'd like to give you a present this year,' she said.

'That's very kind,' I replied, a little embarrassed. 'Thank you very much.'

When I got home that night I put the present with the dozen or so others under the tree and, being a very good boy, didn't open it until Christmas Day.

My parents came up from town for Christmas that year and the three of us spent the morning wearing paper hats and sipping champagne.

'Tree looks good,' my father said. 'Where did you get it?'

'Down by the creek, near where I chucked a dead deer.'

'Probably why the tree looks so healthy,' he replied and we both laughed.

'Aren't we going to open the presents?' my mother asked.

'Of course,' I replied. I poured us all another glass of bubbly and we got started.

After opening the presents we had given one another, I started on those I had been given by patients. The first few turned out to be alcohol of various sorts.

'Very useful. Very drinkable,' I said. 'Lucky all my patients know I'm an alcoholic, isn't it?'

Then I unwrapped Bronwyn's present.

'What on earth is that?' my mother asked.

It was a plastic tube of green liquid and it sparkled as you waved it around.

'Absolutely no idea,' I replied. I put in on the coffee table and left it there whilst we opened the rest of the presents.

Then suddenly it came to me: 'Of course,' I exclaimed. 'How could I not have realised. It's a magic wand. How wonderful.'

'How strange,' said my mother.

The wand hung around the sitting room for several weeks and I often waved it about. It caused much hilarity at a dinner party one night, but eventually I put it away in the old leather sea trunk that had once belonged to my grandfather. It was full of old costumes and props from the years when Linda and I had gone to a few fancy dress parties. I put the trunk back in the wardrobe, but it didn't stay there for long. In fact, it was only a short while later that I pulled it out and opened it up again.

'We're putting on a do for Maggie's fiftieth,' Duncan had said when we were on our own in the kitchen one day.

'What a lovely idea.'

'Yes, the whole family is coming. Maggie knows about it all but she's really worried about being in any photos.'

'Why's that?'

'She just hates having to wear that headscarf,' he said.

I thought for a few moments then suddenly had an idea. 'Leave it with me,' I said, tapping my nose.

The following week, I casually said to Maggie: 'By the way, I nearly forgot. I have a present for you. A present to end all your worries.'

'Oh yes,' she said a bit suspiciously, 'and what might all my worries be?'

'Well, I'm aware that everyone is coming next Saturday.'

'And how would you know about that, I wonder,' she said, looking at Duncan.

'Well, Dr Smarty Pants,' she continued to me, 'since you're so clever, what are my worries?'

'Family photos.'

'And why would I be worried about photos?' she retorted.

'Apart from the obvious one of cracking the lens,' I said, 'I believe you might be concerned about having to wear a gypsy costume to cover up your pate.'

'Hah! You can talk, Dr Billiard Ball,' she said. 'But you're right. I'm not looking forward to that bit.'

'Fortunately,' I said, ignoring the jibe, 'as I said, I have a present for you.'

I reached into my bag and, like a magician pulling a rabbit out of a hat, I produced a luxuriant, shoulder-length, curly blonde wig.

The effect was instantaneous. Maggie dissolved into fits of hysterical laughter. In a trice, the scarf was off and the wig was on. It was awful. Maggie looked absolutely ghastly in it, even worse than Linda had done.

'Paul, this is wonderful,' she said as she admired herself in a hand mirror. 'Where on earth did you get it?'

'From my cross-dressing box.'

'You silly devil. Well, I think it's perfect and I've already decided that I shall wear it to my party,' she said.

It just so happened that the next time I visited Maggie was a week or so after the great event. I didn't need to ask how it had gone, for both Duncan and Maggie had grins from ear to ear. Duncan handed me a thick wad of photos. Maggie, wreathed in smiles and crowned by a mountain of blonde curls, held centre stage in every one.

'We had a wonderful time,' Duncan said. 'Everyone arrived looking a bit glum, as if they didn't know whether they were coming to a knees-up or a wake. But when they came in and saw Maggie, they all fell about laughing, especially the boys, and the party never looked back.'

Not long after the party Maggie started getting headaches and, only a little while later, had her first fit. She then began to deteriorate rapidly.

Brain scans confirmed a large secondary growth and Maggie's medication, of necessity, became more powerful and more complicated.

Through all of this she never stopped smiling and she never stopped encouraging the joke telling either. She lay on her bed, hanging onto life by the thinnest of threads, and listened as Duncan and I tried to outdo one another in poor taste.

And she never stopped worrying about those around her either.

'You're looking very tired again, Paul,' she whispered.

'It's you I'm concerned about,' I would reply.

'Concerned about me?' she would say. 'Why would you be concerned about me? We all know what's going to happen to me. But you . . . you could get better if only you'd look after yourself a little more carefully. Or perhaps let that new "someone" do it for you,' she continued with a smile.

Then one day Maggie stopped smiling. By the time I got to the house her breathing was shallow and her pulse was faint and irregular. It was obvious that her last battle was nearly over. Duncan and I sat on either side of the bed and held her hands.

'It's time,' she said quietly. 'Thank you. Both of you. And you, Duncan, promise you won't die with me. Promise you'll have the courage to live again. And you, Paul, promise me that you'll live again too. Not as you are but *really* live again. None of us are meant to be on our own.'

The three of us sat there in silence for a while.

'Ah, Maggie, I nearly forgot,' I said. 'I have another present for you.'

Maggie must have seen a glint in my eye for she managed a weak smile. 'What have you got now, you crazy man?'

I reached into my bag and drew out a small cylinder of green liquid that sparkled in the light.

Maggie smiled again. 'And what on earth have you brought this time?'

'A magic wand,' I replied, waving it about.

'And what in all creation would I want with a magic wand?' she asked weakly.

'Well,' I said, 'nothing else is working, so I thought we might as well give this a go.'

Maggie's weak laugh brought on a coughing fit. When she had got her breath back she took the wand from me.

'I don't want any jokes today,' she said, 'But I'd like you to tell me a story instead. A magical story.'

I sat for a few moments wondering what to say. And then I had it.

'Funnily enough,' I said, 'I do have a magical story for you. Only a few days ago, I saw lots of fairies and wizards. Heaps of them and, funnily enough, this story also involves a young lady.'

'Now there's a surprise,' said Maggie, managing a smile.

'Just last week,' I continued, 'someone came into my surgery, sat down and simply smiled at me.

'"How can I help?" I asked.

'"I'm feeling very pleased with myself," she replied.

'"I can see that," I said, "but is there anything I can do to help?"

'"Not really. I just wanted you to know."

'"Know what?" I queried.

'"That I am now a world champion! Three World Titles, and you're a part of it."

'"What on earth are you talking about?" I asked her.

'"You are looking at the new World Champion Best Fantasy, Best Large Black and Best Female Back. Isn't it wonderful?" she said excitedly.

'"I don't wish to spoil your excitement," I said, "but I haven't the faintest idea what you are talking about."

'In answer, she turned away from me, lifted her jumper and said over her shoulder: "What you are looking at now is officially the best in the world."

'And there it was, from shoulder to shoulder and from nape to waist, a wonderful and intricate picture of fairies and castles and dragons and wizards.

'"It's certainly very impressive," I said, "but how does it make you a world champion?"

'"Just recently the world tattoo championships were held in Melbourne and I happened to be down in town for a few days staying with a girlfriend. She knew about my tattoo and suggested I enter. I was a bit shy about the idea at first, but then I thought what the hell, so I did. Anyway, to cut a long story short, I entered, and won!"

'"Well, that's great," I said. "But how am I a part of that?"

'She pointed to a fairy on her right shoulder blade and asked if I could see it. I replied that indeed I could.

'"Well that fairy was the very first part of the whole tattoo," she said.

'"I'm still not following you," I said as she lowered her jumper and turned back to me. "You'll have to give me more clues."

"'Last winter I came to you with bronchitis. When you had finished examining my chest you gave me some antibiotics and told me to stop smoking. I didn't stop smoking," she shrugged, "but I did take the antibiotics."

"'And?'

"'And then, when I was leaving the surgery, you said: 'Oh and another thing, the fairy on your right shoulder has an ugly nose.' I was very upset at the time and rather cross with you. But I went straight home and looked at it in the mirror and you were right, she *did* have an ugly nose.

"'I immediately phoned my tattooist and told him what I thought of him. I got him to change her nose to a pretty little turned-up one, and at no extra cost, I might add. That set a new standard in our relationship and from that time on he drew every figure with meticulous attention to every detail.

"'So there you are. I simply wouldn't be where I am today if it hadn't been for you," she said, then gave me a quick hug and left.'

When I had finished, Maggie lay there for a while smiling. 'Promise you'll tell stories about me one day, Paul.'

'Yes,' I promised. 'I sure will.'

Maggie waved her wand about a little and managed to make it sparkle. 'This might be a touch late for this world,' she said, 'but Duncan, will you please make sure that it goes with me to the next one. I'm sure I'll find a use for it there.'

There was a knock on the door and I went and let the boys in. I glanced through the door to see the whole family united for the last time, then quietly stepped outside into the garden.

Maggie died about twenty minutes later.

As she wished, she was placed in her casket holding a bright green wand and wearing a ridiculous curly wig.

I kept in touch with Duncan after Maggie died and, when time permitted, had a cup of tea with him to make sure he was OK. A couple of months or so after the funeral I bumped into him at a social function one evening. I asked him how he was travelling.

'The truth is, I'm torn in two,' he said. 'Part of me is devastated, of course, but another part of me just can't stop smiling. It probably sounds really odd, but every time I think of Maggie's last few weeks I feel really sad and then start laughing. She looked dreadful in that wig, you silly bugger, and as for that dopey wand! So I laugh as well as cry and perhaps that's what she would've wanted.'

He turned away to chat with some other people, then turned back to me. 'Oh, I nearly forgot,' he said. 'I've got a present for you this time. It's in the boot of my car. Come out with me now and I'll give it to you before I forget.'

A little mystified, I followed him out to the car park where he opened his boot and presented me with a large galvanised bird feeder, just like the one in their garden.

'That is beautiful,' I said in astonishment. 'Thank you so much.'

'It was Maggie's idea,' he said, 'but it is really from the both of us,' and he shook me by the hand.

I still bump into Duncan from time to time. A year or two after Maggie died I had taken a break from the morning surgery and was having a coffee in a nice little café that had recently opened up nearby, when I felt a tap on my shoulder.

'Hi, Duncan,' I said as I realised who it was. 'You look great.'

'Yes, I am really well,' he replied. 'Bring your coffee and join us. There's someone I would like you to meet.'

He led me to a table on the other side of the café.

'Paul, this is Jo. Jo, this is Paul,' said Duncan.

'Nice to meet you,' I said, and we shook hands as I sat down.

'I've got one over you.' Jo's smile illuminated her whole face. 'You know nothing about me, but I know all about you. Thank you so much for looking after Duncan as well as Maggie, but you don't need to do that anymore. Your job's over,' she continued with a twinkle in her eye.

'Oh?' I said. 'And how's that?'

'Because,' she replied, 'looking after Duncan will be my job from now on.'

I finished my coffee, wished them well and wandered back to the surgery.

'Maggie keep waving that wand,' I murmured as I picked up my in-tray and called for the first patient of the afternoon.

As afternoons go it wasn't a bad one. Meaghan and Heather both seemed in a funny mood, but everything flowed smoothly enough. I even got away quite a bit earlier than usual as a number of patients seemed to have cancelled their appointments.

When I got home, expecting a quiet evening on my own, I was surprised to find that all the lights were on and when I opened the back door, even more surprised to hear Sumi Jo singing Mozart.

The table had been laid for a banquet for two, something on the stove smelled wonderful and there were candles everywhere.

And there was also Helen.

'I hope you don't mind,' she said, and smiled at me as she got up from the table and poured two glasses of champagne, 'but I thought I would like to make us a meal. Especially on our first evening together at Woongarra.'

She looked stunning.

'But, how, how . . . ?' I gibbered

'Easy,' she replied. 'I phoned the surgery. A very nice lady called Heather gave me directions on how to get here and another very nice lady called Meaghan told me she would make sure you weren't late.'

'Thank you,' I said, and was going to add a whole lot more, but, at that moment, Helen leaned forward and silenced me with a kiss.